Gender, Class and Work

Gender, Class and Work

Edited by

Eva Gamarnikow
David H.J. Morgan
June Purvis
Daphne E. Taylorson

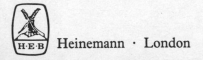 Heinemann · London

Heinemann Educational Books Ltd
22 Bedford Square, London WC1B 3HH
LONDON EDINBURGH MELBOURNE AUCKLAND
HONG KONG SINGAPORE KUALA LUMPUR NEW DELHI
IBADAN NAIROBI JOHANNESBURG
EXETER (NH) KINGSTON PORT OF SPAIN

© British Sociological Association 1983
First published 1983

British Cataloguing in Publication Data

Gender, class and work.
    1. Sexism—Great Britain—History
    I. Gamarnikow, Eva
    305.3'09   HQ1075

    ISBN   0-435-82336-1
    ISBN   0-435-82337-X Pbk

Phototypesetting by Georgia Origination, Liverpool
and printed by Biddles Ltd, Guildford, Surrey

Contents

1   Introduction: Class and Work: Bringing Women Back In
David H.J. Morgan and Daphne E. Taylorson

This volume, together with its companion, *The Public and The Private*, is a selection around some common themes which emerged from the April 1982 Annual Conference of the British Sociological Association titled 'Gender and Society', which was held in Manchester. While this particular selection from the eighty or so papers that were presented at the Conference does not claim to be fully representative, it does capture some important and developing areas of concern within British sociology. This is not perhaps surprising, given that a major inspiration of the 1982 Conference was Margaret Stacey's paper on 'Overcoming the Two Adams' (Stacey, 1981), itself presented at an earlier BSA Conference. Here, Stacey demonstrated the way in which British sociology had persisted in splitting its subject area into two worlds, the public world of class, industry and work on the one hand and the world of the domestic and the private on the other: in short, she argues, the worlds of Adam Smith and Adam and Eve.

The 1982 Conference, with sessions on topics as diverse as class, gender, sexuality, health, medicine, education and work, was an impressive witness to the considerable effort that is now being devoted towards overcoming and challenging this split. The papers included in the two volumes provide a criticism of conventional sociological practice, which continues to marginalise women and downgrade, obscure or sometimes reify questions of gender. It is, regrettably, still the case that the more sociology deals with questions in the public arena – questions of politics, industry and work, organisations and law and order – the less visible are women, for women usually feature prominently only in studies of the private arena – marriage, family and sexuality – studies which still have relatively marginal status in sociological study and theorising. The papers in this volume question this marginalisation of women in two key areas of sociological analysis: class and work.

At the same time, these papers examine the social processes that marginalise women in these two areas in daily life. When over half of even married women are in employment, 'the myth of the male breadwinner' (Land, 1975) seems insubstantial indeed, however much it may continue to be used to justify the allocation of women to marginal positions in the workforce. Yet this myth, and its accompanying myth about the conventional nuclear family as the dominant household form, continues to exercise seductive power over women's everyday existence, as well as sociological analysis, and the papers in this collection document the many and varied ways in which women continue to be marginalised both in the study of class and work and in their daily lives, even where social reality issues a constant rebuke.

The sheer numbers of offers of papers and actual participants, together with the crowded and often animated discussions at the 1982 Conference, might lead a casual observer to conclude that the split between the two Adams had indeed been overcome and that conventional sociology was in retreat. Such an impression might well be premature. The editors of an earlier Conference volume noted:

> The papers in this volume thus deal with aspects of social relationships consistently neglected by sociologists, and ridiculed or denigrated by some. But in so far as sexism constitutes unproblematic, common-sense behaviour in contemporary British culture, it should not surprise us that it appears thus in sociology (Barker and Allen, 1976, p. 2).

Comments from some senior academics prior to the 1982 Conference, and an editorial in *The Times* immediately afterwards, suggest that these attitudes are still flourishing and that, in some quarters, gender is still regarded as a near synonym for 'trivial' or even 'frivolous'. The fragile growth of women's studies in a handful of institutions should remind us of the continuing marginalisation of issues of gender and the inclusion of a couple of questions about women on examination papers hardly constitutes a major topic shift. The number of participants at the 1982 Conference who were unemployed or on short-term or part-time appointments was noteworthy and the marginalisation of women in the sphere of class and work parallels their marginalisation in academic institutions.

The papers in this volume, therefore, deal neither simply nor straightforwardly with traditional women's issues, but focus on mainstream, 'public' issues of class, work and unemployment. They constitute a critique of many abiding practices and assumptions within contemporary sociology and within contemporary society but, more importantly, they address themselves to the task of attempting to overcome these perceived defects. It should be noted that the methods and approaches adopted in this collection are very varied. Middleton presents a historically based argument using a wide variety of sources while Lown provides a more focused historical case study. Payne *et al.* and Britten and Heath make critical uses of survey data while Attwood and Hatton, Cunnison and Pollert use ethnographies and open-ended interviews. Walby makes critical use of official statistics and Heritage's case study combines an analysis of union records with data derived from interviews. The diversity of methods adopted and of levels of analysis should serve to remind us that there is no one 'feminist' method or style. At the same time, this diversity of method should not obscure the fact that all these papers have a common and central area of substantive concern; the examination of the social relationships of gender, the processes by which women are marginalised in work, stratification and employment, and in the sociological study of these areas.

The distinction between the public and private (themes explored in greater detail in the companion volume) highlights the marginalisation of women, both in sociological practice and theorising and in everyday life. This distinction maps on to several other familiar distinctions, such as that between work and home, the traditional spheres of men and women. Yet to hold up the distinction between the public and the private to critical scrutiny is not necessarily to abandon it. The distinction may indeed obscure our understanding of social processes if it be held to signify some relatively timeless opposition between men's and women's spheres. It is certainly a dangerous distinction to use if it be seen as a justification for the exclusion of women from stratification studies; seeing women as enjoying a secondary or derived status in terms of some man and his position in the public arena. The aim should not be to use the opposition as, in some simple way, an explanation for gender divisions between and within home and work. Rather the aim should be to explore the way in which the distinction is used by various people, such as managers, trade union officials and different groups or categories of workers, within the areas of work and employment. We need to explore the way in which the public/private distinction works as ideology, informing social practices both at home and at work. We see the public/private distinction as a culturally available mode of categorisation which is used as a way of justifying, understanding or explaining the world in a variety of contexts. It is these justifications, understandings and explanations, derived from the distinction, that are more of interest than the distinction itself. One important consequence of this shift in focus is to see the sphere of work as being a locus of interaction between the public and the private rather than simply being firmly placed within the public sphere and to which, therefore, women are admitted only as temporary guests.

All of the papers in this volume deal with some aspects of women's work and with the way in which the public/private distinction serves to shape and inform their experience at home, in employment and in the labour market. Middleton, for example, writing of pre-industrial England shows the crucial role that women's work played in the processes of capital accumulation. (He also notes how this importance has been ignored by historians, Marxist as well as non-Marxist.) The bulk of this economically important labour was performed within the domestic sphere. The process of industrialisation and the development of capitalism were supposed to create and sharpen the distinctions between the public and private but all the remaining papers show this distinction to operate in decisive ways, whether we are considering silk-manufacture in the nineteenth century or hairdressing in the twentieth. In the former case (Lown) paternalistic relations at the workplace demonstrated the real continuities that existed between home and work while in the latter case (Attwood and Hatton), such distinctions inform the differential experiences of men and women in the trade and their differing patterns of relationships with their clients.

The papers that deal more specifically with work in this volume serve, among other things, to emphasise the continuing significance of women's participation in paid employment. They illustrate the central role of women in many spheres of employment, occupations and, increasingly, trade unions. They re-affirm several central facts about women in our society, namely that a woman is not simply a summation of a set of domestic identities (wife, mother, daughter, etc.), that her status is not one of a dependant and that marriage is not a life-long career. Moreover, they underline the fact that for most households in this country two incomes do not mean luxuries or 'extras', although the belief that the women's income may be regarded in these terms is shown to persist and to contribute to the marginalisation of her work experience. Discussion of women's work and the struggle for equality in pay and employment has too frequently been conducted at the level of professional women in the world of dual-career families (Fogarty *et al.* 1971a, 1971b; Rapoport and Rapoport, 1971, 1976). The emphasis here has been on the intrinsic rewards and satisfactions to be gained from such forms of employment and in particular the clustering of such rewards around the notion of a career. In the cases described in this volume, on the other hand, the rewards are more tangible and form a vital element in the maintenance of a reasonable standard of living for many households, single-parent and two-parent. Women's work in all its aspects continues to be of importance to the household as well as to the economy.

Thus in real economic terms, women's paid employment is by no means marginal. Yet, as Cunnison and others show, the money from this employment is often marginalised in a variety of ways at home and at work. But the economic centrality of such work is linked to another factor of working-class experience, which contrasts with the nature of work at the professional or middle-class levels: its relative unpleasantness and low status. The work situations described here – and these are the work situations where women predominate – are for the most part routine, sometimes physically demanding, of low status and poorly paid. In hairdressing, for example, women are more likely to be found in the 'shampoo and set' end of the market rather than the glamorous West End salons. There is little, if any, notion of a career for the women working at Churchman's tobacco factory or among school meals assistants or even among bank employees. If women appear to manifest little commitment to the workplace as such, this is to be explained not simply in terms of domestic commitments or family-based identities, but in terms of the demanding and unglamorous nature of the work itself. Women themselves often say in such situations that 'No man would do it' (Pollert), a recognition contributing to the ambiguous role that paid employment often plays in the life of many women and to the continuing marginalisation of these work-experiences.

And what of the men? The term 'gender' refers, of course, not simply to women but to women and men and to the social processes shaping these identities and the interaction between them. While none of the studies deal with men directly, they are present nevertheless, as foremen, as trade-union officials, as managers, sometimes as co-workers, and as fathers, and husbands. They often exist in contrast to the women, as in the contrasting careers in hairdressing or banking. They equally often exist in interaction with the women, in terms of sexual banter and gender-specific references, often reinforcing status and authority differences within the factory or union. The studies remind us that, even in the same or similar occupations, the work experiences of men and women are not the same. It is perhaps a pity that none of the papers presented at the Conference dealt directly with questions of men and masculinity at work; however, the studies presented here provide us with plenty of pictures of men at work as seen largely through the eyes of women workers.

The papers by Attwood and Hatton, Cunnison, Lown and Pollert (and to some extent the paper by Heritage also) all deal, for the most part, with *working-class* women. Theoretically, what is important in each paper is that the object of study is the interaction of class and gender in each case and not either class or gender or, indeed, some simple summation of the two. Pollert seeks to separate the two to some degree by her choice of the terms exploitation and oppression to relate to class and gender respectively but shows, as do the other papers, that in the actual analysis of day-to-day relationships at work the two factors (together with other factors such as age) overlap and mutually influence each other.

While it would be pointless to summarise the subleties of the analysis in each paper, the following general points seem to emerge from these studies:

(1) Class and gender in interaction enter into the processes whereby women are allocated to particular kinds of work, such as the tobacco grading described by Pollert and the school meals workers in Cunnison's study. Similarly, divisions within a particular industry in terms of typical careers are explored by Attwood and Hatton; in a predominantly female occupation most of the prestigious positions and careers are occupied by men. Thus it is possible for the authors to show quite different careers and conceptions of 'getting on' for men and women (and between different categories of women) within the hairdressing trade and to demonstrate how these differences are shaped by a complex set of factors including traditional expectations concerning careers for working-class women, patriarchal controls within the industry and the largely male-defined conceptions of glamour and success. Attwood and Hatton, like Pollert, also show how different expectations bear upon *young* working-class women (although in different ways in each case), showing the importance of introducing age into the analysis. All these case studies provide detailed amplification and confirmation of Walby's more macroscopic and theoretical analysis of labour markets as well as providing many suggestions for further research. Thus the studies are dealing with the processes by which working-class women get working-class women's jobs, and the reinforcement and reproduction of gender and class divisions that follow from these processes.

(2) Each study also explores class and gender consciousness, again seeing this consciousness as a totality rather than as a simple summation of two separate identities. The notion of the 'fractured' or 'splintered' consciousness in the lives of working-class women (developed especially in the papers by Pollert and Cunnison) is one of particular importance in this context. On the one hand the women have a very clear understanding of who is in control and of the nature of exploitation; on the other hand they give assent to such ideological notions as 'the family wage'. What is important in these studies is the way in which they force us to take seriously what working-class women say about their work and family experiences, and this entails neither a simple reporting nor an over-theorising (seeing such utterances as, for example, instances of 'false class consciousness') but rather a sensitive appreciation of the complex and often contradictory social pressures that make such statements intelligible. The experience of work encountered by working-class women and the consciousness engendered by their daily experience is not identical to that of working-class men or of middle-class women. The dialectics of con-

sciousness and experience are different in each case.

(3) The term 'working-class', of course, is itself a very complex summation of a variety of different experiences and traditions. Within the category of women workers a variety of distinctions may be made according to the structure of the industry or sector of the economy concerned, the overall percentages of women employed in each occupation, differences between women workers within the same industry or sector and the extent to which the work experiences are fragmented or individualised, or alternatively, conform more closely to the traditional 'industrial proletariat' model. In short, it makes a difference whether women workers are dispersed in a variety of small-scale enterprises (as is the case for a large section of the hairdressing trade) or whether they are working together in a large factory or office block. The traditional differences between manual, routine non-manual and service occupations captures some, if not all, of the kinds of differences that we need to explore.

One area of particular importance in the lives of working women is the area of routine white-collar work. Lockwood (1958) noted the replacement of white-collared by white-bloused workers in many areas of routine clerical work but did not, in any systematic fashion, follow up the implications of this shift. It is in this sector that we find one of the largest concentrations of female labour and the consequences for class and occupational mobility are explored by Payne *et al.* while the central role played by the feminisation of the labour force within banking (especially for unionisation and union activity) is a key issue in the paper by Heritage. Clearly, we need many more studies of this particularly central area of female employment for developing an understanding of the interplay of class and gender in work contexts.

We have considered the way in which the papers in this volume deal with issues of work and of the interrelationships between gender and class at the workplace. Turning more specifically to the questions of class, it can be seen that all the contributors to this volume either directly or indirectly make plain that we have had to wait a long time before gender has been given a central place in the analysis of social stratification. The defects of traditional social class analysis are now well-known (although this knowledge has not always brought about a corresponding change in sociological practice) and some of the main points of this criticism are outlined in the papers by Britten and Heath and Payne *et al.* In short, stratification was based upon occupation, and the world of occupations was seen as being centrally the world of men. Women were thus either excluded from the analysis of social stratification or were treated as having a status dependent upon that of a man, a husband or a father. The argument that the family or household constituted the basic unit of systems of stratification was taken to mean that the head of the household in some way represented the household and that the head was assumed to be a man. Women, therefore, were either invisible or enjoyed a secondary, derived status in stratification studies.

Whether or not the feminist critique of traditional stratification studies constitutes a fatal blow to such modes of analysis or whether some kind of repair work is possible remains a point for debate. Britten and Heath and Payne *et al.* clearly believe that such repair work is both desirable and possible and they do so not simply as people concerned with rectifying an academic injustice but in order to demonstrate that the inclusion of women in stratification analysis does have important consequences for such studies and their conclusions. Thus Payne *et al.* point to the important patterns of upward social mobility for women. Whether such movements, which are of relatively short distances, are consequential in terms of the lives and experiences of the women indicated by these moves is clearly a question for further research but it is an issue that would have remained unexplored for as long as women remained absent from stratification studies. Similarly, Britten and Heath, through taking women into account, attempt to redescribe the class structure, focusing particularly on the numerical importance of the group containing skilled male manual workers married to routine non-manual female workers which they call cross-class families. Again, this statistical analysis does not tell us much about the way in which such marriages are perceived and understood by the participants but such an investigation clearly opens up many new areas in the analysis of marriage and stratification.

Yet, although the feminist critique of stratification studies has clear and important implications for the study of class, this is not to say that women can be simply incorporated into a class analysis. Whether we adopt some version of a Marxist or a Weberian analysis, in practice our concern is with occupational groupings, their different relations to the mode of production, their different rankings in terms of income, power and prestige and so on. Since most women have, for most of their lives, work and occupational identities, and since most women at some time contribute to the household income, women should clearly occupy a place in studies of class and stratification in their own right. But this is not the whole story and most of the papers in this volume argue the need to go beyond a simple class analysis in considering women in the world of work. Some papers, in particular, argue for the need for the concept of patriarchy.

The debate over the concept of patriarchy, its usefulness or otherwise and its relationship to capitalism, continues to be one of the most contested areas within contemporary feminist thought. Many of these theoretical debates and issues are summarised in the papers by Lown, Middleton and Walby, all of whom favour the retention and elaboration of the concept of patriarchy. There is little doubt that sociology needs to preserve the sense of structured gender inequalities, ante-dating capitalist and class relationships, which the term patriarchy seeks to convey. At the same time, there is a need to avoid the opposite danger of positing a timeless opposition between 'gender-classes', an opposition which may at worst slide into a kind of biologism and at best may provide a rhetorical re-organising of our frames of reference (itself no mean achievement) but without any real or discriminatory explanatory power. As with the more specific issue of class and gender in the workplace, capitalism and partriarchy must be constantly related to each other, both preserving the specificity of the kinds of relationships subsumed on either side whilst being constantly sensitive to the inter-determining play of these relationships in any concrete situation.

The papers by Middleton and Lown represent two attempts to explore the complex interplay between patriarchy and particular social formations. In both papers, the emphasis is on showing how patriarchy works in specific historical contexts, rather than either reducing the analysis to economic class relationships or treating the concept of patriarchy as the sole explanatory variable. In a different, and current, context, Walby's analysis of unemployment points to the defects of many analyses – again both Marxist and non-Marxist – of women in the labour market and points to the need to examine the ways in which an essential part of any such analysis must include accounts of the patriarchal relationships that have, as their consequence, the concentration of women in part-time work, the invisibility of women in many sets of unemployment statistics and the differential impact of economic recession on women and men. Walby points to interesting differences between European countries in these respects, again underlining the need to consider the specific workings of patriarchal relationships rather than treating patriarchy as a blanket mode of explanation.

One feature of many of these papers, and one of the disquiets which gave rise to the elaboration of the concept of patriarchy in the first place, is the questioning of what has been called 'Marxist functionalism'. (Pollert for example uses this term.) Implied here is a kind of parallel to earlier feminist and Marxist critiques of structural-functionalism and the suggestion that some versions of Marxism have taken over features of the Parsonianism which they sought to criticise. This is an approach which views class relationships as dominant and which seeks to explain, for example, family structures and processes and relationships at work in terms of their contribution to the maintenance or reproduction of a capitalist social formation. Such accounts are found wanting in that, among other things, they seem to deny the possibility for any organised or individual opposition, in that they perpetuate oppositions between home and work and the public and the private and, first and foremost, because they subordinate domestic and gender relationships to class relationships. The use of the term 'patriarchy', while it may run into difficulties of its own, serves as a warning light against the dangers of Marxist functionalism.

The other danger with some versions of Marxist functionalism – and this is also a possible danger with analyses in terms of patriarchy – is the playing down of the possibility for change brought about by women themselves. Yet some studies in this volume show very clearly the complex links between consciousness and practice. While these case studies, in different ways, highlight the familiar vicious circles of expectations about and behaviour towards women workers and the continuing double subordination of these workers, they also suggest that these self-same women are capable of breaking out of these vicious circles. There are, as Pollert reminds us, virtuous circles as well, and the fractured consciousness of women workers can sometimes provide the basis for collective action. The experience of taking part in a strike or demonstration may sometimes lead to a return to the status quo, at least in appearance, but may also, as Cunnison's study demonstrates, have effects far beyond the particular issues for collective action, having reverberations within local branches of unions and workplaces. Heritage, in his study of bank employees, also demonstrates how unionisation depended heavily on the increasing feminisation of the industry and was a significant factor in the growth of NUBE. These papers seek to destroy the myth of the 'passive female worker' just as they seek to destroy the myth of the 'male breadwinner'.

Acknowledgements
To Margaret Smith, Joan Stuart, Janet Teimoorifar, Olive Wilson and Gillian Woolley for typing portions of the manuscript, often at short notice.

To Mike Milotte of the BSA Office for effective mediation between ourselves and the publishers.

To Anne Dix and all our colleagues on the BSA Executive for their support and encouragement in preparing these volumes.

2 Patriarchal Exploitation and the Rise of English Capitalism
Chris Middleton

In recent years various feminist authors have suggested that work performed by women in the home may constitute *exploited* labour. This idea has been broached in a number of Marxist–feminist contributions to the domestic labour debate, the radical feminist materialism of Christine Delphy, and in a series of empirical studies documenting patterns of household resource allocation. In this paper I shall offer a very brief appraisal of the arguments in each of these accounts (essentially summarising criticisms already made by others) as a background to an examination of a particular historical case-study, the process which Marx referred to as 'the so-called primitive accumulation of capital'. In discussing this example I shall reflect on two main issues:

(1) In what respects are existing Marxist accounts of primitive accumulation deficient?
(2) Is there any evidence, direct or otherwise, to suggest that this primitive accumulation was based to some extent on the patriarchal exploitation of women's labour within the households of the emerging class of capitalist entrepreneurs? (I should add that exploitation will be provisionally defined here in the traditional Marxist sense of the word, as the appropriation of surplus labour.)

Theories of household exploitation

(1) Many contributors to the domestic labour debate have held that the work proletarian women perform for their families benefits capital by increasing the level of surplus value. There is some disagreement regarding the precise mechanism by which capital is understood to achieve the appropriation of surplus labour performed in the home – housework can be seen as actually producing surplus value (Dalla Costa, 1972, p. 52), as enabling capitalists to pay wages at a level *below*

that of the value of labour-power thereby increasing the margin of surplus-value (Harrison, 1974), or else as *depressing* the value of labour-power essentially by reducing the amount that the proletarian household needs to spend on commodities (Gardiner, 1975b, 1976; Fox, 1980). But whatever their disagreements over the mechanics of the process each subscribes to a common view that proletarian housework is exploited by capital.

(2) The thrust of Christine Delphy's argument diverges sharply from that of the Marxist–feminists whose views I have just outlined. While she would agree that women perform surplus labour in the home, she believes that it is appropriated by *men*, not by capital (Delphy 1976; 1977). Her essential proposition is 'that marriage is the institution by which gratuitous work is extorted from a particular category of the population, women-wives' (1976, p. 77). She claims that domestic services, child-rearing and other goods are produced in a family mode of production which gives rise to patriarchal exploitation, and that the marriage contract is a form of labour contract which ensures that domestic work has no value. For the majority of women, therefore, marriage results in the total appropriation of their labour-power, and it is this material exploitation within marriage which constitutes the oppression common to all women.

(3) The domestic exploitation of women has also been implied in a number of empirical studies documenting the inequitable distribution of resources within households and families, and especially as between husbands and wives (Oren, 1973; Pahl, 1980; Land, 1980; Whitehead, 1981; Maher, 1981; Delphy, 1979). There has been a concern, first, with questions of resource control, that is with the arrangements for the authoritative allocation of resources to individual family members or for different household purposes; and second, there has been an attempt to determine which members typically benefit most from this distribution both in terms of the unequal allocation of funds for individual personal expenditure and of differential access to and use of 'collective' household assets. Given this focus on patterns of consumption it might be thought that these studies had no direct bearing on the question of household labour exploitation. However, the two spheres cannot be separated so easily, for the reciprocal (though not necessarily equal) exchanges of labour between household members can only be evaluated if opportunities for consumption are taken into account. Moreover, as Ann Whitehead has emphasised, patterns of household resource allocation arise out of and are dependent upon the organisation of the sexual division of labour, and she strongly implies that the family or household is a site of exploit-

ation in the Marxist sense (Whitehead, 1981, pp. 90–1).

How then should we assess these three very different perspectives on the exploitation of women in the household? A key problem with the Marxist–feminist theories of domestic labour is their essential incapacity to explain the widespread identification of housework and childcare as *women's* work. They have found it difficult to relate the process of capital accumulation to the sexual division of labour that exists both inside and outside the home, and they have consequently tended to sidestep the specifically feminist questions regarding the social relations of gender. Moreover, the particular contributions to the debate which I summarised earlier have been handicapped by two closely linked shortcomings: a tendency to incorporate functionalist assumptions into their analyses (seeing domestic labour as 'essential to' or 'necessary for' capitalism), and an associated failure to translate their insights into an appropriate programme of historical and empirical research. There is, in fact, no a priori reason why domestic labour should invariably increase the level of surplus-value extracted in a capitalist economy. Whether it does so or not will depend on quite specific historical and conjunctural determinants. In principle, therefore, it is a matter that can only be decided by empirical investigation, and should not be adduced as a central tenet of the theory (Molyneux, 1979a).

Delphy, of course, could never be accused of subordinating feminist issues to other concerns. Her argument is unequivocally about gender exploitation. Yet I doubt very much whether her theoretical work adds much to our understanding of this material relation.[1] In her general theoretical writings she exhibits a gross insensitivity to the substance of historical change, and her dogmatic stance on the universal character of the marriage contract totally pre-empts the possible findings of comparative and historical research. Whatever obstacles the domestic labour debate may have encountered, its great strength has always lain in its commitment to a systematic and historically grounded exploration of the structural links between proletarian housework and exploitation in the market sector. Delphy, in stark contrast, has quite deliberately severed the analysis of women's exploitation within the family from that of the process of capital accumulation. To my mind, this constitutes a basic flaw in her position.

The urge to keep feminist and Marxist accounts distinct and separate represents a powerful, though regrettable, strand in recent feminist thought (e.g. Hamilton, 1978; Hartmann, 1979). But to reject that call is not to suggest that our interest in the domestic exploitation of women should be subordinated to a prior concern with a limited conception of capitalist class relations; still less that the analyses of either class or gender exploitation can be reduced to each other's terms. It is perfectly possible to envisage instances of domestic exploitation that have no *necessary* implications for capital accumulation – say, where a man exploits the subordinate members of his household while absorbing the entire surplus in higher levels of personal consumption. But even in this case, where market and domestic exploitation seem maximally separate, any explanation of the domestic exchange that failed to consider the broader context would be woefully incomplete – just as accounts of market exploitation are inadequate if they fail to take cognizance of the effects of domestic labour. The grounds and nature of women's exploitation in the household have varied historically, not least because of changes in the relations of production that men experience. An understanding of that variation will require an *integrated* analysis of the major relations of production and reproduction in any given social formation (Barrett and McIntosh, 1979).

A bifurcated approach does not seem to be either a necessary or an intended feature of most of the studies of household resource allocation. Indeed, most of the women doing research in this tradition appear to be broadly committed to the kind of research agenda I have just been advocating. Nevertheless, with the important exception of the study of state policy in relation to the family (see especially, McIntosh, 1979), a split does seem to have developed in practice. Not unnaturally, perhaps, the research has concentrated heavily on the processes of decision-taking within households and the typical distributive consequences which these have for variously placed members of the family. There has been little attempt, as yet, to integrate this research agenda with theoretical analyses of domestic labour's links with capital accumulation.

Fortunately the conceptual and theoretical problems encountered in analysing the relationship between primitive capital accumulation and the household exploitation of women appear relatively straightforward when compared with those that beset the analysis of subsequent stages of capitalist development. For we shall be dealing here with the household labour processes of an embryonic capitalist class where (if my conjecture is correct) surplus labour performed by subordinate members of the household was appropriated directly to fuel accumulation, rather than, as in the case of proletarian domestic labour, being mediated through people who appear on the labour market as wage-labourers who are themselves exploited.

Even so, a couple of preliminary theoretical clarifications do need to be made. In the first place a distinction has to be drawn between the *exploitation* of labour and the 'mere' act of appropriation. For instance, a man might appropriate the labour of subordinate members of his household, being able to command its performance and/or having disposition over its products, and yet return the full worth of that labour to them – say, in the form of goods for consumption. In this case appropriation would not have entailed expropriation, and so exploitation could not be said to have occurred. The distinction seems important for without exploitation (of a class, of subordinate household members, or whatever) accumulation becomes a virtual impossibility. In the era of high feudalism, for example, male heads of peasant households appropriated most of the household product, but there was in general no economic surplus beyond that expropriated by the feudal landlords which might serve to fuel a primitive accumulation from within the ranks of the peasantry.

On the other hand, as we have seen, a surplus expropriated within the household may be consumed entirely within it too. The absence of accumulation is therefore no guarantor of the absence of patriarchal exploitation. Indeed, it might not be unrealistic to surmise that where, as in medieval peasant households, the prerogative of the dominant male was so firmly entrenched, exploitation of this non-cumulative kind would very likely be widespread. However, in our present state of knowledge this would be to indulge in sheer speculation.

Theories of primitive accumulation

Marx introduced his discussion of primitive accumulation with the following passage:

> The accumulation of capital pre-supposes surplus-value; surplus-value pre-supposes capitalistic production; capitalistic production pre-supposes the pre-existence of considerable masses of capital and of labour-power in the hands of producers of commodities. The whole movement, therefore, seems to turn in a vicious circle, out of which we can only get by supposing a primitive accumulation (previous accumulation of Adam Smith) preceding capitalistic accumulation; an accumulation not the result of the capitalist mode of production, but its starting point (1954, p. 713).

If we accept this view, primitive accumulation can be seen to have a two-fold character. On the one hand it includes 'the creation of a class of free-labourers, free in the double sense of having no feudal obligations and also being free from, "unencumbered by", any property of their own' (Saville, 1969, p. 266) (a development which has been exhaustively discussed else-where). On the other it involves the amassing of resources which, in so far as they may be used to hire the newly freed labourers, can be transformed into capital in the strict sense.

A focal point of recent controversies in Marxism around the transition from feudalism to capitalism has concerned the exact nature of this process of primitive accumulation (Dobb, 1963; Hilton, 1976; Wallerstein, 1974). In stark terms the dispute can be presented as a disagreement between those who saw capitalism as having made its mark in the guise of wealthy, urban-based merchant capitalists owing the bulk of their fortunes to plunder especially in the overseas colonies, and those who have endorsed Dobb's initial claim that the revolutionary transformation in relations of production depended on a class of indigenous petty-proprietors, located as much in the countryside as in the towns, who accumulated capital through small-scale accretions to their property. Most of the early contributors to the debate supported this second interpretation and, while it cannot be said to form the whole story, subsequent research has produced a good deal of evidence to corroborate that judgement.

For a century after the Black Death the land hunger which had previously afflicted the English peasantry was transformed into a chronic shortage of labour. Land became plentiful and the quality of soil under cultivation improved as marginal tracts were allowed to return to waste. The number of small-holding families, supplementing their income through wage-labour, was drastically reduced. All strata of peasants prospered, but above all it was the age of the middling peasantry who relied heavily on family labour. While the richer yeomanry shared in the general well-being, opportunities for expansion were limited by the shortage of labour available for hire. Nevertheless, this was not an economy geared simply to self-sufficiency, but one where markets were already well-established and, as Hilton has commented, 'the fact that the country was not devastated by war must, during the long period of the prosperity of the middle peasantry, have made possible accumulations of wealth such as would not have been possible elsewhere' (1978, p. 282). By the sixteenth century, however, we can observe a marked change. The number of small-holders and of landless labourers is on the increase again. Hoskins has noted that 'a class of capitalist peasants who owned substantially larger farms and capital resources than the general run of village farmers' was beginning to appear all over the Midlands counties (1957, p. 141). According to Dobb the century saw:

> a considerable growth of independent, peasant farming by tenants who rented land as enclosed holdings outside the open-field system. Among these there developed . . . an important section of richer peasants or yeomen, who as they prospered added field to field, by lease or purchase, perhaps became usurers to their poorer neighbours, and grew by the end of the century into considerable farmers who relied on the hire of wage-labour, recruited from the victims of enclosures or from the poorer cottagers. It was by this class of rising yeomen farmers that most of the improvements in methods of cultivation seem to have been pioneered (1963, p. 125).

A small surplus, in an era of rising prices, could offer a sufficient basis for expansion. No large outlays of capital were required (Campbell, 1942, pp. 69–70; Dobb, 1963, p. 64).[2]

The precondition of this development lay in the peasant struggles over the form of feudal rent whose victory, in England, was sealed by the decades of plague and population decline. It had been a struggle over the share-out of the surplus product – a resistance to labour services on the lord's demesne so that more of the household's labour could be devoted to the family holding, more of the surplus product retained. While the transformation of labour rent into money rent did not alter 'the basic nature of feudal rent as direct appropriation of unpaid surplus labour by the landlord', one author rightly speaks of it 'stimulating the growth of independent commodity production and differentiation within the peasantry' by way of fixing this surplus labour to a constant magnitude (Merrington, 1976, p. 179). It enabled the peasantry to accumulate resources in a small way on the basis of mainly family labour, with the more successful of them eventually able to capitalise those resources by employing cheapened hired labour in production for an expanding market.

Much capitalist industry likewise developed out of small beginnings and, contrary to popular belief, was not especially centred in the towns. In the later Middle Ages the basis of urban production lay with a class of small, independent craft producers, organised into gilds and dependent on the labour of family, journeymen and apprentices. It appears that, at this time, women were expected to participate in their husband's business activities, and they were admitted to all but 5 out of 500 English gilds though not as full members (Hogrefe, 1975; Lacey, 1981). Dobb in fact argues that the margin for saving in this petty mode of production must have been narrow, and that the source of capital accumulation should be sought elsewhere, in the rise of a class of privileged burghers who in the thirteenth and fourteenth centuries cut themselves off from production and began to engage exclusively in wholesale trade (Dobb, 1963, p. 86; Thrupp, 1948). Certainly, this mercantile element had an important part to play in primitive accumulation, but its role was limited essentially to the redistribution of an existing surplus through windfall profits and the political exploitation of monopolies and trade. It did not have the capacity to create a surplus by itself.

By the late fifteenth century several of the great export merchant companies, notably in the wool and cloth trades, were making a determined effort to appropriate a greater share of the surplus produced in the local markets with which they traded. In order to lower the price at which they had to purchase, an attempt was made to multiply the number of producers in competition with each other. The gilds spread their tentacles into the surrounding countryside. They fastened on to domestic production forcing producers into a private relation of dependence by obliging them to take work 'put out' to them. Yet even with this development the really revolutionary impetus seems to have come from small capitalist entrepreneurs rising from the ranks of the craft producers themselves. Recent research by Joan Thirsk has shown that this development was not confined to the wool cloth industry even though that remained paramount both in terms of total output and the number of workers employed. She has confirmed the remarkable spread in the late sixteenth and seventeenth centuries of home-based industries producing a wide range of miscellaneous wares of varied quality, pattern and price (Thirsk, 1978). Among these must be counted a large number of essentially agricultural industries. Of course, industrial development at this time was not confined to domestic production (Nef, 1932; 1934–5; Coleman, 1975; Jack, 1977; Dobb, 1963, pp. 139–41), but the importance of these numerous small projects for the expansion of the capitalist economy has been consistently underestimated. It is not so much that they pioneered major new industrial techniques as that they facilitated manufacture and small-scale capital accumulation under conditions that were free from the traditional restrictions of the craft and merchant guilds, effecting a geographical redistribution of industrial production in the process. They provided the broad base on which British industry arose.

> The virtual freedom accorded to rural industries permitted a wide range of manufacturing enterprises to exist alongside one another, some large (employing 10 or 20 people on the premises), but much more frequently small (employing the family members and perhaps one servant) (Thirsk, 1978, p. 107).

Entrepreneurs who wished to expand their ventures would require only modest capital resources. Their one unavoidable expense would be the cost of hiring labour, and for most of the sixteenth and seventeenth centuries even this cost lagged behind other prices as compared with the ratio before the great Tudor inflation. Small *urban* craftsmen, meanwhile, were finding it increasingly hard to establish themselves on an independent footing in the face of a stringent policy of exclusiveness being pursued by the richer sections of the craft guilds.

The importance of household labour for significant sections of the embryonic capitalist class is thus widely recognised by historians of all shades of opinion. Apart from the occasional passing reference, however, the question has never been asked whether household labour actually contributed to capital accumulation. This omission is particularly anomalous in the case of Marxism given its fundamental premise that an economic surplus is always the product of somebody's unrecompensed labour and not merely the function of some intersecting marginal utility curves. One might justifiably have expected Marxist historians, through a consistent application of historical materialism, to have become curious about the labour processes which made small-scale primitive accumulation possible. Unfortunately, however, they have shown a persistent reluctance to apply economic concepts to relations of production that have become embedded in intimate and perhaps affectionate personal relationships. With a due sense of propriety they have taken off their mucky boots as they pass through the front door.

There is nothing particularly novel about this reticence. Notwithstanding Engels, Marxism has from the very outset had a tendency to conceive production in capitalist economies in a somewhat limited fashion. Olivia Harris has recently remarked how, even in Marx's own writings, the emphasis on the 'social' character of commodity-producing labour implied, at least, that other kinds of labour not geared to the production of commodities was somehow 'less social'; and she records that this hint became palpable in Luxembourg's work where non-commodity economies were described as 'natural' (Harris, 1981, p. 67). In distinguishing between a social sphere of production and the natural domestic economy of the household, capital accumulation came to be identified as belonging exclusively to the former domain. Consequently, any contribution that women may have made to capital accumulation has been conceived in strictly 'orthodox' class terms. Capitalism has been analysed as an economic force whose impetus invariably came from outside the family or household. The possibility that certain classes of women may have been absorbed into the accumulation process through relations of production *within* the household, and structured according to gender, has not even been aired.[3]

Accordingly, the account of how small accumulations of capital were amassed has been less than satisfactory. Marx, in his chapters on the genesis of the capitalist farmer and the industrial capitalist simply evaded the problem (Marx, 1961, pp. 742–4 and 750–60). Dobb is rather more explicit. He writes that it was a matter of,

> a growth in the resources of the small man sufficient to cause him to place greater reliance on the results of hired labour than on the work of himself and his family, and in his calculations to relate the gain of his enterprise to his capital rather than to his own exertions. [To this development] the rapid price changes of the sixteenth century with their consequent depression of real wages and 'profit inflation' contributed in no small measure; to which no doubt must be added substantial gains from usury at the expense of their poorer brethren (1963, p. 126).

The predictable consequences of the failure to analyse household labour relations are all too apparent in this passage. The argument has, in fact, been ceded to the categories of 'bourgeois' political economy: small entrepreneurs must, it is presumed, have originally accumulated their capital through a combination of hard work ('their own exertions'), thrift and politic responses to market opportunities. Qualities of the kind described may well have been relevant to the pace, and indeed the possibility of accumulation, but without the household labour of wives, servants and other subordinate kin one wonders how there could have been any surplus production to accumulate in the first place.

Women's household labour and primitive accumulation
It would certainly be a mistake to think of primitive accumulation based on household labour and small-scale capitalist enterprise based on free wage-labour as simply consecutive phases of economic development. Not only was the transition from one form to the other very gradual and uneven, but for a long time accumulation in many household-based enterprises was possible only on the basis of a flexible and pragmatic manipulation of different types of labour resource. To some extent, indeed, these familiar distinctions do violence to the real character of household systems of production. The sharp dividing line between domestic service and agricultural or industrial employment did not exist, and even the demarcation between family labour and hired wage-labour was not as well-defined as it might appear at first sight. Workpeople were often described indifferently as labourers or servants, so that the latter term could refer not only to household menials but also to field and industrial workers including some who were not even resident with their employers. In the case of women and girls, however, to be employed as a servant almost always meant a form of household service. Women were more likely than men to be incorporated into a household labour force as living-in servants, and this probably meant that their time was more completely at their employer's disposal. Certainly, they were required to be adaptable and to work at a wide variety of tasks both inside and outside the house, and few were able to acquire the occupational identities which some men were beginning to possess (Hilton, 1975; Emmison, 1976, pp. 147–64; Scott, 1973, p. 39–52).

In the opinion of contemporary male writers on good husbandry the value of an industrious and thrifty wife, properly trained in all the various arts of housewifery, was hardly capable of overstatement, and for no group was this more evident than the middling strata of independent farmers and craftsmen. 'To thrive one must wive' was the counsel of one popular sixteenth century author, for 'husbandrie otherwise speedeth not well' (Tusser, 1557). Did yeomen and men of similar rank keep such economic calculations uppermost in their minds when choosing a wife, or were they moved by more emotional and sexual impulses? We can still only conjecture (MacFarlane, 1970, pp. 94–7; Stone, 1977, pp. 292–7; Wrightson, 1981, pp. 66–88). But there can be no doubt that the advice was generally sound. A hardworking and provident wife was an indispensable material asset to any budding entrepreneur. If prosperous yeomen employed several women servants as well, it was not so that their wives and daughters could enjoy more ease and leisure; it was rather because there was too much work for them to cope alone.

The ways in which women's labour could augment the material wealth of the household were diffuse, but they can be dealt with conveniently under four headings. In the first place there was domestic work and production for home consumption – activities which were so interfused that they cannot sensibly be disentangled. The feeding and clothing of a substantial household was a complex business involving the processing of much farm produce before it could be stored or consumed. They include dairying, cheesemaking, brewing, baking, preserving, pickling, salting meat, spinning yarn, making and mending clothes and many more, and this was in addition to the work women did in the fields, the garden and in the yard looking after pigs and poultry (Scott, 1973). Mildred Campbell, the leading historian of the English yeomen, was convinced that it was this labour in conjunction with the field labour of men which enabled the class to profit from the long inflation.

> Rarely, if ever, did it happen that the yeomen did not have enough food to supply their own households, and wool with which to keep themselves in warm clothes. Hence the rise in the prices of these staples affected their expense outlay to a much less degree than it augmented their incomes . . . . They were also, because of their simple standard of living, spared much of the burden of increased costs that fell upon the gentry who found that clothes, house furnishings, and other articles procured from the outside were rising steadily in price (1942, pp. 186–7).

Moreover, by working the land, a rural wife or daughter could free a husband to engage, perhaps full-time, in some entirely separate sphere of production, with the prospect particularly of establishing himself in some rural industry (Thirsk, 1961; 1978; Middleton, forthcoming). In larger households the employment of female servants could likewise release the energies of a wife for profitable market-oriented activity, or to be used as a cheap substitute for hired day labour. The costs of expanding in this manner were minimal, not least because the wages of domestic servants were kept so abysmally low. In particular, the Statute of Artificers (1563), by prohibiting the unmarried person from 'living at one's owne hands', undermined in those areas where the regulations were zealously enforced the last vestiges of bargaining power which domestic servants might have possessed (Kelsall, 1938). The justices were especially anxious to force unmarried women into household service and in these circumstances it was not hard to keep pay low. On leaving her own household a girl would be ordered to enter the household service of another and would find herself in a situation where she earned little more than her keep – 'subsistence gained through domestic work, the paradigm of the woman's role in the household' (Scott, 1973, pp. 41–52).

Women were also heavily engaged in the production of goods for sale, ranging from simple extensions of domestic production (making more bread or ale than was needed by the immediate household; selling off vegetables or cheeses when there were some spare etc.), through to the systematic and regular production of agricultural surpluses or involvement in one of the rural industries. Producing for markets was not a new experience for English peasants. Even at the height of the feudal era there had been a not-inconsiderable market in farming surpluses and the products of home-manufacture. Commodity production had been a necessary counterpart of the commutation in rents (Middleton, 1979, pp. 152–5). But with the progressive development of the cloth industry from the fourteenth century and the later proliferation of rural industries, coupled with a marked increase in the stratification of farming families, this sort of activity acquired a new importance in the peasant household economy.

In large part the increase in productivity came through the provision of work for an under-utilised labour force. Whatever the range of activities involved in domestic production, for example, the amount of land held by a family or the availability of by-industrial work would be critical in determining the degree to which women could be productive. Thus the differentiation within the peasantry that took place during the Tudor and Stuart reigns, while it may have reduced the productiveness of women in many land-poor households, gave more work than ever to the women in yeomen families, as the number of stock they kept increased, their gardens were enlarged to meet the demand for cash crops and so on. As for the new industries, these did not at first rely on a landless proletariat, nor did they depend on a full-time specialised workforce. They were carried on rather by craftsmen who held land sufficient to provide food for the household and who often even had a surplus to sell. 'Industrial employment was thus an additional source of income, supplying more ready cash, but occupying the family for only part of the time' (Thirsk, 1978, p. 110). It is evident, therefore, that the greatest effect was felt by households in districts where labour had been chronically *under*employed – for the most part, that is, in the pasture farming areas of England rather than those predominantly given over to arable cultivation (Thirsk, 1961; 1967, pp. 2–16; Middleton, forthcoming).

It seems plain that the accumulation of capital by this sector of the population must have depended on the combined incomes of a number of commodity-producing activities. There is clear evidence, for the sixteenth and seventeenth centuries, of the importance of by-industry for households lower down the social scale, where it could make all the difference between mere subsistence and a modest acquisition of personal property (Everitt, 1967, pp. 425–9). How much more value, then, may it have yielded to yeomen households whose women were placed in a much stronger position in relation to the market? In the wool trade, for example, the spinner who owned her own wool could usually gain the full value of her labour by selling directly to the small clothier or weaver, rather than dealing through a middleman; if she were not wholly dependent on her spinning for a livelihood she could hold back the yarn to sell it in the dearest market; and even if she owned no wool of her own, but had to purchase it from the packhouse, she might still procure for herself, her children and her servants the greater part of the spinning work available, even at the expense of the poor (Clark, 1968, pp. 97–124; Scott, 1973, pp. 154–7).

This example indicates the fine line that sometimes existed between simple commodity production and wage-earning – the third possible source of income for women. On the whole, however, although there is some evidence of women working for wages, it was a very marginal source of income for women in substantial yeoman and craft-based households as their labour could usually be deployed more lucratively in other forms of production.

Finally, women – and especially wives – could act as assistants to the household head in the performance of his occupation. Direct cooperation of this kind was probably not typical of yeoman marriages in arable areas because of the conventional sexual division of labour that barred women of that class from participation in fieldwork (Campbell, 1942, p. 256); but in pasture farming districts the work of men and women in the care of livestock was obviously closely interlinked. It was in the towns, however, where the duties associated with domestic work were anyway much lighter, that wives were most frequently recorded as assistants or even partners in their husband's craft or trade, and they are sometimes found carrying it on after his death. The degree and kind of their assistance varied: sometimes a wife would be engaged in the preliminary or finishing processes of production, sometimes she would act as his buyer or selling agent, sometimes as manager of the household funds; and in some instances she appears to have acquired sufficient skill and knowledge of the trade to be able to instruct apprentices on her own account. By dint of these various means a wife's work could augment the household's income by acting as a substitute for hired labour, increasing the scope for specialisation, or helping to expand her husband's business. The fact that some guilds passed regulations specifically to prohibit the expansion of man's . trade by using his wife's labour in this way is perhaps the best evidence there is that such strategems were sometimes employed (Hutton, forthcoming; Scott, 1973, pp. 53–63).

In summarising the argument of this section it is worth stressing the fundamentally integrated character of the household economy. It would be quite artificial, for example, to posit that the production of commodities added to the surplus product whereas the production of goods for home consumption was necessary 'subsistence' labour. The household budget has to be treated in its entirety and, in the light of the evidence referred to above, I think it is safe to conclude that had it not been for the labour of women in the household, primitive accumulation by this 'revolutionary' route could never have taken place.

A case of patriarchal exploitation?

Finally, I wish to come back to the question of exploitation. Would we be justified in claiming that primitive accumulation by this method was built on the *exploitation* of subordinate household labour?

The master–servant relationship can be dealt with quite straightforwardly. There can be no doubt that, by any Marxist definition, household servants (most of whom, remember, were female) were exploited in the course of primitive accumulation. Though a living-in servant may have enjoyed a reasonable standard of food, clothing and accommodation by the standards of the labouring population, she was virtually coerced into service, was worked extremely hard for very little reward and, above all, was deprived of the product of her labour, beyond that needed for her maintenance, by a man who belonged to a family other than her own. She could not, in short, expect to enjoy the fruits of accumulation. Marriage, it would seem, was not the only or even the major instrument for the exploitation of women in this kind of household economy.

Any problems that arise in using the concept of 'exploitation' are clearly connected not with the master–servant relationship, but with that between a household-head and the rest of the family who worked under him. Put simply, even if we accept that family labour was necessary for primitive accumulation, can we seriously regard that labour as exploited inasmuch as family members shared in the benefits of accumulation – in a rising standard of living, in more generous marriage portions for daughters and, eventually, in increased scope for bourgeois women to lead a life of leisure? We could, I suppose, settle the matter a priori through a dogmatic assertion of definitional principles: men accumulated surplus wealth on the basis of family labour; therefore, the latter must have been exploited. But to affix conceptual labels without some reference to their social context and without some awareness of the *purposes* of the analytical schema of which they form a part, would seem to be a peculiarly arid activity. If we wish to resolve this difficulty in a reasonable and empirically-grounded way we must consider an aspect of exploitation which was not made explicit in our opening definition, namely that it entails some notion of the exercise and maintenance of a *power relationship* by which the surplus product is forcibly appropriated. It would therefore be sensible to reformulate our earlier question about primitive accumulation in the following way: 'Did the household labour of women, inasmuch as it contributed to accumulation, enable the emerging class of male capitalists to preserve or extend their domination over female members of this class?' The short answer is that it most probably did.

Consider first the nature of marital authority in this class. There has been a tendency of late for British historians to suggest that wives of this rank enjoyed a practical equality with their husbands grounded in their economic complementarity and cooperation (Wrightson, 1981, p. 93; see also, Power, 1975; MacFarlane, 1978). The claim is based on quite inadequate evidence: the unquestioned indispensability of women's work, marital quarrels over household finances, the fact that husbands often (sometimes?) consulted their wives over matters of family importance, the apparent care with which husbands made provision for their wives' widowhood. Sociologists who profess the discovery of a symmetrical family in modern Britain are able to support their claims with a much more substantial body of evidence than this, but few feminists would accept their arguments. Yet the meagre findings for the sixteenth and seventeenth centuries have to be placed in the context of a public and religious culture that was far more paternalistic than that which is prevalent today. Integrated and interdependent these household economies may have been; but to suggest that they were founded on a marital *partnership* is to invest language with an uncommon degree of flexibility. Authority, in fact, was strictly patriarchal. Essential powers of decision-taking, especially in regard to the disposition of resources, resided with the household-head – though it may well be that the exercise of those powers was influenced by genuine sentiments of love and consideration.

Under the feudal mode of production this structure of male domination had been anchored in the attempt to regulate women's *fertility* under the specific conditions of peasant landholding that characterised that system. In that context, the assertion of patriarchal control over family labour and decision-taking can be viewed as essentially derivative (Middleton, 1981). But, with the growth of the capitalist accumulation, the patriarchal centre of gravity shifted (at least, it did in the class being discussed here). It was the male head's appropriation of household labour which became pivotal in maintaining the edifice of patriarchy as the old bases of domination began to crumble.

In a persuasive essay on attitudes towards wage-labour in the sixteenth and seventeenth centuries, Christopher Hill has argued that the 'independent' Englishman identified liberty with something which he regarded as his birthright, but which wage-labour was presumed to deny. This birthright was his property in his own person and labour. As Hill develops this theme, however, it becomes apparent that for women the birthright was more than a little equivocal. 'Liberty', he writes, 'included the concept of property in one's own labour (*and that of one's family*).' What great tales can be told in a parenthesis! (Hill, 1967, p. 350, emphasis added.)

But the full significance of men's appropriation of women's labour can best be appreciated if we look at what was happening to openings for *independent* female economic activity. As Alice Clark demonstrated over sixty years ago, the scope for such activity by women in the middle ranks of society was being progressively narrowed (Clark, 1968). Women were being eliminated from a range of occupations, trades and crafts where they had previously operated with some degree of independence. Clark rightly attributed this process of exclusion in many instances to the advancing capitalistic organisation of industries and agriculture. But, in this event, capitalism was not operating in a 'sex-blind' fashion. The new industrial projects were actually *expanding* the range of opportunities for men with little capital, outside the traditional centres of craft, industry and trade. Women were unable to capitalise on the new possibilities because their surplus labour was being systematically drained off by their husbands or fathers. At the same time, in so far as they continued to engage in production, whilst losing many of their traditionally separate spheres of labour, they fell increasingly under the supervision of men (Bloch, 1978, pp. 238–45).

This shift in the basis of partriarchal power was crucial for its survival within the capitalist class that emerged from the ranks of petty producers. For whereas it is virtually impossible to imagine the establishment of a relatively stable structure of peasant landholding, under conditions of feudal exploitation, unless the patriarchal regulation of female procreativity is secured, there does not appear to be a similar *necessity* for the systematic exclusion of women from the ranks of capitalist employers or associated professions. The fact that so few women were able to resist the strategies of closure should thus be seen as a result of the rising male bourgeoisie's success in concentrating capital into its own hands; and it was the initial appropriation of household labour during the phase of primitive accumulation which made this patriarchal victory possible.

Undoubtedly, we will need a great deal more empirical documentation of this process before it could be argued with complete conviction, not least because there are certain pointers to alternative interpretations (e.g. the exclusion of women from some guilds may have preceded the main impact of capitalisation; there is a possibility that wives and daughters may have retained their own earnings in certain circumstances; and women, especially widows, may have had some role in the provision of credit for capitalist entrepreneurs, etc.). Nevertheless, I am fairly confident that the weight of the evidence will bear out the general conclusions of this paper.

It is only by exploring the possible connections between patriarchal exploitation and capitalist accumulation in particular historical conjunctures that we may rescue the former from serving merely as an article of faith and term of censure, and so transform it into a concept which has explanatory power. Using the concept of patriarchal exploitation in this paper has opened up possibilities on two fronts: it helps to fill a gap in the Marxist theory of capitalist accumulation; and it suggests a way in which the structure of male domination has shifted in the transition from feudalism to capitalism. An understanding of how patriarchy has developed historically may help eventually to turn moral censure into effective political practice.

Notes

1. In contrast to her general theorising Delphy's studies of concrete social relations are often subtle and certainly more nuanced (see, for example, Delphy, 1979).
2. We should not exaggerate the pace or uniformity of change, however. There was much regional and even local variation. In Gloucestershire, Tawney and Tawney found a system of family farms with little hired labour in 1608 (1934–5, p. 53).
3. A similar criticism can be made of the work of major non-Marxist historians who have studied the history of women's work. cf. Clark (1968), Pinchbeck (1981).

3 Not so much a Factory, More a Form of Patriarchy: Gender and Class during Industrialisation
Judy Lown

Introduction

As anyone attempting to analyse the ways in which women experience subordination knows, to start talking in terms of 'patriarchy' is to enter a conceptual minefield. The term has occupied a central place in feminist thinking over the last few years and has been subjected to a variety of interpretations and applications (Beechey, 1979). Among those who have been particularly pre-occupied with analysing the relationship between gender and class, a number of theoretical schema have been suggested.

One approach has been to attempt a reconciliation of analysis of class relations with those of male dominance through the conceptualisation of 'capitalism' and 'patriarchy' as coexisting systems (Hartmann, 1976; Eisenstein, 1979). Alternatively, it has been argued that the use of the term 'patriarchy' is inappropriate to conditions of modern industrial society and should be reserved for specific situations characterised by the direct exercise of authority by fathers and husbands over wives and children and by older men over younger men (Young and Harris, 1976; Edholm, Harris and Young, 1977; Cockburn, 1981; Fox-Genovese, 1982). In its place, concepts such as 'sex-gender system' (Rubin, 1975) and 'andrarchy' (Cockburn, 1981) have been suggested to cater more suitably for the pervasiveness and longevity of systems of male dominance.

Inherent in many of these debates is an assumption that the location of the 'original causes' of male domination is of prime importance: that once these have been established the link between a pre-defined system of class relations and the persistence of unequal gender relations can be traced. The main problem with this approach is that it inevitably leads to a search for the sources of male dominance *outside* of the social relations between men and women themselves (Friedman, 1982).

Even where attention has been focused on relationships specifically centring on women's experience, such as those of reproduction,

(McDonoagh and Harrison, 1978; O'Brien, 1981), it has proved difficult to avoid the kind of dualistic notions of social relations which characterise so many accounts. These dualistic models generally rely on making a distinction of some sort between economic hierarchies which are rooted in the mode of production and gender hierarchies which are shaped in the sphere of familial and reproductive relations, and it is the economic hierarchies which are usually afforded ultimate analytical pre-eminence.

To avoid the deterministic, and sometimes reductionist tendencies of these models, my use of the term 'patriarchy' is posited on the possibility of economic and familial relations being a *single process* with no causal variable lying beyond the privileges and advantages accruing to those who benefit from such a process.

The concept of 'patriarchy'

One of the reasons why many approaches continue to separate the 'economic' from the 'familial' is because of a pre-occupation with causation. When radical feminists first started employing the concept of 'patriarchy' (Millet, 1969; Rich, 1977) they recognised that a search for origins was empirically impossible. The accusation from Marxist feminists that writers such as Millet were adopting a transhistorical usage of the concept 'patriarchy' is unfounded since these early writings made it clear that one of the central concerns was the historical development of different patriarchal forms (Friedman, 1982b).

What the critics of this perspective seem to ignore is that the concept of 'patriarchy' is being employed as an analytical tool with which to identify the nature of political relations between men and women. If it is theoretically tenable to analyse historical and cultural variations of 'economic class' relations it should be acceptable to look for the varying forms of political relationships between men and women. Such a project only becomes unacceptable when theoretical primacy is attributed to relationships of an 'economic class' nature. Radical feminists continue to emphasise that it is power relationships between men and women which they wish to explore and that it is for this purpose that 'patriarchy' provides a central analytical tool (Barry, 1979; Dworkin, 1981; see also 'Interview with Andrea Dworkin' in *Feminist Review*, Summer 1982).

Rather than conceptualise patriarchy in terms of an outmoded familial form, my argument is based on the notion of unequal power relations of gender and age forming a central axis of historical and social change. When patriarchal relations are recognised as a pivotal organising principle of society, and not just a facet of one particular historical formation, the need to distinguish conceptually between 'the economy', on the one hand, and 'the family', on the other, becomes irrelevant. Power relationships between men and women cut across every aspect of social existence, and, being located historically, are subject to change. Only by exploring the material conditions of women's lives can the changing nature of these political relations be understood.

It is from these premises that I wish to illustrate the relevance of the concept of 'patriarchy' to an understanding of social stratification in modern industrial society. I shall begin this exercise by turning to some of the recent attempts by feminists to reconceptualise such archetypal notions as 'the family', 'class', 'sexuality' and 'violence' and by measuring these reconceptualisations against the historical record.

I am limiting this particular exercise to one particular industry in one particular geographical area – a Courtaulds silk mill in the town of Halstead in North East Essex. Furthermore, only a small proportion of the total body of data can be presented here.[1] The argument therefore inevitably remains at a very schematic level. In focusing primarily on the nature of the power relationships involved, however, it is aimed at identifying some of the historically changing circumstances in which relations of domination and subordination between men and women can occur.

Deconstructing familiar concepts

One of the major contributions towards rethinking our conceptual apparatus has come from writers of various disciplines who have emphasised the need to distinguish between 'households' as forms of living arrangements and 'families' as particular constellations of ideals and attitudes (Rupp *et al.*, 1980; Rosaldo, 1980; Chaytor, 1980; Thorn and Yalom, 1982). These writers underline the importance of avoiding twentieth century assumptions about the experiences and meanings of lives lived in previous centuries. Special attention has been drawn to the way in which 'household' and 'family' were not coterminous ideologically and structurally in past times in the way they are assumed to be in present-day industrial society.

To employ the concept of patriarchy is not to limit the boundaries of analysis to locales where fathers have direct rule over their wives and offspring but rather to recognise that relationships of male supremacy are located in the socio-cultural significance of familial relations as an organising principle of societies. The 'traditional' patriarch within pre-industrial households was *not* the biological father to all over whom he had authority. Young apprentices, stepchildren and servants of both sexes, as well as the wife and immediate offspring, could come under the familial authority of the male father/master (Flandrin, 1979; Chaytor and Lewis, 1982; Kussmaul, 1978). Likewise, feudal lordship, so often characterised as patriarchal, was frequently typified by the lord acting as a surrogate father to sons of his vassals living as pages at his court (Roberts, 1979). The relationship in each case was both economic *and* familial. What distinguished the position of all those who came under the authority of the paterfamilias was the relationship of *dependency* in which they lived. They occupied a separate and distinctive category in pre-industrial conceptuali- sations of the social order, deriving their status from their dependency on their masters, fathers and husbands.

Intrinsic to this status was the provision of services to the men upon whom they were dependent in order to ensure daily survival. As with the conditions of existence of all relationships of dependency, those who occupied the superordinate position also relied on the services of their dependants for their own survival and status and were faced with certain obligations themselves. Being in a more powerful position rendered the fulfiment of these obligations, however, a matter frequently of individual will and widespread variation. It was a superordinate position, moreover, which was supported by and reflected in the political institutions and customs of society (Fox-Genovese, 1977; see also Clark and Lange, 1979).

Dependency, therefore, had far-reaching implications for these defined within its parameters. On this account, marriage also becomes integral to, not separate from, economic analysis. Research on earlier periods has begun to explore some of the political implications of the marriage contract (Shanley, 1979), and radical rethinking of history and economics has been urged by writers sensitive to the ramifications of the material nature of the marital relationship (Kelly-Cadol, 1975; Kelly, 1979; Delphy, 1980; Leghorn and Parker, 1981).

Patriarchal authority was not something which was 'dismantled' by bourgeois revolutions (Fox-Genovese, 1982) but constituted a structure and set of principles which were embodied in varying institutional and customary forms. As such, it must be analysed as part of the material arrangements of the society and subject to historical change in the same way as other material forms.

This was a traditional form of authority, then, that characterised not only productive and reproductive arrangements but stood at the centre of all institutional arrangements, significantly political, legal and religious arrangements, and which was to continue as a focal organising principle throughout the process of industrialisation and despite the increasing ideological equation of 'family' with blood relationships between parents and offspring. Indeed, this very change in the definition of 'the family' forms a major plank in the strategies adopted to ensure the continuation of patriarchal power in an era when gender relationships, and political and social stability generally, were being severely threatened.

The pursuit of strategies aimed at legitimating their superordinate position is a prominent characteristic of holders of traditional forms of power (Newby, 1975). The continuation of the economic, political and social benefits which men gained in pre-industrial society largely depended upon a whole chain of exchanges and obligations in which marriage provided a crucial link. Marriage played a central role in the movement of people and property from one household to another whereby men acquired status and prestige through the property and wealth so accumulated and women derived their status from their relationship to men (Chaytor, 1980).

Regardless of the multifarious activities in which women participated in order to help sustain the households in which they lived (Clarke, 1982; Hufton, 1975) they lacked the opportunity to develop the same sort of 'work identity' which men gained through their formalised systems of apprenticeship and the public and political recognition of their work status (Davies, 1982). The strong identification of women and girls as familial dependants, whether they lived in the house of their own father or husband or as a servant in that of someone else's father or husband, largely ensured their continued subordination, although occupying such a position in the social hierarchy did not preclude instances of rebellion and defiance.

New insights have also been brought to bear upon the concept of 'class'. Again, feminist historians have been significant, for instance, in drawing our attention to the need to examine the differential experiences of male and female members of both the working class and the middle class and the role of gender definitions in influencing those experiences (Alexander, 1976; Burman, 1979, Davidoff, 1973, 1979; Taylor, 1979; Ryan, 1981). What these studies have highlighted is the need to avoid subsuming gender relations under those of a pre-defined system of class relations and the importance of analysing processes of distinctively male interests and privileges. They reveal, above all, the need to examine the processes whereby gender and class are constructed *simultaneously*.

In other words, we can no more talk about 'the economy' as if it had fixed and unambiguous boundaries as we can do about 'the family'. Only by looking through a single lens at these 'two worlds in one' (Pleck, 1976) can we begin to distinguish more clearly the actual nature of many of the interests standing at the centre of historical and social change.

The third area of feminist research to enable this adjustment of sights on examining our past has been in the area of sexuality and physical violence. Significant here, of course, has been the increasing emphasis on these phenomena as social constructions (*Signs*, 1980; Barry, 1979; Brownmiller, 1975; Friedman and Sarah, 1982) and their role in the social control of women. Hitherto relegated to the realm of 'natural' differences, these areas of inequality have, again, focused attention on the need to specify behaviour and meanings that distinctively benefit men at the expense of women.

What all these attempts at deconstructing familiar concepts share is a common concern to re-examine the analytical boundaries between the 'public' and 'private' spheres. A major problem facing all feminist scholars has been the difficulty of working in disciplines that have themselves developed concepts and whole systems of thought that reflect and reinforce these boundaries. Built into these systems of thought is a conflation of the 'general' with the masculine, a restriction of the notion of 'the material' to the realm of 'the public' and a blindness to the social and historical significance of gender.

It is as inappropriate to think in terms of patriarchy being a redundant concept as it is to regard capitalism as a thing of the past. In this respect, the questioning of the term 'patriarchy' is reminiscent of the search for new conceptualisations of modern stratification systems in terms of 'post capitalist' developments and the 'managerial revolution' (Dahrendorf, 1959; Burnham, 1941). To explore and understand modern-day social relations of patriarchy is no more futile than an examination of the contemporary dynamics of capitalist social relations.

What is difficult, of course, is to analyse the social relations of both within a single focus. This is a procedure made even more complex by the fact that patriarchal relations are generally regarded as being of a different order than capitalist relations and as being more pervasive both historically and cross-culturally.

In this respect, we are only beginning to discover ways of thinking about these issues simultaneously. The most fruitful avenue so far, however, must lie in the increasing attempts to collapse the analytical division between 'the public' and 'the private'. If we do this, patriarchal power can be characterised in terms of organising and rationalising social relations based on male superiority and female inferiority which, *at one and the same time*, take an economic and familial form, and which pervade the major institutions and belief systems of the society.

The particular constellation of social relations is obviously historically and culturally specific, but a major key to locating the significance of patriarchal power lies in an understanding of the nature of traditional authority. We have been led to believe that, on a societal level, traditional authority has given way either to impersonal capitalist control or, to retain the Weberian terminology, to rational–legal systems of authority. These notions are, of course, predicated on the whole public/private dichotomy and fail to recognise the ways in which traditional authority has not only survived but actually shaped the changing relations of industrial society.

One important vehicle through which such a process can be illustrated is the phenomenon of paternalism.

Patriarchy and paternalism
The social and historical significance of paternalism has been the subject

of revived academic interest of late (Roberts, 1979; Stearns, 1979; Joyce, 1980). The role of paternalism in securing and maintaining social stability has been of particular concern. Characterised in terms of rights and duties pertaining to relationships based on authority, property and social rank, paternalism has been identified as a crucial means of rationalising the social order at different periods throughout the pre-industrial era (Roberts, 1979). Originally associated with a social hierarchy shaped out of relationships to the land, increasing interest has been shown in the way in which paternalism figured as a key feature among certain industrialists of the nineteenth century.

Three factors are identifiable as merging to produce a resurgence of paternalist relations during the nineteenth century; the perceived threat to the social order contained in the processes of industrialisation and urbanisation, the continuation of rural cultural ties into urban settings, and the aspirations of the ascendant industrialists to cultivate among themselves a 'gentlemanly ethic' whereby they could compete with the landed aristocracy as legitimate superordinates in the local social hierarchy.

What is significant about these developments is that paternalism relies heavily on an appeal to personal ties of dependency and that these ties are interpreted in familial terms. In Roberts' words, 'To be a paternalist was to act towards dependants *as a father does to his wife, his children and his servants.*' (emphasis added).

Is what we are witnessing in the paternalist practice and philosophy of nineteenth-century manufacturers, therefore, an attempt to reconstitute patriarchal relations, hitherto located primarily in the household/workshop, within the factory and its environment? Can we identify a process whereby familial relationships were not simply being utilised as a system of accommodation into the factory system (Hareven, 1982) but were actually being used as an organising principle of workplace relations?

If this was the case, traditional authority, far from being left behind in the home, was being carried into market relationships as well, and constituting a primary factor in the shaping of gender and age hierarchies in the society as a whole and for future as well as contemporary generations.

A distinctive feature of this new form of paternalism was its appeal not only to ties of dependency based on the peculiar combination of industrial property holding and rural cultural bonds but its strong association with the new domestic ideology, which stressed the primary identification of women with home and children and men as breadwinners, and its relationship to a legal and political system which marginalised and subordinated women's access to property and citizenship rights. (For instance, married women had no claim to their earnings until the 1870s and, of course, no woman could vote until after the First World War.)

In many ways these developments were a continuation of the traditional marriage and authority relationships of pre-industrial times, the essential feature of which, as we have seen, is *dependency*. Women, children and servants were always a separate category. They never had the same legal, educational, religious, political or property rights as men. They never had access to the equivalent 'work identity' as men. They were always expected to provide services for men.

In the nineteenth century, domestic ideology provided a useful legitimating source of control, but when this failed, ideas sanctioning the need to keep women in their 'natural' place and constrain their 'unnatural' behaviour could make way for physical coercion and restraint. Thus it is not unusual to find that a blind eye was frequently turned towards the use and threat of physical violence by men towards women.

It is not difficult, therefore, to see why paternalism with its strong emphasis on locality, community, and totality of relationships had such an appeal to manufacturers in the nineteenth century, and not just to manufacturers either. The distinctively male interests tied up in paternalism are visible in so far as it was a theme embraced by figures as different as romantic poets such as Southey and Coleridge, Peelite MPs such as Gladstone and Palmer, country squires such as Lord John Manners and Sir John Trollope, and political radicals such as William Cobbett (Roberts, 1979).

Paternalism has, of course, been noted for the deferential nature of the relationships it embodies. Writers who have been reworking the notion of deference, however, emphasise its normative and relational characteristics (Newby, 1975). It is a form of social interaction, associated with the exercise of traditional authority, which contains possibilities of both subservience *and* rebellion. Its origins lie in 'the processes of legitimation by tradition of the hierarchical nature of the social structure by those in superordinate positions' (Newby, 1975). In other words, it is the *outcome* of the stratification system and not the source of it. Those occupying superordinate positions have to manage the tensions that arise in a hierarchically ordered social structure and the way in which they do this depends upon their own sources of power.

This distinction aids a conceptual clarification of the terms 'patriarchy' and 'paternalism'. While the two are often conflated, we do need to distinguish between, on the one hand, a hierarchical system whereby adult men occupy superordinate positions of power over women, children and younger men, namely *patriarchy*, and the forms of social interaction that occur in such hierarchical systems whereby the power of those in superordinate positions (i.e. men) is legitimated, namely *paternalism*.

In this respect, we should not equate paternalism with patriarchy (Fox-

Genovese, 1982), but we should certainly trace the links between the two and extend our scope of analysis to examining the many and varying forms of legitimation that holders of patriarchal power adopt, of which paternalism is but one. A reluctance to let go of an analysis which attributes ultimate causation of women's subordination in contemporary capitalist societies to the 'need' of 'capital' to extract surplus value serves to hinder this endeavour. The constant reification of capitalism obscures the historical reality of both capitalists and workers as gendered beings with differing interests and stakes in the material features of employment *and* marital arrangements. Viewed from this vantage point, capitalists as capitalists were not the only beneficiaries of nineteenth-century social and economic change.

Without looking for determining factors beyond the advantages accruing to men from the maintenance of a familially defined social and economic order, then, an area characterised by the presence of a large manufacturing concern at the centre of a 'village folded within a town' (Joyce, 1980) can be analysed in terms of the sources of power available to the industrial elite in maintaining its superordinate position and the consequences of the strategies adopted for the lives of men, women and children in the locality.

In developing this argument through the use of material relating to just one nineteenth-century silk mill, the intention is not to plead any typicality for the circumstances described. Rather key problems concerning the kinds of contestable issues that surrounded the lives of those involved in the mill will be discussed. Aspects of industrialisation that usually remain hidden can thus emerge. In particular, as well as documenting the differential effects of factory life for men and women, it will be argued that women in fact *cushioned* the effects of industrialisation for men. The ways in which women experienced industrialisation *enabled* men to secure a better deal out of the social and economic changes taking place. The processes by which this took place were by no means even, but they can only be understood by perceiving the essentially *patriarchal* interests at stake for men in both middle-class and working-class positions. The shape those interests took depended greatly, of course, on the particular configuration of class and gender characteristics prevalent for men occupying different positions in the social structure.

It is an elaboration of the issues through which such interests can be explored which is the main aim of the remainder of this paper.

The Halstead silk mill: gender at work
The mill that provided the material for this exercise was one established by Samuel Courtauld, the founder of the Courtauld empire, which now is one of the ten biggest multinationals originating from this country. As part

Table 3.1   Courtauld employees at Halstead, 1861

	No.	Approximate weekly wages	Age	Most frequent Marital status
Males				
Mill manager	1	£1000 p.a. (+ 3% profits)	Over 30	Married
Overseers and clerks	26	15/- to 32/6	Over 30	Married
Mechanics and engine drivers	6	17/- to 25/6	Over 30	Married
Carpenters and blacksmiths	3	14/- to 21/-	Over 30	Married
Lodgekeeper	1	15/- + handlm. produce	Over 40	Married
Power loom machinery attendants and steamers	16	14/- to 15/-	Over 20	Married
Mill machinery attendants and loom cleaners	18	10/- to 15/-	Over 20	Married
Spindle cleaners, bobbin stampers and packers, messengers and sweepers	5	5/- to 12/-	Between 14 and 25 and over 40	Single Married
Watchmen	NA	7/- to 10/-	NA	NA
Coachmen, grooms and van driver	NA	5/- to 10/-	NA	NA
Winders	38	2/- to 4/6	12–15	Single
Total males	114			
Females				
Gauze examiners	4	10/- to 11/-	Over 30	Married
Female assistant overseers	4	9/- to 10/-	Over 30	Married
Warpers	16	7/6 to 10/-	Over 20	Married
Twisters	9	7/- to 10/-	Over 20	Married
Wasters	4	6/6 to 9/-	Over 20	Married
Weavers	589	5/6 to 8/-	Over 17	Single & Married
Plugwinders	2	6/- to 7/6	Over 20	Married
Drawers and doublers	83	4/- to 6/-	Over 17	Married
Winders	188	2/- to 4/-	12–17	Single
Housekeeper	1	NA	NA	NA
Schoolteacher	1	NA	NA	NA
Total females	901			

Total males and females: 1015[a]
(Actual total in 1857:   1089)

Note: [a] The figure of 1015 represents the total number of employees upon whom it was possible to construct reliable employment profiles from the business records. The figure of 1089 refers to the actual total of employees recorded as present in the year 1857.

Sources: Courtauld Registers of Employees, 1830–1919 (E.R.O. DF 3/3/1 to 3/3/10): Wages Book, 1852–1876 (E.R.O. DF 3/3/27; Letters Book of Mill Manager, 1873–1890 (E.R.O. DF 3/3/22); Memo Book, 1873–1896 (E.R.O. DF 3/3/24).

of his business ventures into the silk industry, he set up a mill in the town of Halstead in Essex in 1825. Although initially powered by water, steam-engines were being introduced by 1828 with a total labour force in this mill alone of 390 in 1838. The firm specialised in the manufacture of black crepe for the ever increasing and reliable market in middle-class mourning attire. The majority of the hands employed in the mill were female. For most of the nineteenth century the proportion of females employed was never less than 75% and in the 1860s it was close to 90%.

After the early days of heavy reliance on workhouse labour, Courtauld began to draw more and more on women and girls, both single and married, living in cottages in the locality. He was also recruiting a small number of men, however, so it is useful to look at the different kinds of jobs into which females and males were being directed.

By the 1860s two distinct hierarchies of labour can be detected, one consisting entirely of females and the other almost entirely of males. Table 3.1 shows the occupational categories and the approximate wage levels, ages and marital status of each group.

The majority of the men were clearly in jobs that involved the maintenance of the machinery and the supervision of the workforce. By far the largest group of women were employed on operating the powerlooms at wage levels which were approximately half those of the male attendants and less than a quarter of some of the male overseers. Moreover, most of the women were paid piece-rates whereas the men received a flat-rate, and mobility patterns were primarily horizontal for women while they were vertical for men.

The factory was not without its disputes, however, and it was women, on every occasion, who were central in the action. In May 1860, the powerloom weavers went on strike over a speed-up in production which adversely affected their piece-rates. The *Halstead Gazette* reported a meeting held by the women on Market Hill near the mill and commented on the fact that a woman was addressing the crowd. On this occasion, however, the women were unsuccessful. Samuel Courtauld reacted by directing an immediate lock-out and the dismissal of between 20 and 50 of those who had been 'foremost in this shameful disorder'.

A similar dispute in the early 1870s was more successful as, at this time, Courtauld was facing increased competition for labour from domestic service which was attracting many younger women away from the mill. Concessions were actually made and piece-rates improved.

Paternalism and the 'domestic ideal'

That the employers felt uncomfortable about women's employment in factories is clearly evidenced in a number of comments that they made, of which George Courtauld II's statement in a letter written in 1846, is typical:

Among the girls and young women the various evils of ignorance are not only much aggravated by their being brought together in large numbers and to some extent compelled to associate – but the nature of their employment takes from them even the poor preparation they might have received at their homes for the duties of wives and mothers.[2]

In order to continue relying on large numbers of cheap female hands and, at the same time, to enable them to construct women as essentially domestic creatures, the Courtaulds undertook a number of strategies aimed at facilitating the combination of employment with domestic duties by the women.

In the first place, they undertook a number of philanthropic projects based on 'improving' the welfare of the women and girls in their employment. In December 1850, an infant nursery was set up to look after the young children of the married women. Children of between one month and 2 years were accepted and a sum of fourpence a day charged. In the same year, regular monthly 'Maternal Meetings' were set up and run by Mrs Clements, the wife of the Baptist minister in Halstead. Married women from the factory were particularly encouraged to attend to learn about domestic chores, health and hygiene with the help of such journals as the *Mother's Friend* and *Readings for Mothers' Meetings*.

Meanwhile, the young single women who worked at the mill were being recruited into the evening school which was started in 1847. The school mistress was a 'middle class' woman called Mary Merryweather, who taught a curriculum including health and hygiene, nature study, geography, letter-writing and moral stories.

Other attempts at paternalistic enterprises included the setting up of a boarding house, called Factory Home, in 1849 to provide lodgings for girls who came from the surrounding villages and to attract them away from lodging with 'a class of women particularly adverse to morality' who 'positively helped to instruct and encourage them in abandoned courses'.[3] Courtauld had no luck with employing women of 'bad morals' in his mill. In a classic demonstration of the 'double standard' (Thomas, 1959; Trudgill, 1976), women but not men were dismissed for sexual 'offences', many of which were no doubt a product of the low wages and vulnerable conditions in which women lived. Such 'offences' included suspected prostitution, having illegitimate children, helping to procure abortions and living with men while unmarried.

At the same time, paternalistic practices were being directed at the men too. The Mechanics Institute was set up under Courtauld's auspices in 1849 and the men were encouraged to attend not only the meetings and lectures organised there but to also take part in the temperance movement, of which the Courtaulds were supporters.

As Unitarians, the Courtaulds fully espoused the values of hard work and the educative and moral duties of the wealthy captains of industry (CFL, 1916; Coleman, 1969; Holt, 1938). There are clear links to be drawn here with the Evangelicals' attempts to reconstruct everyday morality based primarily on a reconceptualisation of the position of the woman in the household (Hall, 1979).

Principles of rationalism and moral revitalisation projected Samuel Courtauld into the role of a kind of surrogate father/patriarch as far as running his firm was concerned. He was both protector and moral arbitrator. He shared the familiar middle class notion that poverty was not an economic problem but a moral one (Summers, 1979), and that, in putting the houses of the poor in order, the 'virtuous ladies' of his class had not only a moral but a 'natural role' to play in the form of philanthropic and charitable activities.

Running through all their paternalistic activities was a persistent attempt to construct femininity and masculinity in their own image. It is almost as if by trying to proselytize to others the Courtaulds were trying to convince themselves. They needed to find a secure position for themselves in the local social structure, as members of the industrial *nouveau riche* establishing themselves in an area where they had to compete for credibility with the local landed aristocracy. As part of this endeavour, Samuel Courtauld bought the former manorial estate of Gosfield Hall in 1854, together with 2000 acres of agricultural land.

The notion of 'the family' in this context served as a favourable arena in which the Courtaulds could seek to effect their duties and obligations to the labouring poor. Paternalistic provisions helped to bridge the contradictions of depending upon a labour force stocked primarily with people whom the employers essentially conceptualised as belonging to the home.

It was probably in these areas of struggle, however, that women were able to offer the most resistance at times. The firm's nursery had to be closed down after less than three years since the women simply refused to use it. They preferred their own means of childcare, such as paying a young girl 1/6 a week or leaving their infants with elderly female relatives or neighbours. Co-residence patterns were very similar to those identified in other industrial areas during this period (Anderson, 1971) and were mostly constructed around kin connections between female members of the household.

The Factory Home also had to be closed down after seven years through lack of use. After several incidents where the girls rebelled against the discipline in the Home, even burning copies of the rules which were pinned up in every room, the numbers lodging there gradually dwindled until no girl could be induced to live there.

The other form taken by strategies aimed at facilitating the domesticity of the female workers was the ease with which women were allowed to enter and leave the workforce. Although three-quarters of the female workforce had no absences of any significant length recorded, the remainder had employment records which were punctuated by short periods of temporary absence. The most common reasons stated for such absences were marriage and childbirth, moving away, domestic service, soft-silk weaving at home, or looking after relatives. What such characteristics show is that the rhythm of household life-cycles – marriage, having children, how many children there were and how old they were, whether there were aged parents present, what sort of employment other members of the household were engaged in – had far more influence on their employment record at the mill than it did for male employees. It was *women* who were expected to take time out from the mill.

Yet no one questioned women's right to be employed in the mill. As far as the women themselves were concerned they always had worked and they were simply continuing to do so – it was the location and conditions which were largely changed. In the case of Samuel Courtauld, he was not going to add his voice to those objecting to women's factory employment as long as he was benefiting from it.

With respect to the husbands and fathers of the female silk-workers, it was not in their interests at this stage to object to women's factory employment in the way that working-class men in some other industries and regions were. As far as the men who were predominantly agricultural labourers were concerned, and the other men engaged in low paid labouring jobs, they were benefiting from both the economic contributions of their wives and daughters to the household and, at the same time, the ability of their female kin to stay at home or adopt other forms of employment for short periods when circumstances required it. As for the small core of male workers in the mill they too had no fear for their jobs since the women and girls were so clearly segregated into a separate hierarchy of labour and they too were benefiting from the marginalisation of women 'freeing' them to combine both wage labour and domestic and other household based duties. In other words, working-class men were benefiting from the 'double burden' being borne by most of the women.

Despite the resistance which the women were able to offer in the face of particular forms of wage control, factory discipline and domestic training which confronted them, they were still being deprived of a primary 'work identity' and were, in the long term, suffering even more far reaching losses in terms of their access to and status in the local labour market.

Disputes outside the mill

Contestable issues were also being raised beyond the mill gates concerning resources and responsibilities connected to household and kin duties.

Reports of court proceedings in Halstead in the 1860s document a number of cases of violence being used by men against women in disputes concerning paternity and the welfare of children.

A woman was particularly financially vulnerable when there was no male wage-earner in the household. Her earnings were unlikely to be sufficient to maintain young children as well as herself. One in six of the households in Halstead in 1861 were headed by women and 38% of these were silk-workers.[4] These women did not share the same sort of earning power and status as the male heads of household. The existence of patriarchy does *not* require every head of household to be male.

There is no doubt then that all the women living in Halstead – even those with access to jobs in the mill, commanding higher wages than women not employed in silk – were in a vulnerable situation as far as financial survival was concerned. The lowness of their wages forced them into further dependence on men. In turn, the possibility of men deserting their wives increased the likelihood of the burden of dependence of children and elderly relatives falling on women. Even in situations of poverty, which was widespread among Halstead inhabitants, it was frequently the wife who bore the greatest burden (Oren, 1973). As we have seen from the employment records, it was women who took time off for the care of elderly or infirm kin.

We must remember too that the period in question is before the passing of the Married Women's Poverty Act in 1870, so women still had no legal right to their earnings. Both before and after the Act, control over earnings may well have provided another area of dispute between men, women and children in households. Other court cases occasionally mentioned a dispute over rent or money, but altercations over the actual control and distribution of income inside households might well have evaded the intervention of the courts although other researchers have revealed useful material on this issue (Tomes, 1977–78).

Physical abuse by husbands of their wives was commented upon by Mary Merryweather as a common occurrence. She remarks upon the fact that,

> If we said to a poor woman who came for relief, 'I hope your husband is kind to you', the answer often was, 'well Ma'am, he don't pay me', [beat me], implying that she was grateful for that amount of goodness.[5]

These are all areas of control and conflict which rarely receive serious analytical attention in histories of factory life and underline another aspect of the distinctiveness of women's experience of industrialisation. Furthermore, these areas of dispute focusing on household and kin responsibilities and women's physical and sexual integrity highlight other important spheres in which men's *patriarchal* interests manifested themselves. In the rearrangement of productive relationships men's status in the household and control over women's labour and bodies was also a crucial issue at stake.

Conclusion

It is not, then, exclusively the *different types* of experience as between men and women which should concern us. What is of significance, particularly in the feminist project of clarifying our theoretical understanding of various forms of women's subordination, is the light shed by historical studies on the nature of *social relations* between men and women.

Through examining struggles which cross the analytical boundaries between household and workplace, 'private' and 'public', the interconnections between kin and household organisation, on the one hand, and production, on the other, become much clearer. In the case of the Courtaulds' mill, we can see how, with paternalism acting as a major vehicle for such reconfigurations, adult men, whether as capitalists or workers, emerged from mechanisation and factory organisation with authority and control in varying degrees and types over female kin and non-kin and over younger males. New hierarchies took shape, with the factory itself becoming an embodiment of 'family' ideals and the employer as father/patriarch at the head. Patriarchal relations were being reformulated in both the home *and* the workplace.

Essential to the task of analysing these kinds of developments is the possession of conceptual apparatus which can specify different types of power interests which are present in the creation and recreation of gender and class.

Historically, unequal gender hierarchies have been located in stratification systems whereby adult males occupied superordinate positions to which women, even if they were titular heads, could not aspire. Great variations in household arrangements and authority patterns have existed, of course (Berkner, 1975; Goody, Thirsk and Thompson, 1976; Harris, 1981) but the social and jural protection afforded to men has ensured the widespread exclusion of women.

Incipient conflicts of an 'economic class' nature had many of their roots in tensions surrounding patriarchal interests *vis-à-vis* the widening gap between journeymen and masters in the guild system (Clawson, 1980; see also Lazonick, 1978). The growth of workshops and the increasing power of the masters was a threat to the social and economic significance of journeymen as patriarchs. The social, economic and political standing of men was synonymous with their position as patriarchal heads.

In the social and economic transformation which was to alter the productive and reproductive arrangements of emergent capitalist societies, patriarchal interests were at the very centre of the struggles reshaping the class and gender hierarchies.

Intrinsic to men's attempts to secure a livelihood was the maintenance of their status and power as patriarchs. This was at stake in their competition with women for wage labour as much as their interest in securing jobs – because economic status meant patriarchal power: the two were inseparable.

The case of the Halstead mill outlines only one instance of the ways in which such struggles were fought out. But a study of factory employment does underline the ideological concerns of the period and some of the key processes underlying the construction of gender and class. If it doesn't aid generalisation, it adds to our knowledge of historically specific circumstances in which gender and class interact. Central to the Courtauld experience was the realignment of patriarchal interests whereby a gender and occupational hierarchy was being negotiated which structurally marginalised women's economic status and ideologically restricted them to the realm of the 'domestic'. Moreover, the Courtauld experience highlights the way in which patriarchal interests were maintained even in the face of the fact of women's employment outside the home.

To conceptualise the developments in the Halstead silk industry in terms of patriarchal interests is by no means to connote monolithic and all-powerful dimensions to male power. The degree of success or failure of patriarchal interests in particular instances depended, as we have seen, on specific constellations of circumstances in which the relative amount of resources and bargaining power available to women was especially significant.

The ramifications, however, reach beyond the small town of Halstead in the latter decades of the nineteenth century. With the increasing penetration of capital into former agricultural economies all over the world the need to analyse the interconnections between changes in household and kin organisation and production have been accentuated. The distance in time and geography between nineteenth-century Essex and twentieth-century countries of the Third World may seem gigantic but the conceptual equipment needed to make sense of the gender and class relationships in both may be much more similar than we sometimes allow ourselves to think.

Notes
1. For a fuller presentation of the historical data see Judy Lown, *Gender and Class during Industrialisation: A Study of the Halstead Silk Industry in Essex 1815–1900.* Unpublished Ph.D. thesis, Department of Sociology, University of Essex.

2. S. A. Courtauld (ed.), *Courtauld Family Letters, 1782–1900* vol. vii, 1915, p. 3193, emphasis original.
3. Mary Merryweather, *Experiences of Factory Life*, London, 1862, p. 43.
4. This information on households comes from records constructed on a 20% sample of Courtauld employees from the 1861 Halstead census enumerator's books.
5. Merryweather, p. 19.

Acknowledgements
I owe many thanks to Leonore Davidoff for all her help and support during the writing of this paper, and should also like to thank Katherine Clarricoates, Cynthia Enloe, Annabel Faraday, Scarlet Friedman, Catherine Hall, Jane Lewis, Jo Sutton, the editors of this volume and the participants of the workshop at the BSA 'Gender and Society' conference in April, 1982, where this paper was first presented, for all their helpful suggestions and comments.

I am also grateful to the Courtauld family whose business records, which formed the source material for the bulk of this research, are deposited at the Essex Record Office, and to the University of Essex library staff who enabled me to use the nineteenth-century census enumerator's records at the university library.

4 Women, Men and Social Class
Nicky Britten and Anthony Heath

Introduction

The treatment of women in classifications of social class has become something of a scandal. As Delphy has pointed out, a double standard has generally operated in the sense that if a woman is single, her own occupation is used as the criterion of her class position; but if she is married, it is her husband's occupation which is used instead (Delphy, 1981, p. 116). Even when married women's own occupations are taken into account, those who are not employed are attributed their husbands' occupations, so that a crucial factor – the presence or absence of economic independence – is obscured. It follows that the measurement of a woman's class position must take into account the question of her economic dependence or independence as well as the character of her job (if she has one).

Against this it might be argued that in practice the great majority of married women in Britain, even those with jobs, actually are dependent on their husbands and that the distinctions drawn by Delphy, whatever their conceptual validity, are nonetheless of little empirical consequence. In Britain the majority of employed married women are working part-time and their economic participation may have a somewhat impermanent and intermittent character as they enter or leave the labour force in response to the needs of childcare or the demands of a husband's career.

On this view then (a view which has been orthodox up till now), marriage entails a real change for most women as regards their economic independence; their jobs become a secondary rather than a primary means of economic support and it is thus entirely appropriate (or at any rate has been until recently in Britain) to classify single and married women on different principles. The issue is partly an empirical one, although it must be said that a classification that at least recognises the possibility, however rare, of cases where the woman's occupation was the primary source of economic support for herself and her family is conceptually superior to one that ruled out that possibility by definitional fiat.

However, it is by no means clear that we should restrict ourselves to the economic aspects of class alone. Measures of social class such as the

Registrar General's are frequently used as indicators of 'social background' in studies of health, fertility, or educational attainment. This particular usage, we would argue, implies a broader conception of social class which includes normative and relational as well as economic aspects.

If this is the use to which we wish to put our classification of social class, the position of women cannot simply be dismissed a priori. We must attend not only to the pay and conditions of women's occupations but also to the social correlates and consequences of their employment. Viewed from this broader perspective women's occupations and their correlates may well 'cut across' those evident among men, and women's occupations may therefore become important as indicators of the family's social class background. What we propose to do in this paper is to use data from one of the national birth cohort studies, the Child Health and Education Study, and from the British Election Survey to explore the relation between husbands' and wives' occupations and to investigate the possibility and usefulness of a combined measure of family social class.

Sources of data

(i) Child Health and Education Study (CHES)

A recent survey that provides information on the occupations of both women and men, and on their families, is the Child Health and Education Study. This is a longitudinal survey of all children born in the week 5–11 April 1970 (see Chamberlain *et al.* 1975; Chamberlain *et al.* 1978; Osborn and Morris, 1979, 1982). Data have been collected at three points in time: in the first week after the birth of the children, at age 5, and at age 10. These cover a wide range of topics concerning the social circumstances, health, education, and behaviour of the children. In 1980 detailed information was collected on, among other things, the parents' occupations, their joint income, and household composition. Each parent was asked about their current employment situation (to identify the housewives and the unemployed for instance) and for details of their present or last job. Details of employment status (self-employed, manager, supervisor, and so on) were also obtained.

Since the study is child-based, these questions were asked of those adults who were residing in the same household as the study child at the time of the interview, unless the child was at boarding school or in institutional care. The majority (85%) of children were living with both natural parents in 1980, and a further 14% with one natural parent. However, stepparents, foster parents, adoptive parents, cohabitees of natural parents, or grandparents were recorded as 'parent figures' if the corresponding biological parent was absent from the household. This implies that the other children in the household were not necessarily sisters and brothers of the study children, and also that the other children may not all be children of the present mother figure. For convenience, we shall refer to the parent figures as husband and wives, although in a small proportion of cases this will not be strictly accurate.

This paper reports material from the 1980 sweep when the children were 10 years old, and is based on a sub-sample of 7000 children who have been analysed before data for the remaining families are available.

(ii) British Election Study (BES)

The 1979 survey of the British Election Study at the University of Essex was carried out after voting day on a representative cross-section of the electorate in that year. This paper reports material based on 596 respondents who were married men and 663 who were married women. Respondents reported their own and their spouses' occupations, and the party they themselves had voted for (for more detailed information see Crewe, Robertson and Sarlrik, 1981).

The main difference between the two samples is the age distribution of the BES respondents compared with that of the CHES parents. While the CHES sample consists of the parents of 10-year-old children, the BES respondents are aged 18 or over, and are registered on the electoral roll. The former are thus likely to under-represent the extreme ends of the BES age distributions, and this may account for the greater proportion of housewives married to manual workers in the BES sample.

(iii) Occupational classifications

The occupations of the CHES parents were coded according to the Registrar General's social classes (OPCS, 1970) as follows:

I   Professional etc. occupations
II   Intermediate occupations
IIIN   Skilled occupations – non-manual
IIIM   Skilled occupations – manual
IV   Partly skilled occupations
V   Unskilled occupations

The occupations of the BES respondents were coded using the market research classification as follows:

A   Higher managerial and professional
B   Lower managerial and administrative
C1   Other non-manual
C2   Skilled manual
D   Unskilled manual

The main difference is likely to be between Class IIIN and Category C1. The latter is the larger of the two and includes a number of occupations that are classified as Class IIIM or IV by the Registrar General, such as telephone operators, waitresses and waiters, caretakers and street vendors.

The employment of women and men

We shall begin by using the data to look at the employment patterns of the men and women in the sample, first of all looking at them separately rather than as members of 'couples'. We shall then put the two distributions together thus giving the occupational profile of families as opposed to individuals.

The current employment distributions of the men and women (given in the margins of Table 4.1) show the expected patterns. Over one-third of the women are housewives, while among those who are employed there is the familiar bimodal distribution; the employed wives are concentrated in junior non-manual occupations (Class IIIN) and in semi-skilled manual ones (Class IV). The only other category in which they are over-represented is unskilled manual work (Class V); they approach parity in Class II, but are grossly under-represented in Classes I and IIIM.

The occupational distribution of the husbands is also bimodal, but the peaks occur 'higher up' the class structure. Men are concentrated in inter-mediate, not junior, non-manual occupations and in skilled, not semi-skilled, manual ones. If we use the familiar dichotomous model of the class structure, dividing it into a 'middle' (Classes I, II and IIIN) and a 'working' class (IIIM, IV and V), we see clearly that in each of them women are heavily weighted towards the bottom.

The same phenomenon whereby women are disproportionately concentrated at the lower levels of a class can also be seen within the individual Registrar General's classes. This is shown in Figure 4.1, for Classes II, IIIN and IV. In this diagram occupations have been ordered according to their Hope–Goldthorpe scale values (Goldthorpe and Hope, 1974). These values are taken by Hope and Goldthorpe to represent the social standing or 'general desirability' of occupations and are thus a kind of latter-day equivalent of what used to be known as occupational prestige scales. Their respondents were asked to rate the 'social standing' of male incumbents of particular occupations, even for typically female jobs such as secretaries. Strictly speaking, therefore, they should not be used to rank women's occupations. However, it is notable that no British occupational grading has been devised specifically for women's occupations, and in any event it seems likely that, if respondents had taken the gender of incumbents into account, the scores of typically female jobs would have been even lower than they are in the Hope–Goldthorpe scale. This implies

Table 4.1 Husband's current work situation by wife's current work situation (actual numbers given)

Wife	Class I	Class II	Class IIIN	Class IIIM	Husband Class IV	Class V	Unemployed, sick, etc.	Houseworker	No father figure	All wives
Class I	15	18	1	5	1	0	0	–	5	45
Class II	78	321	77	197	46	8	28	–	70	825
Class IIIN	118	353	141	556	113	25	25	1	98	1430
Class IIIM	8	50	22	172	51	9	7	–	22	341
Class IV	34	152	95	625	187	38	34	1	80	1246
Class V	4	34	25	224	73	30	24	–	20	434
Unemployed, sick, etc.	18	27	9	59	7	5	16	1	20	162
Houseworker	171	446	156	884	253	64	215	3	198	2390
No mother figure	2	11	2	23	4	1	4	8	–	55
All husbands	448	1412	528	2745	735	180	353	14	513	6928

Source: Child Health and Education Study

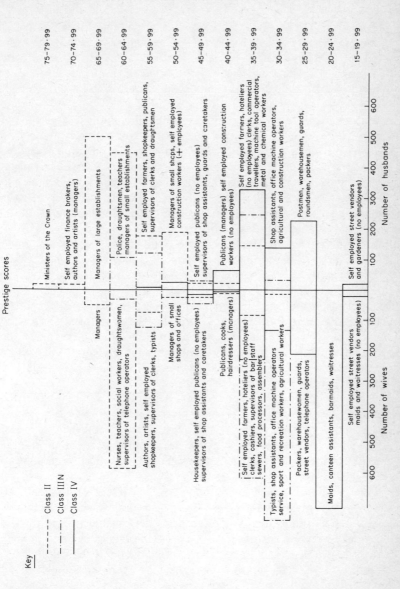

Figure 4.1 Prestige scores of wives and husbands in Classes II, IIIN and IV Source: Child Health and Education Study

that the disparity between women's and men's jobs shown in Figure 4.1 is a minimal estimate of the difference in 'occupational standing' between the sexes.

Within each class we find that women and men typically hold different kinds of jobs, and it is the jobs that the women hold which tend to have the lower scores. Thus in Class II we see that the great majority of women are nurses, teachers, and social workers while more of the men are managers, particularly of large establishments. It is the latter who have the higher scores.

In Class IIIN, the vast majority of women fall within a narrow band of low prestige scores, particularly as typists, shop assistants and office machine operators. The almost complete absence of male shop assistants, and the relatively small number of male clerks and commercial travellers, is also striking. This will in part reflect the age distribution of the men in our sample. By the time they have 10-year-old children most men are to be found elsewhere – many of them of course having been promoted to the managerial positions of Class II or the supervisory ones of Class IIIN.

The general absence of women from Class IIIM is well-known, and again the bulk of the women are in the typically 'female' jobs of hairdresser and cook in the service sector of the economy rather than in skilled industrial manual jobs such as fitters, welders and so on. Similarly in Class IV the women are concentrated at the lowest level as maids, canteen assistants, barmaids and waitresses – 'female' jobs in the service sector and ones that are now classified by the Registrar General as non-manual. The men in contrast are in the higher-scoring manual categories of Class IV such as machine tool operator and chemical worker. In Class V all the women are at the lowest prestige level.

Thus the higher scores of the men's jobs are due in part to the fact that men are more frequently in the higher-scoring jobs with supervisory responsibilities, being more often employers, foremen or managers. And it is also partly because routine personal service jobs score lower than the comparable industrial manual jobs, women being found more often as typists, shop assistants or waitresses.

These within-class gender differences could be of some importance for class theory. It suggests that, for example, the typical woman in Class IIIN may be in a position with very different pay, responsibility, conditions of work and promotion chances from the position filled by the typical man. The usual practice, then, of regarding the manual/non-manual divide as the major 'break' in the class structure separating the middle and working classes is thus called into question in the case of women's jobs. The woman in the lowest level of Class IIIN, that is the female typist, shop assistant or office machine operator, might be regarded as occupying what is essentially a proletarian position which has more in common (with regard to its economic conditions) with the manual occupations of Classes IV and V. The same argument might also be extended, although perhaps with less plausibility, to the female clerks and cashiers.

When applied to shop assistants and office machine operators we find the argument highly plausible. Indeed, we would argue that it is to these types of female worker that Braverman's (1974) proletarianisation thesis most clearly applies. His argument is highly questionable with respect to men, but there can be no doubt about the existence of an immense mass of female wage workers in white-collar offices.

We would, then, wish to question the use of the Registrar General's schema, and particularly Class IIIN, in the classification of women's occupations. We do not ourselves have data on the working conditions of individual occupations, but following our interest in the broader normative and relational aspects of class we looked at the kinds of women (distinguished according to their educational qualifications and spouses' occupations) in the different component categories of Class IIIN. In particular we were interested in differences between the female clerks and cashiers on the one hand and the typists, shop assistants and office machine operators on the other, whom we expected to be more proletarian in their schooling and affiliations.

The differences between these two groups of notionally junior non-manual women are in the expected direction. The higher prestige occupations were associated with higher family incomes and women in these jobs were more likely to have non-manual husbands than women with the lower prestige jobs. But the differences are not so marked as to warrant (in the absence of further research) a thorough-going reorganisation of the Registrar General's schema. The difficulty, we suspect, is that the component categories of Class IIIN may themselves be unduly heterogeneous. We therefore regard it as an unavoidable 'second-best' at the moment to maintain Class IIIN intact, and the consequence of this, we suspect, will be to overestimate the number of 'cross-class' families which we shall be discussing later in this paper but at the same time to underestimate their distinctiveness.

Families in the class structure

At this point we shall turn from the distribution in the class structure of women and men treated as individuals to that of families. Our basis for this part of the analysis is Table 4.1 which cross-tabulates the current work situations of the wives and husbands in the CHES sample.

One of the striking features of Table 4.1 is the extremely uneven distribution of families in the class structure. Many of the cells in the table are very sparsely populated (or are quite empty), while almost half the families are concentrated in a mere 6 of the total 81 cells. The central

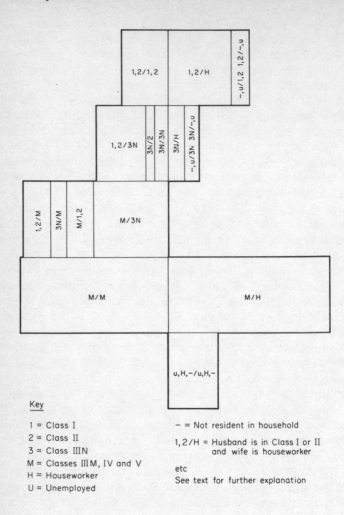

Figure 4.2   Map of the class structure
Source: Child Health and Education Study

features of the distribution of families in the class structure are thus easily
sketched: first, there are families with only one breadwinner, typically a
male in intermediate non-manual or skilled manual work. These families
constitute 32% of the present sample. Secondly, there are families where
both spouses are engaged in paid non-manual work, the woman's job
typically being of subordinate character. These 'homogeneous non-
manual families' constitute 16% of the sample. Third, there are the

families in which one spouse is in manual work and the other is in non-manual work, most commonly a skilled manual man married to a non-manual woman. These are the ones which we shall term 'cross-class families' (since their members fall on different sides of the conventional manual/non-manual divide). They constitute a further 20% of the sample. Fourth, there are the homogeneous manual families (another 20% of the sample), the most common combination being that of a skilled manual man married to a semi-skilled female.

The remainder of the sample consists of families without a breadwinner. These are the 'lone parent families' and ones where both spouses are either unemployed, sick or houseworkers. They constitute 12% of the sample, an important but often neglected group.

The general distribution of families in the class structure is presented graphically in Figure 4.2. Here the main cells from Table 4.1 are drawn with their areas being made proportional to the number of families contained in each (the most sparsely populated cells being combined with adjacent larger ones). The top 'layer' of the diagram can be thought of as the apex of the class structure. Working from left to right across the top layer we begin with families where both parents are in Class I or II occupations. These will be our 'dual career' families. To the right then come the more traditional 'single career' families where the man is the breadwinner and the woman is the housewife. At the extreme right are those families in which one spouse has a Class I or II occupation and the other spouse is either unemployed or absent.

The second layer of the diagram again contains non-manual families, but this time those in which one or both parents is a routine (i.e. Class IIIN) non-manual worker, usually the woman. As in the top layer we have placed families with two breadwinners on the left and those with only one on the right. In the usual social class classifications which ignore women's occupations these 'dual-earner' families in the second layer would of course be categorised according to the man's job and many of them would thus have been allocated to the top layer of the diagram. In the next section of this paper we must therefore check whether our inclusion of women's jobs 'makes a difference' – are there genuine differences between our top two layers in their patterns of behaviour over and above their actual work lives? In short, what do we gain by including women in our measure of social class background?

Most interesting from this point of view is our third layer, which contains the families we have labelled 'cross-class' (i.e. the ones that straddle the manual/non-manual divide). All the cells in this layer would be classified elsewhere in a conventional social class schema, and it is this layer which is crucial in our attempt to redescribe the class structure. The critical cell is also the largest – it is the one containing skilled manual men married to routine non-manual women (the clerks, secretaries and shop assistants). And on the view that women are peripheral to the class structure it is one that would normally be placed, on the basis of the man's occupation, in an unambiguous manual category.

In our analysis, on the other hand, the unambiguous manual category consists of the fourth layer of the diagram and consists of families where the paid work of both husband and wife is exclusively manual. As we have observed already, these are in the great majority of cases families where a skilled manual man is married to a semi-skilled manual or domestic worker. (So few women are in Classes IIIM and V that they have been combined with Class IV in the diagram.)

The fifth layer consists of the families where there is nobody in paid employment.

Do women's jobs 'make a difference'?

Figure 4.2 presents our map of the class structure. We must now consider how useful a guide this map is to the character and behaviour of the families concerned. From the currently available CHES data we can look at family size, family income, and the educational qualifications of wife and husband. These are all shown in Table 4.2. From our second data base, the British Election Survey of 1979, we can look at the voting behaviour of married men and women (Table 4.3). These two data sets should enable us to get a reasonably detailed picture of the way in which our different categories of family differ.

The biggest differences in Table 4.2 are to be found between the layers. Here the most interesting (and trustworthy) comparisons are those between the four big cells running down the centre of Figure 4.2. At the top comes the cell containing the dual career families (the 1,2/1,2 cell); below them in the second layer come the non-manual families where the women are in subordinate occupations to those held by their husbands (the 1,2/3N cell); next down in the third layer come the cross-class families with manual men married to routine non-manual women (the M/3N cell); and lastly in the fourth layer we have the homogeneous manual families (the M/M cell). These four cells in a sense provide the backbone of the class structure. Their large size means that we can be reasonably confident about the differences we find. And the comparisons should be particularly illuminating because at each move down we change only one of the spouse's jobs while holding the other's constant.

We turn now to the first column of Table 4.2 which shows the distribution of family income, the only variable bearing a direct relationship to the joint social class classification. Having a second earner in the family clearly does make a difference, as shown by the gradients within layers. What may be more surprising, in view of women's low wages

Table 4.2 Family characteristics by family social class

Family social class[a]	% of families earning over £99 per week[b]	% of families in which the husband had any qualification	% of families in which the wife had any qualification	% of families with more than two children	N =
1,2/1,2	**92**	**90**	**87**	**36**	**432**
1,2/H	86	83	69	45	617
-, U/1,2 and 1,2/-, U	53	77	83	38	161
1,2/3N	**94**	**85**	**75**	**24**	**471**
3N/2	94	86	77	35	78
3N/3N	89	74	60	33	141
3N/H	65	70	58	44	157
-, U/3N and 3N/-, U	16	63	60	29	134
1,2/M	79	78	56	34	282
3N/M	78	70	49	27	142
M/1,2	83	64	65	42	257
M/3N	**79**	**64**	**57**	**29**	**694**
M/M	**67**	**46**	**25**	**45**	**1409**
M/H	46	50	28	56	1202
-, U/M and M/-, U	15	44	25	40	286
U,H,-/U,H,-	3	33	22	60	465

Notes: [a] For key to nomenclature see Figure 4.2.
[b] Thus in the first cell we record that of the 432 families in which both wife and husband has a Class I or II job, 92% earned over £99 per week.
Source: Child Health and Education Study.

compared with men's, is that the type of job the wife has does have an impact on family income. When the husband is in Class I or II, the family income is much lower if the wife has a manual occupation than when she is in non-manual work (compare cell 1,2/M with 1,2/3N). This is also true for the families where the husband is in manual work (compare cell M/M with M/3N) and again when he is in routine non-manual work (compare cell 3N/M with 3N/3N). In this sense women's employment does seem to 'cut across' conventional (male oriented) class lines. Thus we see that the homogeneous manual families in the fourth layer of the diagram fall distinctly lower with respect to family income than any of the 'cross-class' categories in the layer above. While the man's job may prove to be the main discriminator, the kind of work the woman does is undeniably

Table 4.3   Voting behaviour by family social class

Family social class[a]	Married men			Married women		
	Conservative %	Labour %	N =	Conservative %	Labour %	N =
AB/AB	59	21	34	71	21	34
AB/H	63	19	62	73	12	67
AB/C1	54	25	48	64	15	33
C1/AB	(9)	(1)	12	(9)	(4)	15
C1/C1	62	24	42	72	20	50
C1/H	57	19	37	64	23	56
AB/C2D	(4)	(2)	7	(5)	(6)	14
C1/C2D	(9)	(8)	21	(4)	(6)	12
C2D/AB	(9)	(3)	17	(4)	(4)	12
C2D/C1	41	40	91	38	40	97
C2D/C2D	36	55	89	37	50	98
C2D/H	33	52	136	36	55	175

Notes: [a] See p. 48 for occupational classification.
[b] Where N $\langle$ 25, percentages have not been calculated but the raw numbers are given in brackets.
Source: British Election Survey.

associated with differences in family income.

A somewhat similar pattern emerges in the second column. Not surprisingly men's qualifications are more closely associated with their own jobs than with their wives'. However the much greater prevalence of qualified men in cross-class families than in the homogeneous manual ones (compare cell M/3N with M/M) suggests that there is a real and interesting difference to be explored here. In the first place it demonstrates the presence of 'assortative mating' – manual workers with educational qualifications are more likely to marry 'white blouse' than 'shopfloor' wives. And secondly it suggests strongly that these cross-class families may be distinctly different as 'learning environments' for children. As a social background measure the cross-class family begins to look a promising addition to the usual class schema.

This is reinforced by the third column. Again we find that the women's qualifications are strongly associated with their own occupational levels, the cross-class families therefore having more qualified women than the homogeneous manual ones. But this column also gives further evidence of assortative mating. There is a much higher preponderance of qualified women among the 'white blouse' workers married to men in Classes I and II than among those married to manual workers (compare cell 1,2/3N with

M/3N). Overall the third column produces the clearest evidence so far for definite differences between the four major cells which provide the backbone of our structure. The dual career families at the top would seem to offer the most 'educogenic' environment for children and then there is a marked gradient as we move down the hierarchy.

Some kind of gradient, although on occasion a rather uneven one, is evident in all three columns as we move down from top to bottom of the class structure. The difference between the top two layers tends to be rather small, and the gaps widen lower down. But this changes when we come to the last column and family size. Looking at the four major cells (1,2/1,2, 1,2/3N, M/3N and M/M) we have the familiar U-shaped relationship between social class and family size with the largest families in the top and bottom layers of the diagram. But there is also evidence that family size is related more closely to the woman's occupation than her husband's. Of those families where the husband has a Class I or II or manual job, those in which the wife has a routine non-manual job have the smallest families (compare cells 1,2/1,2, 1,2/M with 1,2/3N and cells M/1,2, M/M with M/3N). These results hold good even when parents' qualifications are controlled for. It would seem unwise, therefore, to omit women's occupations in any future analysis of the relation between social class and fertility.

Finally, we come to voting behaviour and Table 4.3. This time the major division appears between the second and third layers of the table with the top two layers being in general rather similar. But important differences persist between the cross-class and the homogeneous manual families in the bottom two layers. In particular we see that the voting behaviour of the manual men varies quite dramatically according to their wives' occupations. When married to women in professional, managerial and administrative jobs they show a marked propensity to vote Conservative (cell C2D/AB); when married to women in routine non-manual jobs they divide evenly between Conservative and Labour (cell C2D/C1); and when married to women in manual jobs they show the traditional support for Labour (cell C2D/C2D). The explanation may be assortative mating or the direct influence of wives on their husbands, but the crucial point is that wives' occupations are associated with clear differences in their husbands' behaviour and that the cross-class category in particular proves to be a large and distinctive one that would otherwise have been submerged in the usual social class classification.

As an overall guide to class differences, then, our distinction between the four main cells of the diagrams, paying attention to women's as well as to men's jobs, would appear to be a valuable one. We must emphasise, however, that all we can offer at the moment is a summary description of class differences. We cannot yet make specific causal claims about, for example, influences on voting behaviour. However it remains the case that sociologists need and use summary classifications of the class structure or of class origins. These classifications often are valuable precisely because variables are correlated and these correlations reflect a complex pattern of social relationships which cannot neatly be parcelled out into 'independent' and 'dependent' variables. What we are trying to do in our social class schema is to map the basic structure of socio-cultural differences. It is our claim that our revised map which takes account of women's occupations seriously provides a simple and better map of the basic structure than one which classifies families solely according to the male breadwinner's occupation.

Conclusions

We have seen that the classification of social class which takes women seriously is both easier and more effective than conventional wisdom has allowed. The concentration of women in Classes IIIN and IV, and the fact that Class IV women are typically married to manual workers, means that we do not need to complicate the usual class schema inordinately, the crucial addition being that of a category of cross-class families in which typically a male manual worker is married to a female non-manual worker. Moreover, the members of this cross-class category, both women and men, display characteristics and behaviour which are by no means identical to those of the homogeneous manual families to which they are usually assimilated. The cross-class family is a large and important category within the contemporary class structure which class theorists ignore at their peril.

Acknowledgements

The Child Health and Education Study is directed by Professor N. R. Butler, to whom we are most grateful for advice and encouragement, as we are to Dr M. N. Haslum, the senior research officer of the ten-year study. Brian Howlett and Richard Brewer gave invaluable assistance with the data preparation.

We are also grateful to Mr D. Robertson of St. Hugh's College, Oxford, for use of the British Election Survey data.

5 Trends in Female Social Mobility
Geoff Payne, Judy Payne and Tony Chapman

Introduction

The sociology of social mobility has virtually no female dimension. The classic empirical work, Glass's *Social Mobility in Britain* (1954), did not include an analysis of the female part of the study, while the more recent Nuffield Survey of England and Wales excluded women completely (Goldthorpe, 1980a). Although a small number of sociologists are now working on the problem (as instanced by Britten and Heath's paper in the present volume) the only published information presently available consists of brief treatments by Payne, Ford and Ulas (1979a) and Heath (1981a, b), together with some studies carried out in other countries (Treiman and Terrell, 1975; Duncan and Perrucci, 1976; McClendon, 1976; Rosénfeld, 1978; and Sewell, Hauser and Wolf, 1980). British researchers, such as Keeling (1980), Britten and Heath (in this volume) and Bruegel (1982) have had to make do with secondary analysis of surveys primarily concerned with other issues such as family expenditure, child health and education. And yet the limitations imposed by an absence of knowledge about female social mobility have been known for some time (see Acker, 1972, p. 943), the topic even reaching the letter columns of *The Times* in January 1980.

The Scottish Mobility Study (SMS)[1] on which the present analysis draws, has been little better than its predecessors in its coverage of female mobility. Up to the present, all but one of the twenty-odd SMS articles and conference papers have dealt with mobility as if it were an exclusively male phenomena. Indeed, the present work deliberately builds on an earlier paper dealing only with male respondents, which was presented at the previous year's BSA Conference, by applying the model developed there to data on females. Thus the present paper begins to redress the imbalance by using a male-derived framework in which to demonstrate the different natures of male and female mobility.

Perhaps, the most useful way of perceiving this difference is to start with two well-known facts about women in contemporary society. First, a large majority of women experience the unpaid work roles of housewife and mother: men do not. Second, a very high proportion of female employment is concentrated into routine white-collar work (see for instance Britten and Heath in the present volume, Hakim (1979) and below). Male employment is more widely spread throughout the occupational hierarchy. Both of these facts restrict the opportunity for a woman to be upwardly mobile. Her employment career is shortened and interrupted by her domestic roles, so that she cannot compete for jobs on equal terms with males. And her opportunities for paid employment are restricted to a narrower range of jobs.

The first of these well-known facts raises a major problem for mobility analysis. Although the number of women in paid employment has been increasing during this century (Brown, 1978, pp. 62–3; Westergaard and Resler, 1977, p. 98), fewer women than men are in full-time employment. Without occupations, women cannot be allocated to social classes on the same basis adopted for men. Even if some women *are* in full-time paid employment, their class position is open to dispute. Because mobility is basically measured as occupation, it is not possible to be occupationally or socially mobile without having an occupation. The immediate task must therefore be to consider how a woman's class position is to be defined, because an adequate account of movements between classes or occupations is dependent on a prior adequate (i.e. non-sexist) account of classes and occupations *per se*. Once the question of class position (for both mobility origins and destinations) has been at least operationally resolved, the consequences of female concentration in routine white collar occupations will become clear.

When the analysis of mobility focuses on occupational rather than class processes, as in this paper (see Payne and Payne (1981) for this emphasis on occupation) unpaid female roles such as housewife and mother must either be treated as non-occupational, or possibly as reserve positions in which a woman's former occupational identity is not entirely lost. In other words, to substitute her father's or husband's occupation (Acker, 1972, p. 937; Oppenheimer, 1977; Ritter and Hargen, 1975; Parkin, 1971) is not acceptable, as this would be to shift out of the occupational frame of reference and into that of class, while at the same time diverting attention away from the more general economic position of women as potential members of the labour force in their own right.

However, if a married woman as housewife does not have an active occupational or class role of her own, she must (i) be excluded from an analysis of class mobility; or (ii) have her husband's class identity attached to her; or (iii) be identified by her former occupational identity when she last worked; or (iv) be identified by some combination of (ii) or (iii) (the Britten and Heath solution).

As observed above, option (i) has in practice been the one chosen in most mobility studies to date, and is the one on which we are seeking to improve. There are problems in using just the husband's class, as in option (ii): this ignores the social persona which the woman retains from her earlier life. Equally, option (iii) is not without its disadvantages: if a woman has not worked for 30 years, her identity is given by an occupation that was relevant a very long time ago, but which may even have ceased to exist under present-day technology.

These options have been expressed in terms of a woman's own adult identity, that is, in terms of her mobility 'destination'. A parallel set of choices exists for her mobility origins, where the problem becomes one of deciding how to include her mother as a factor in deciding the classification of her family of origin (a problem which applies equally to the mother of male respondents). The eventual choices will largely depend on the way the family is seen to operate as a unit of production or consumption, although none of the options is without some disadvantages.

Whether we adopt a life-style model or a narrower class-based view for an analysis of mobility, we also need to be clear about the ways in which a family bestows an 'identity' on one of its junior members. There are several mechanisms of inter-generational 'inheritance' which can in turn be related to occupational outcomes. Among the best-known half a dozen or so, the most commonly researched is education, by which we mean that the family background is a major determinant of the qualification level attained by the offspring. By the same token, direct inheritance of property, and job aspirations are two other recognised means of 'transferring' family background to the child. However, these are not so much an outcome of a life style or status, as the products of the underlying class attributes of the parents, which have also created their life style. Three further but less well-researched mechanisms are self-presentation, informal job contacts, and household location.

While these six mechanisms are not an exhaustive list, they serve to demonstrate two points. First, these mechanisms on the whole depend on the parental class or occupational position. The extent to which each of the six mechanisms is equally dependent on both parents, and the extent to which each parent influences the offspring of his/her own gender are empirical questions which require more research. In short, we cannot easily amalgamate male and female roles on the basis of existing knowledge unless we restrict our notions of the linking mechanisms between origins and destinations.

However, as previously indicated, the present authors do not see the family of origin problem as being the main focus. The larger and arguably more significant gap in our knowledge is the mobility career of women as individuals in their own right, rather than as members of a family unit. Of course, we need to know something about origins in order to make sense of this, but it is better to solve part of the problem by side-stepping the origins issue than to be trapped so completely in the logical pitfalls of criticism that no empirical analysis is possible.

One way out of this dilemma – and it is no more than choosing the lesser of the evils – is to make an arbitrary distinction between origins and destinations, which will allow us to present some new evidence. If we retain the practice of identifying the family of origin by the father's occupation, two advantages do accrue. First, we by-pass the problem that in many cases (e.g. between the wars) the mothers were not in paid employment and so had no occupational identity. Second, we can make direct comparisons with earlier, male-only studies that used the father as the class identifier. Even though these are flawed, British sociology is not so generously endowed with empirical studies that we should rush to discard those we do have. Further, if we use the same origin measure (despite its flaws) we can concentrate on current careers as the source of any gender differences in occupational attainment (see below, p. 65). However, the chief disadvantage that has to be taken on board if we adopt this measure is that the modifying influence of the mother is unquantified, an influence which in terms of doing paid work has been growing steadily.

As for destinations, it is proposed that as far as possible, a woman should retain a separate identity. As both a single person and a married woman in paid employment, this is easy to operationalise. When a married woman ceases to work in this way, she can be classed either as retaining an occupational identity but temporarily not available for employment, or just possibly as adopting her husband's class until such time as she opts to resume paid work. This offers the main advantages that again we by-pass the problem of classifying the role of housewife, while setting up a position in which the woman's occupational identity is given the same logical priority as the man's. Against this it can be argued that we have not been consistent in the way that we have treated origins and destinations, and that the class position of the housewife has still to be clarified.

As noted earlier the typical paid work role for a woman is routine white collar (e.g. Hakim, 1979; Payne *et al.*, 1979a). In the SMS data on first job obtained on entering work, almost one in three of women (compared with one in thirty men) were shop assistants, or office workers (Hope–Goldthorpe category 2304) while another one in six were clerical specialists (category 2303).

In other words, just over half of all female employment on entering work was of a routine white-collar kind. Or was it? To label this work as 'white-collar' is already to locate it as on the non-manual side of the manual/non-manual distinction, a location which is currently subject to debate (e.g. Goldthorpe, 1980a; Westergaard and Resler, 1977; Wedderburn and Craig, 1974).

In previous analyses of the SMS data, two alternative conventions have been followed. For male respondents, clerical specialists (Hope–Goldthorpe category 2303) have been treated as non-manual, whereas sales personnel and general office workers (Hope–Goldthorpe category 2304) have been treated as manual (the latter comprise about 3% of male first jobs and less than 0.5% of current male employment). However in an earlier paper which argued that female mobility opportunities at their current employment point were lower than males' (Payne *et al.*, 1979a), sales work was re-classified as non-manual. This was because the ambiguity of its position was recognized, and treating it as non-manual 'loaded' the data against the authors' case in order to avoid any accusation of data manipulation. To be consistent, this second convention has been retained here, for both males and females.

In the following discussion, the data are drawn from the 1975 Scottish Mobility Study survey of males aged 20 to 64 and resident in Scotland (cf. Payne *et al.*, 1979a; Payne and Payne, 1981). When the household details indicated that the respondent was married or living with a woman, information was collected about her. Thus the term 'female social mobility' as used in an empirical sense in this paper refers to women presently married to or living with men aged 20 to 64, or more specifically to those women who in addition started work between 1930 and 1970, i.e. a group with some slight concentration towards the middle of that age-range.

Trends in male and female mobility

Figure 5.1 shows the distribution of non-manual jobs among people starting work at different points between the years 1930 and 1970. The upper line is a plot of the percentage of jobs obtained by women which were non-manual, while below it is the percentage of female jobs which were filled by women upwardly mobile from manual working-class family backgrounds. The lower pair of lines show male first jobs in the same way. These graphs have three main features: (i) the female lines show higher percentages than the males; (ii) the two pairs broadly resemble each other; and (iii) the pattern of upward mobility echoes that of the non-manual percentages in both cases, apart from the later part of the time series.

Taking the latter two findings first, it can be seen that, allowing for some small variations, non-manual occupations show a decade of expansion, a decade of stagnation or contraction, a further decade of expansion, terminating in the 1960s with a sharp hiccup in growth affecting women more severely than men. In each pair, this pattern is repeated for the rate of upward mobility, except that in the last decade the symmetry disappears. For women, the mobility rate falls more steeply than the non-manual employment line, while for men the upward mobility rate flattens

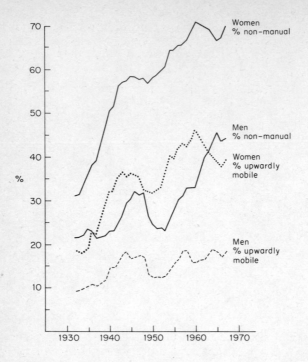

Figure 5.1 5-year moving averages for non-manual employment and mobility on first entry to the labour market

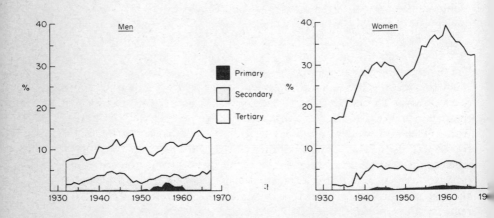

Figure 5.2 Proprotions of upward mobility in three industrial sectors (5-year moving average for first job)

out while non-manual opportunity continues to rise. In other words, although upward mobility rates (calculated as movement across the manual/non-manual line at first job) are much higher than in the 1930s and 1940s, the share of non-manual occupations going to the children of *non-manual* fathers increases in the 1960s.

The pattern is not what one might intuitively expect. Given what we know about the Depression, we would not anticipate a growth of non-manual opportunity in the 1930s, nor would we expect to find the 1960s were a time of increasing social closure. The Scottish economy was already depressed in the 1920s, largely as a result of its dependence on the old staple industries of coal, iron and steel, shipbuilding and textiles. Male unemployment rose from 15 to 25% in the 1930s, and in some of the old staples, it was to exceed 40% and remain so until the war.

However, this period also saw both increases in productivity due to technological innovation (even in the old staples) and considerable economic concentration. Larger units of production required more extensive and complex administrative structures, and permitted greater division of labour with new technical specialism. In other words conditions were right for an expansion of non-manual opportunity even in industries which had a poor economic performance. It would seem that young workers benefited from such changes while older workers were more likely to remain unemployed, trapped in occupational specialisms which were not needed and, being adults, probably more expensive to employ. In as far as the occupational requirements of new technologies and scales of organisation generated more non-manual jobs, it follows that increases

in non-manual employment and upward mobility do not seem to be incompatible with high unemployment, with rising productivity or with marked changes in the nature of capital (Payne and Payne, 1981, pp. 11–12).

These observations seem to apply to both genders.

On the other hand, gender differences begin to emerge during the Second World War and its aftermath in the late 1940s. The first peaks in the non-manual employment in Figure 5.1 are reached during the war, with women reaching a plateau by the middle of the war, and young men by the end of it. The former workers remain at that level until 1950, whereas the men suffer a decline before their recovery starts perhaps two or three years later. The similarity between these profiles is a product of the war; the difference lies in gender responses in time of war. The removal of a significant proportion of the adult male labour force into the armed services, together with the setting up of a state-controlled wartime economy, created a demand for labour which women and very young men filled. The data in Figure 5.1 deal only with civilian jobs: school-leavers taking these jobs between 1939 and 1945 found themselves entering jobs that under normal circumstances would not have been open to them. This part of the time series reflects not so much a change in total opportunity due to an expansion of the non-manual sector, as a temporary change in recruitment practices.

Conversely, in the immediate pre-war years, the opportunities for young men and women were depressed by demobilisation. The claims of demobilised armed forces personnel, together with the log-jam of those who had come onto the market during the war and were now firmly in post, made the next few years more difficult for those just starting work. In this respect, young men suffered more than young women, presumably because more older women left work to become mothers (so creating vacancies) and men were more directly affected by the demobilisation factor. As the 1950s progressed, the upward trends in both non-manual opportunity and upward mobility re-established themselves.

Leaving aside the last decade of the time series for the moment (see below), the broad similarities of the plot in Figure 5.1 suggest that some general process of economic change has similar effects on both males and females. Given that we have been dealing primarily with what Lee has recently called 'systematic' major changes in employment (1981, p. 61) this is perhaps not too surprising, but it is nonetheless of interest that gender does not at this level seem to play such a major part that the long-term external changes are obscured by the differences in male and female experiences.

However, to return to the first of our initial three observations, the female graphs show consistently higher percentages, a basic difference which requires investigation. In the early part of the period, the female upward mobility percentage is about 30%: by the war years this has increased to 35%, and thereafter up to the 1960s it is nearer 40%. In the final decade it declines to below 40% again. From 1940 on, a majority of women entering work did so as non-manual workers, and from the mid–1950s this was running at two in every three. This pattern mirrors the census data for the same years. Nearly 70% of women were currently in non-manual work in 1971 (i.e. their occupation at the time of census, not the occupations of women first entering work in 1971). In contrast, the majority of males started work as *manual* workers, and only in the last 15 years did this drop *below* 2 in every 3.

What we have here is a very simple but often overlooked fact, that employment opportunities determine mobility. If over half of all daughters are employed in non-manual work, and only about one-third of all daughters come from non-manual family backgrounds (as defined by their *male* parents, then there is a structural mismatch. Even if all daughters of non-manual families get non-manual jobs themselves, this still leaves about one in four of all jobs that are non-manual and have to be filled by recruiting from manual families. Although male respondents are also more likely than their fathers to be non-manual workers, due to the occupational transition effect (Payne, Ford and Robertson, 1977) this is nothing like so marked as in the case of women.

On the face of it, it would seem that rather than women being discriminated against, they have an occupational advantage over men which extends to social mobility (where the female percentage increases from a 10% difference to 30% at its peak in the early 1960s). However, the picture is not quite as simple as that. As we saw earlier, women are not employed in the same non-manual occupations as men. Men outnumber women in Classes 1 and 3 (professional and managerial, supervisory and self-employed), while women outnumber men in Classes 2 and 4 (semi-professional and routine clerical work). There is however very little difference in the overall totals in these four classes (27.4% and 26.9%). It is only when category 2304 is added to the non-manual count that the large difference between men and women emerges. This category adds a further 30% to the female total. It follows that the previous apparent advantage of women must be qualified, in that the mobility experience involves a movement to the lowest and most marginal of the non-manual categories.

There is therefore in a double sense a distinctive mobility experience for women. It will be recalled that the distributions of parental origins for the men and women are the same, because they are basically contemporaries. The distinctive mobility patterns are therefore a product of the pattern of destinations, that is to say the distribution of occupational opportunities for men and women. Whereas an average of less than one in three men was upwardly mobile on starting work, the figure for women was closer to two in three. Even if that status were temporary (until marriage) or somewhat illusory (as it was only marginally non-manual) it must still be regarded as an experience of upward mobility, given the logic underlying previous analyses of male mobility.

By the same token, the period of the 1960s showed a marked change in mobility opportunities for both genders. Whereas non-manual opportunity continued to rise for men, but their upward mobility tailed off, for women there was a slight *fall* in the proportion of non-manual jobs obtained, and a drop of nearly 10% in the rate of upward mobility. The fact that something affects both genders suggests a systematic change, but it is not clear what it is. The arguments used to explain earlier changes do not hold true. There is no war dislocation, and the authors know of no evidence that employers modified their patterns of recruitment which in some way discriminated against people from working-class backgrounds. On the contrary, we would have anticipated quite the reverse, as the 1960s have been perceived (not just by a generation of sociologists now entering middle-age) as a decade of greater openness when working-class etiquette, dialect and mannerisms became more acceptable. The 'swinging sixties' were the years in which British social mores underwent their biggest changes this century, but the present evidence suggests a rigidification of the class structure at the macro level.

Components of mobility

In our previous paper, we argued that the male mobility pattern in the 1960s could be explained by a change in the *type* of non-manual employment that was available in the various periods of time series. The essence of the argument is that manufacturing industries and the service sector have different profiles of non-manual jobs and recruitment policies, and in the 1960s the service sector dominates the picture. The manufacturing (or secondary) sector has fewer non-manual jobs, but fills proportionately more of them with men from manual backgrounds. The tertiary sector has far more non-manual openings, but has always tended to hire the sons of non-manual fathers. The reason for this is slightly complicated. The service sector involves more highly technical, knowledge-based occupations, while the state part of it at least is organised on a bureaucratic basis. That is to say, job applicants are expected to have formal educational qualifications. The sons of non-manual workers do better out of the schooling system, and therefore are able to fill more of the available places in service industries. Whereas the manufacturing sector makes a considerable contribution until 1960, thereafter so many of the new non-manual opportunities are concentrated in the tertiary sector that mobility opportunities cease to increase (Payne and Payne, 1981, pp. 15–21).

The basic model can be applied to the female data, but from the outset it is clear that an identical pattern will not emerge. This is because we already know from Figure 5.1 that whereas for men, non-manual opportunity increased while mobility stabilised, for women non-manual opportunity decreased as did mobility. If the shift to tertiary sector dominance is the cause, it would seem to have hit young women harder.

The distributions of mobility within the three main industrial sectors – primary, secondary and tertiary – are given in Figure 5.2. The numbers of non-manual occupations and upwardly mobile people in the primary sector are so small that there is little to discuss. Were we interested in 'non-mobility' it would be a different story. With such small numbers, no clear gender differences can be detected.

The 1960s saw over 10% of all men being upwardly mobile in the tertiary sector, and less than 5% upwardly mobile in secondary industries. Apart from the wartime peak, this pattern is not repeated elsewhere in the time series: the 1930s and late 1940s could be said to run closer to 7 and 3%. Among women the secondary sector contributed a steady 5 or 6% to the mobility rate from the 1930s while the tertiary sector's contribution climbed from 15 to 40% by 1960 (with a drop in the late 1940s), before it dips in the final decade.

Among the men, manufacturing industry accounted for between about one-sixth and one-third of all mobility, with the tertiary sector providing between two-thirds and five-sixths. On the other hand, tertiary industry contained more non-manual jobs: during the 1930s these were about 18% of all jobs, or a little over 1 in 3 of all tertiary sector employment. Secondary industry non-manual jobs were only about 4% of all jobs, which was only about 1 in 8 of that sector's jobs. There was not a great deal of growth in recruitment to manufacturing industry because of the war, but more of the jobs were non-manual, about 1 in 5. In contrast, tertiary sector recruitment to non-manual jobs increased only slightly.

However, in the post-war period, while the overall balance between the sectors did not change much, the proportion of secondary industry jobs which are non-manual fell from just over 20% in the war to less than 10% by the early 1950s before recovering towards the end of the decade. In service industries, the fall is much less pronounced, and occurs a few years later. Thus the availability of non-manual jobs becomes relatively more concentrated in this latter sector. In the final decade, secondary industry begins to contract, even though more of its jobs are non-manual ones. But tertiary industry both continues to grow and to increase its already larger proportion of non-manual jobs by at least as fast a rate. The net effect is to shift the overall balance of non-manual jobs even further into the tertiary sector, so that by the late 1960s nearly 80% of all non-manual jobs are in that sector, compared with under 75% in the late 1950s.

The importance of this will be apparent when one considers the rate at which each of the two sectors fills its non-manual jobs with recruits from manual backgrounds. In secondary industry at least half of the jobs provided upward mobility for almost all of the time series: in a majority of years it ran at over 60%, and at its peak during the war it reached 75%. But in tertiary industry, the level fell more often below 50%, and rarely topped 55%. In the final decade (when as we have just seen, this sector comprises 80% of all non-manual jobs) the rate fell to around 40%. The overall pattern of mobility is therefore largely accounted for by the size of the sectors, the number of the non-manual jobs in each sector, and the recruitment 'rules' that apply in each sector.

If we now turn to the first jobs *of the women,* a parallel analysis shows how far these explanations are general or gender-specific. Before the war, tertiary industry dominated the mobility picture completely, with between 18 or 19 out of every 20 upwardly mobile people, and similar levels of the available non-manual employment. During the war, manufacturing began to contribute about 4 to 6% to the overall mobility rate, a level which has remained more or less constant ever since. Similarly its share of all non-manual jobs has remained stable at around 15%, with a slight rise of a few percentage points in the 1960s. This has been achieved mainly by an absolute increase in numbers of non-manual jobs while total employment in manufacturing has contracted. It follows that non-manual jobs are a bigger proportion of that sector's employment: well over a third during the 1960s compared with a quarter just after the war and less than one-tenth in the 1930s.

The female upward mobility profile for the secondary sector resembles that for males: it seldom drops below 50%, and is more typically around 55%. However, the war saw less of a peak (about 65% in the later stages) and the 1960s tend to run at closer to 50%. In other words, the sector offers slightly poorer mobility chances, job for job, for women than for men, even if the broad profile is similar.

The tertiary sector is another matter altogether. Its total size, its share of all non-manual employment, and the proportion of its jobs that are non-manual all show an almost unbroken rise from 1930 to 1960. Only the years 1950 and 1951 break the succession. By the late 1950s, 85% of service sector jobs were non-manual (compared with about 50% in the early 1930s) which represents just over half of *all* employment for women (less than one-third in the early 1930s).

We already know that retailing and basic grades of office work are major sources of female employment, sources which are by definition predominantly tertiary sector activities. The characteristic profile of female employment in service industry should not, then, come as a surprise. It does, however, point to the fact that whereas men have experienced a small but marked shift towards tertiary sector employment, women have had this as a more typical feature of their occupational opportunities. If we were to ignore the reality of this concentration in routine white-collar work, and look just at the remaining female non-manual employment, it would show a profile which is not too different from that of males.

In the real world, however, the two elements of female employment cannot be separated, and the complete picture of mobility is dominated by the pattern of the tertiary sector. However, its own recruitment outcomes differ from those in manufacturing but not in the same way as for men. Here upward mobility is generally *higher* than in manufacturing with 55% being the base line, rising to 65% in the war and the 1950s. In the final decade of the time series, the rate descends to 55%. This last coincides with a levelling-off of the sector's growth in employment, in its share of all non-manual employment and in the proportion of its jobs that are non-manual. Again, job for job, it offers better mobility chances for women.

Modifying the sectoral explanation

The most obvious result of comparing male and female workers in this way is that the explanations proposed for changes in male mobility cannot be directly applied to female mobility. There is not the same shift from secondary to tertiary sectors, nor do the recruitment practices within each sector operate in the same way for both genders. Given that women do different jobs and are employed to a much greater extent in tertiary industry, this is to be expected. However, if the empirical patterns are dissimilar, this does not necessarily invalidate the basic model. Indeed, what is common to the two accounts is that tertiary industry holds the key to explaining mobility rates.

More theoretically, we find that it is informative to disaggregate total mobility into its constituent elements which are the product of the proportions of non-manual opportunities, and the way these are filled, within major industrial sectors which are themselves expanding and contracting. For men, the service sector does not become dominant until the 1960s, when its style of limited recruitment from the manual class stops any further rise in male mobility rates. For women, this sector is consistently more important throughout the time series, and when service industry ceases to expand its first job recruitment, mobility drops off too. This understanding of the basic structure of mobility draws, albeit a little tenuously, on ideas of sectoral shift during the development of modern capitalism, and the notion of occupational transition in advanced economies (Clark, 1957; Payne, 1977; Browning and Singleman, 1978).

In other words, mobility rates are accounted for by the demand for labour of various kinds under the particular economic conditions of any given period. The mobility experiences of the present adult population have been determined by the shift from primary sector employment to tertiary sector employment, and by the occupational transition from predominantly manual labour to non-manual labour, which characterises late industrialism and the emergence of post-industrial society. Such an explanation of mobility rests primarily on these macro level economic processes, rather than on ideas about class closure – whether conscious or unconscious (e.g. Parkin, 1971; Johnson, 1972) – or on educational reform as a mechanism of enhancing working-class opportunities for career achievement (e.g. Glass, 1954, p. 24; Floud and Halsey, 1961, pp. 1–2; and discussion on males in Payne, Ford and Ulas, 1979b).

These latter explanations are not to be seen as incorrect or irrelevant, but rather as taking a secondary place. After all, it is one thing to identify the growth of the tertiary sector as lying at the heart of the matter, but another to discover the distinctive practices in the tertiary sector which determine its contribution to mobility rates. In this paper it is not possible to do more than speculate, but one aspect of tertiary industry seems a likely candidate. Much of the sector is public, that is, it takes the form of a government-controlled bureaucracy (health, education, welfare, administration, etc.). Following the line of classical bureaucracy theory, one might therefore expect a more formal approach to recruitment, relying on paper qualifications. If this were true, we would expect non-manual employees to be better qualified than in other industries, and – because the children of middle-class families do better than those of the working class in the education system – the mobility rates to be lower. A preliminary analysis not presented here suggests that both male and female non-manual employees are indeed better qualified than in other industries, while mobility rates are lower for men and for the 'non-routine white collar' part of female employment (some data for males are given in Payne and Payne (1981) and further work is in hand).

Conclusion

An account of female mobility must draw on two interconnected kinds of explanation, one dealing with occupations and mobility in general, and the other with gender-specific features of employment practice. The former, what might loosely be called the 'occupational needs' of modern capitalism (such as the growth of non-manual occupations and the shift to the tertiary sector) can in theory be supplied by recruiting men or women. In practice, women have been hired for some jobs such as shop assistant or routine office work to an extent that is less to do with 'occupational needs' than with gender attitudes. As women moved out of the private domain into the public, they were channelled into a subset of occupational roles. It can be argued that the development of capitalism was dependent on having those roles filled, but it is not evident that capitalism required them to be filled so overwhelmingly with female labour.

The distribution of employment destinations for women is different from that for men, so that what passes for upward mobility must also necessarily be different. This is one of the strengths of taking an *occupational* rather than a *class* mobility perspective, in that knowledge about gender employment patterns can be integrated into a discussion of mobility. For example, it seems likely that the higher rates of female mobility in the tertiary sector reflect not just its greater number of non-manual jobs but that compared with manufacturing industry there are many more non-routine non-manual jobs for women in the service sector. In other words, in manufacturing industry, almost all jobs for women are routine office work: in the service sector, although low level jobs predominate, there are relatively more jobs of a higher level. We might also speculate that the trends of the late 1950s and 1960s owe a great deal to two uniquely female employment trends. On the one hand, the revolution in the distributive trades which spawned the supermarket cut opportunities for shop work, while on the other, older married women came back onto the labour market in increasing numbers, to compete with the school-leaver for available jobs.

This sort of pattern calls for more analysis. The authors are well-aware that the present paper is only a preliminary exercise which cannot hope to be a full answer. A more detailed analysis of the components of the non-manual class, looking at category 2304 in particular, and of the components of tertiary industry, looking at differences between construction, distribution, transport, public administration, and banking, is in hand.

Despite the methodological limitations of an imperfect sample, a 'male' occupational grading scale, and a rather crude solution to defining family origins, the analysis has nevertheless been useful as a test of several ideas both in mobility and in stratification theory more generally. On the credit side, the analysis of overall trends showed that some changes had an effect on both men and women, even if the effects were not identical. The predominance of the tertiary sector as a non-manual employer stands out in this respect. The general approach of disaggregating mobility rates retains its utility.

On the debit side (if one can think in these terms), several features dear to recent sociology look decidedly less robust. The manual/non-manual distinction has been seen to have considerable limitations as a tool of research on female occupations. A doubt has been raised about the suggested tightening link between educational qualifications, occupational attainment and mobility. And indeed the basic idea of sectoral shift has been shown to require heavy qualification to allow for gender.

This paper thus provides some basic information about female mobility, and how it has changed, to fill a gap in our sociological knowledge, as well as making a small contribution at a conceptual level. Mobility analysis is a good example of a paradigm which worked quite well in a world where women did not work. When women moved out of the domestic world into public life, mobility research and in particular that branch of it which defines its focus as class mobility and spurns the examination of occupational attainment was faced with a dilemma which it has so far largely ignored. As the opening sections here showed, we have not yet solved some of the conceptual difficulties, but examination of the *causes* of mobility, both male and female, nonetheless still remains a fruitful area of research.

Note

1. The Scottish Mobility Study was carried out under the direction of Geoff Payne, and financed by SSRC Grant No H2173 to Professors M. P. Carter and R. Moore, Department of Sociology, University of Aberdeen. The original 4887 male interviews represent a response rate

of 81% in a survey covering the whole of Scotland except for the Outer Islands. Further details of the sample are available from the authors, who wish to acknowledge the assistance of the research team in Aberdeen from 1973 to 1977, and in particular Graeme Ford.

6 Participation in Local Union Organisation. School Meals Staff: a Case Study[1]
Sheila Cunnison

General introduction

Anyone who has been looking at television and newspaper reports of strikes and sit-ins over the past few years can hardly have failed to notice the number of women involved. To take a few instances: the grand London demonstration of NUPE[2] in 1979 against the Government's 5% pay norm, the successful sit-in led by women at the Lee Jeans factory near Glasgow, the recently ended sit-in at the Plessey factory at Bathgate, and others (Edwards, 1982). Going back earlier there was the now famous equal pay strike by the sewing machinists at the Ford Motor company in 1968, the city-wide strike of garment workers in Leeds in 1971, the widely reported Fakenham sit-in of 1972 and the less well-known one at Imperial Typewriters in Hull in 1975.

Surely all this is evidence that women are now playing a full part in their trade unions? In a sense they are. When it comes to industrial action women are perhaps becoming more active, more ready to 'vote with their feet' as they put it. In terms of membership the percentage of women in trade unions has risen dramatically during the past three decades, from 16% in 1950 to 27% in 1975 (Hunt, 1975, p. 8). The part played by women in mainstream union organisation however has altered little: men still retain control over the routine running of unions, from branch level upwards, even in the unions comprised mainly of women.

Yet there are changes, not such sweeping changes as in women's membership, but smaller advances: more women emerging as shop stewards, more activists at the branches, more women on committees, and more women taking their places as paid officials. Progress is not steady; it may come in sudden onrushes, but mostly it is slow and halting. One reason lies in the reluctance of women to come forward; another lies in the often unwelcoming response to them of unions where male power is entrenched, and where little attempt is made to accommodate to women's traditional responsibilities.

This paper is based on research among school meals staff from 1978 to 1980 and is part of a project in which comparison was made with school teachers and their local unions. It examines the changing role in their unions of one particular group of women, school dinner ladies. The intention is to bring within a single frame of reference the social life of the home, the work situation and the union branch. First of all I look at how the jobs of dinner ladies were structured and at how they saw themselves and their union. Then I recount what happened when the women called on the union for help. Next I turn attention to how the unions catering for the dinner ladies are structured, and how the officials see women. Finally I tell the story of the changing awareness of the women in the 'Winter of Discontent',[3] the emergence of the first-ever dinner-lady shop steward in a city and the formation of a branch where membership and official positions were dominated by women.

As is increasingly recognised, any discussion about women's role in the unions must consider women's role in the family and its difference from that of men (Stageman, 1980; Coote and Kellner, 1981). However, this is sometimes taken to imply that women's low involvement in routine union organisation can be explained by a lack of free time, especially in the evenings when most union meetings are held. This is an over-simplification and misses an important point: it is not so much the extent of domestic obligations which matters, as the way in which they are perceived, the priority accorded to them in competition with obligations connected with work and wage earning (Wilson, 1963; Hunt, 1980, Pollert, 1981; Cavendish, 1982); and the willingness or not of women to organise their lives so that these latter interests and obligations can be accommodated. Indeed I have been surprised in the course of my research by the number of women with family responsibilities – though rarely women with babies and very small children – who still find time for union work.

The research method that I used may be broadly called ethnographic. I studied two work situations in fair depth, joining in each for a period of three months. First I became a participant observer in a school kitchen, and then I joined the teaching staff of the same school. Over a two-year period I became involved with local union organisation, attending meetings of the trades council and a variety of other union and political gatherings. I sought out and interviewed activist women from a variety of unions, concentrating on those that catered for the occupations of the women from the workshops I studied.

Introduction to the workplace: the structure of the job
Between 800 and 900 dinner ladies were employed in the city in just over one hundred schools. Most were in small kitchens with staffs of less than

10, but I worked in one of the larger kitchens with a staff of a cook–supervisor and 13 others. In this kitchen between 200 and 300 meals were cooked daily in two batches, one for schools without their own kitchens and one to be eaten on site. For the senior schools there was always a choice of at least two main dishes, two kinds of potatoes, two other vegetables and two puddings, and there were a few salads.

The kitchen was run by the cook–supervisor (later referred to as supervisor) with the help of a senior cook, an assistant cook, eleven general assistants and me, an unpaid volunteer. All the workers were women. Prospects for promotion beyond supervisor were bleak; most of the new entrants to the administration these days are young women with college qualifications. No qualifications were required of the general catering assistants, but a woman promoted to senior cook was expected to attend day release courses and become qualified. The supervisor had the whole responsibility of getting meals out on time to an acceptable standard. But payment for qualifications and responsibility were minimal and the difference between her pay and that of her staff was reckoned in pennies per hour. The assistant and senior cook also got a slightly higher wage than the general assistants who took home around £40 for a 30-hour week. Four of the general assistants worked a 30-hour week, two a 25-hour week, and five a 12½hour week. The latter took home around £14. The work was rushed, though it varied according to menu.[4]

How the women saw themselves
The women's emphasis on home and family is apparent. There are however conflicts and contradictions in their self-images. They are splintered images where incompatible ideas are found in uneasy coexistence: for example the belief that men and women should be paid the same money for the same work exists alongside support for the 'family wage'. Traditionally women work more in the private domestic arena and men in the public; women contribute more direct labour to the private household, men more money. Yet women are now bringing in an increasing share of household income. Because of this we might expect them to be more involved than they are in their trade unions. But women's commitment to paid work is generally more fragile than that of men. They do not become so readily involved in trade unions as men because they perceive their jobs as being less important than their domestic life which is the major source of their social identity. However, there are different ways of being committed to work, and commitment to work does not always lead to greater union involvement. Though some kind of strong commitment to work is probably a necessary condition for involvement in trade union activity, it is not a sufficient one.

Money is arguably the most important factor which ties people to their jobs. Most of the dinner ladies really liked their jobs and saw themselves as socially useful. But the 58-year-old woman who came in for two-and-a-half hours a day to serve school dinners spoke for all when she said, 'Let's face it, we're all here because of what there is at the end of the week.' The 13 dinner ladies permanently employed in the kitchen were all nearing or over 40; all had children; all except one were married and that one was cohabiting. How did these women feel about their earnings? What function did they see them as fulfilling in the family?

Marginalising women's earnings: low earnings
With one exception, the dinner ladies brought less money into the household than did their husbands. Because of this they saw themselves as financially dependent on their men, and saw the need for the men to earn more than women: they supported a family wage. They saw their jobs as financially less important than those of their men, and partly as a result of this, saw themselves as having the main responsibility for housework and childcare. Several different social mechanisms supported these views. First the wages were low, the job was routine, part-time, and mainly classed as unskilled. Next, all the women save one had stayed at home for some time after their children were born, thus becoming wholly dependent financially on a man when they themselves felt most vulnerable through having children dependent on them. This period lasted from 2 to 10 years, and in one case 30 years, and its effect was to reinforce the women's belief that men with families needed to earn more than women.

The husbands earned more. One was a scrap merchant, one taught at a trade school, two were craftsmen; the rest, who were unskilled men, earned more through working shifts or overtime. The long absence from home of the latter threw domestic responsibilities clearly on to the wives' shoulders. Women accepted this because of the higher earnings and because long hours were often a formal or informal condition of men's employment. The result was that women had less opportunity to work outside the home and had to weigh domestic commitments carefully against benefits from working. For example, the woman who later became the shop steward had four children, she needed money quite badly but had to wait until her older children could be responsible for supervising the younger ones' breakfasts before she could take a full-time job starting at 7.30 a.m. – her lorry driver husband might be away from home or in bed when it was time for her to leave for work.

The woman who earned more than her man and the one who had stopped work for only a matter of months to have her baby were the same person, the supervisor. Now in her fifties, she was an unmarried mother who lived with, but refused to marry, her child's father. While her child was still a baby she had gone out to work and studied at evening classes to obtain a qualification. Though she lived with a man she retained her financial independence. She and he each kept their own money separately. He paid her a certain amount for food and half the rent. All other recurrent outgoings were shared, even the pocket money of their child. Yet this woman still considered it her role to furnish and equip the home, and it remained a major focus of her life. She chose exactly what she wanted and bought it. It was hers, but he usually gave half towards it. This woman was committed to work: it provided her livelihood. She was a member of NALGO, but she was an individualist who had made her own way without any help from others. She had attained a secure job: she was one of a handful of salaried rather than waged supervisors in the city. She had never had any help from her union and she had no time for it though she did pay her dues. Her role was largely managerial, but she was accepted by the women in the kitchen as one of themselves. While the supervisor did not provide the other women in the kitchen with a pattern for trade union activity, she did provide a model of sturdy independence of her man and of her immediate bosses.

None of the other women retained the level of financial independence they had had before they married: they did not earn enough money. Paid in cash, all the women laid immediate claim to some of their earnings as their own. Some of this they saved in weekly diddleums (i.e. savings clubs); some they spent on catalogues; some they used as pocket money to give them that little bit of independence so they did not have to ask their husbands for everything. The rest they took home.

Most of them got an allowance (their 'wages') from their husbands for the housekeeping, and they put their money to this. Some women said that the household income was jointly managed. Sometimes this appeared to mask male control as when, even though weekly outgoings were jointly discussed and apportioned, all savings were kept in his bank account and in his name. In another case joint control seemed nearer; both were paid in cash which was pooled and used as needed, but each was allowed pocket money. Anything over was saved towards whatever the family needed next; she appeared to make the most of these decisions as they revolved around house and children.

Marginalising women's earnings: earmarking and extras
Consciously or unconsciously the women usually accepted the management of children and the interior of the house as their responsibility. Sometimes money earned by the women was earmarked for particular outgoings, either by the women concerned or by joint decision of the couple. Such money was usually put towards things for the house, for the children or for holidays. Men's money was earmarked for the infrastructure of family life, rent or mortgage, electricity and gas.

Even when the woman's money appeared to be engulfed in family finance and general living standards, it was still often thought of as being spent on 'extras', for instance a car. Only two-thirds of the couples owned a car and only half went on foreign holidays. When one of the husbands had been out of work the wife reported that they had 'lived' off his dole money, even though she had a part-time job. She spent her earnings on bingo, on her daughter's dancing lessons and on more and better food. A server who had one adult child at home paying board and a husband in a salaried job said most of her earnings were put towards a second foreign holiday. However, the woman who later became the shop steward, said that her working just meant that the family could live better, implying her money was all swallowed up in what might be called necessities. Yet even she said that her own special gain from working was a colour telly, her 'pleasure' as she put it, implying that it was a luxury, an extra.

Earmarking or just thinking about women's income in terms of extras immediately puts their jobs into a position of secondary importance. The perceived use of women's money for household and children's needs both underlines the symbolic importance of the house and stresses women's domestic role at the expense of their breadwinning role. These findings about women's earnings are similar to those documented by Pauline Hunt (Hunt, 1980).

Gossip and domesticating work
The social climate in the school kitchen reinforced women's domestic role. Peeling potatoes, making pies, washing up, matched the work done at home. More important, the relationships of the women with one another were expressed through their common family and domestic roles rather than through their work roles.

The kitchen was a close community of women in constant interaction, sharing a common teapot and table. It was, as the supervisor explained on my first visit, a place where people helped one another, not only in their work, but also by giving succour in times of bereavement and sharing pleasures when times were good. Concern and care on the part of the women about one another's families were apparent. Problems such as those arising from children's unemployment, elderly parents or men at sea, and the pleasures from engagements, weddings, births and so on were all the subject of common interest and conversation. Such matters formed the staple backdrop to the life of the kitchen.

Not only domesticity but also femininity and sexuality were part of the social climate. Personal appearance was a focus. Catalogues were the occasion for talk about clothes and make-up. Hair was important, its setting, styling and tinting. Despite their ages there was only one grey head among the staff. Body weight and body shape concerned them. All wanted to be slimmer. Soon after I started work the whole kitchen except the servers went on a diet – not for the first time. There was a competition to see who could lose the most weight. In this dieting there was very little concern with health; the aim was to conform to the conventional and media image of the slender woman. These kinds of common interest in family, home and appearance may well have been deliberately fostered by the supervisor as a means of maintaining unity in the face of problems at work. But a consequence was the domestication and feminisation of the work environment, and an expression of the position of women as secondary earners.

Finally to sexuality. A driver used to visit the kitchen twice daily. His role was defined by the women as one of aggressive but joking sexuality. My first encounter with him was a bear-hug and question about what I was doing that night. He was often to be seen creeping up behind someone to seize her round the waist and tickle her. Verbal banter, protests and laughter ensued. Outside the work situation, however, he was a mild and quiet chap. Inside, the women had put him in this role, thereby setting positive emphasis on their own sexuality in a context outside marriage. It was perhaps a common act of assertiveness. It gave rise to a lot of fun, but it was of little relevance to improving the women's position as wage-earners.

How the women saw the union
In 1978, except for a few temporary workers, all the women were in a union. The staff of the kitchen were all NUPE except for the supervisor who was in NALGO and one woman in the G & M – at first she was not sure whether it was the T & G. The NUPE members were all represented by a caretaker from a nearby school; the G & M woman was also represented by a caretaker, but she did not know who he was. All had been in the G & M but had left it because they felt they were neglected, particularly in that they were not learning about trips and social evenings arranged by the union, or discovering such only after the events had taken place. Now that they were in NUPE they did not go to branch meetings, but they did attend occasional social events and did get union news from the caretakers there.

Next I consider how the organisation of work influenced the way the women looked at the union. Three important points characterise the organisation of school kitchen work. The workforce was fragmented, the work was controlled by the bureaucratic and centralised administration of the local authority, and the supervisor was a focal point. It was her responsibility to prepare meals on time and to standard, and to this end she could call on any woman to do any job. Relationships with the authority were very cool; it was a case of 'us' and 'them'. The small numbers, the ethos of pulling together and the power of the supervisor all led to highly personalised work relations, and it was these rather than organised trade union opposition which drew the kitchen together against the office.

The women deemed the union irrelevant to the day-to-day problems in the kitchen. Everyday problems were thought of as the concern of each worker, to be solved by herself or in conjunction with the supervisor. While I was at the kitchen only one woman, the one who later became the shop steward, ever suggested going to the union over a problem. We all took her remarks as a joke. The main function of the union was seen as representing the women in pay negotiations. The fact that wages were negotiated centrally meant there was no occasion for the women to become directly involved over this issue themselves, as often happens in manufacturing. The other function of the union, in the women's eyes, was to solve exceptional problems when they themselves, or their supervisor, had failed, or to tackle any problems that arose about the behaviour of the supervisor herself. This attitude of seeing the union as only relevant *in extremis* began to change later with the advent of industrial action during the Winter of Discontent. However before I began work in the kitchen some of the women had actually taken a problem to the union. It remained unsolved for over eight months, until just before I left.

The women go to the union
Most school kitchens are staffed according to a scale unilaterally set by the Ministry of Education in 1952 (NUPE, 1979a). The scale lays down the total number of woman-hours per kitchen, according to the number of meals produced. This total is reviewed at regular intervals, usually after the beginning of each term, and as the number of meals goes up or down there is an increase or decrease in the number of hours available. How changes in the number of hours are apportioned is the responsibility of the office, but usually it is arrived at by a joint decision on the part of the office and the supervisor and sometimes the women.

In 1977 the number of children at the school in question taking meals fell and the total hours of the kitchen were reduced. All workers, except the supervisor, took an equal cut. Thus the six 30-hour workers, the two 25-hour workers and the five $12\frac{1}{2}$-hour 'servers', who only came in to serve meals and wash up, each lost one-quarter of an hour. For the 30-hour women this meant an extra loss of 'service pay', an increment paid only to those who worked 30 hours or more. Later the numbers taking meals increased, but not to the earlier level. The hours of all the workers, with the exception of the five servers, were restored. The servers were still cut by one-quarter of an hour a day. Later when I questioned the authority about this divisive action the reply that was they thought it unfair to deprive the 30-hour women of their service pay. No explanation was given regarding the 25-hour women.

The servers were angry. With their small earnings they said that they noticed a cut far more than the others. They pointed to the furious pace at which they worked, bent over sterilising sinks of nearly boiling water. It wasn't one you could keep up all day, they argued. And they claimed to work harder than the others. They complained to the supervisor. She said there was nothing she could do: they had to accept it. But she phoned the authority. Someone came from the authority and she too said there was nothing to be done. When the servers told her they could no longer get through their work, she told them to leave it. And they did. They no longer got down on their hands and knees and scrubbed the floors of the serving areas, a job done at the end of every week. They showed me the floors and pointed out the stubborn grease spots which were not removed by the daily wet mopping. Leaving the work bothered them; they took pride in keeping their service areas spotless, the stainless steel surfaces washed and polished till they glowed, and the floors scrubbed.

Relations between the servers and the rest of the kitchen deteriorated. They had been poor for some time. The small size of the staffroom meant all could not eat together, so the supervisor, cooks and assistants ate first and the servers later. The servers felt the others were favoured by the supervisor; they complained that they had to eat all the left-overs, so the supervisor decided to reserve staff dinners for the two groups of women separately. Still the servers could complain that their dinners were kept hot too long.

The loss of wages brought matters to an open quarrel. The design of the staff quarters meant that anyone going to the toilet had to walk to it through the staffroom. One day the senior cook tried to enter the staffroom while the servers were having dinner. A server slammed the staffroom door in her face, and the senior cook retaliated by throwing her out of her diddleum club. After that tempers simmered down, but there was under-lying resentment. Finally the servers decided to go to the union. Unknown to them the meeting they decided to attend was one where the branch was to vote on a pay offer. The male officers started the meeting. The women tried to speak, but they were ruled out of order; first it was minutes, then it was correspondence, then the pay claim. The officers recommended rejection of the claim. Angry because they could not get a hearing, the women voted for acceptance and their numbers carried the vote. This made the men, in their turn, angry with the women.

The women left the meeting disillusioned. They had not known how to get their problem put on the agenda or how to raise it under 'any other business'. They felt they had got nowhere. However, they had made contact with their shop steward, a caretaker, who promised to look into their grievance and to come back to them. But he never came. Though his school was only five minutes away, the women never considered going to find him. They had paid their dues and expected a service.

I went to see the steward and while there I mentioned the problem in the kitchen. He was surprised; he said he had put the matter to the secretary who had visited the kitchen and settled the affair. The women denied such a visit. The steward said he would get in touch with the secretary again. He also gave me a copy of the Ministry of Education scale relating hours allowed to the number of meals, and I took it back to the servers. They worked out that according to this scale the kitchen was eligible for more hours than it was currently allocated and so there was no need for anyone's hours to be cut.

A little later I saw the secretary of the branch. He had now got in touch with the union office about the problem. But he too expressed surprise that the women had been still aggrieved. He had heard of the trouble much earlier and thought it had been settled, presumably regarding it just as a matter of quarrelling women who could not agree.

In a few weeks the hours were restored. Because work had been left undone, there could be no compensation for loss of earnings. But the servers, before highly critical of their steward, now said he was 'not so bad'; he had at least got their money back. But the fact remains that the hours should not have been taken away in the first place and could have been more speedily restored.

The whole episode took about eight months, most of the delay springing from the union side. It illustrates both the failure of the steward to act on behalf of his members' interests, and the alienation of the women from branch procedures. It suggests divide and rule tactics on the part of the local authority, and in so far as the supervisor agreed to the way the cut in hours was distributed among the women, it suggests connivance on her part.

How the union officers saw the women

National policy and local union structure

The G&M and NUPE were the main unions organising school meals staff in the area. Nationally though both have directed a certain amount of interest towards women members, NUPE's campaigns have been much more vigorous. This reflects the fact that by 1978 the union had become 75% female.

NUPE's journal from 1970 to 1978 showed increasing emphasis on women as subjects of articles and photographs and as objects of recruitment. The cause of nurses' pay was taken up nationally in the form of a Nurses Charter in 1968 and again in 1974. In the late 1970s there was a drive to recruit school meals workers. Their concerns were taken up and a Working Party was set up which reported in 1979 (NUPE, 1979b). There was a national drive on the training of shop stewards, especially women. NUPE has also campaigned for nursery education and an improved deal for childminders. However most of the women in the kitchen remained unaware of these efforts: the union journal never entered the kitchen. What they did know was that their union had recently got them a rise and for that they were grateful.

More relevant to understanding the role of women in their local union is an assessment of the local union situation and the opinions of local branch and paid officials. The G & M dinner ladies belonged to an education branch some 2300 strong. It contained over 2000 men including about 80 school caretakers; the rest were mainly women – cleaners and school meals staff. The proportion of men to women was thus roughly ten to one. NUPE education workers, because of the smaller numbers, were organised into a general branch containing in addition workers in parks, cleansing and school crossing patrols, wardens of sheltered dwellings and civilians employed by the police. In this branch the proportion of men to women was approximately one to two. In both branches men held all the offices. Branch meetings were not very well attended in either union, but those who did go were nearly all men.

A few women attended the G & M meeting intermittently. One regular attender and very active unionist was a school cleaner. She was interested in politics and in various schemes to help local youth. Her husband was an active member of one of the socialist parties and she supported him in his work. But she herself was also very concerned for the interests of working-class women in jobs like her own.

The views of the branch secretaries

When interviewed the branch secretaries, both school caretakers, spoke of women as being basically uninterested in the union, concerned only with earning their own money. A union secretary might be expected to see his members in terms of the labour expended for their employer and the rate of pay received in return. Not so the branch secretaries. They insisted on defining women in a similar way to the way women themselves did, but with a difference. They exaggerated the role of women as secondary and dependent earners; they talked of most women only coming out to work for 'pin money' and for 'beer and cigarettes' quite belittling their contribution to family upkeep. While the NUPE branch secretary had gone out of his way to encourage and take women on union demonstrations, he still despaired of any serious commitment on their behalf to the branch itself.

The officers of the G & M were more extreme in their attitudes towards women and openly advocated a family wage. They claimed that the women in their branch supported them in this, as had been shown on an occasion some years back when the women voted against equal pay. In an interview with the G & M branch secretary, he complained of the 'frivolous' issues brought up by women. One of these concerned uniform. Women were supposed to wear skirts and tights beneath their nylon overalls, white pinnies and paper caps. In the winter it was often bitterly cold in the early morning; standing with hands in cold water peeling potatoes, one's legs were exposed to an icy blast whenever anyone opened the door. Ventilation was poor in many of the kitchens and in the summer it became swelteringly hot. Women asked to be allowed to wear trousers in the winter and to go barelegged in the summer. But the authority thought that this would not look nice when it came to serving the dinners, though the children could see very little through the hatch. The only concession the authority made was that women working in certain areas were allowed to wear trousers in the early part of the morning.

The practice of the G & M branch, sanctioned by the paid officials, was to hold monthly meetings. These were mostly attended by men and issues relating to them were discussed; about 20 men usually attended. But when an issue affecting the majority of women came up, such as whether or not to continue free school meals, a mass meeting was held for them, on grounds that there were too many to be accommodated at a normal branch meeting. The officers found these meetings difficult to run, and complained of the unruly behaviour of some of the women and the fact that many did not understand procedure and so did not vote at the correct time, with the result that votes had to be taken more than once.

The chairman of the branch said that the practice of separate meetings for men and women had been introduced after a meeting when the women had outvoted the men on an issue about Saturday working. The men did not want it to happen again. Women were not made welcome when they attended the monthly meeting and if they tried to press a viewpoint they were greeted with remarks such as 'I'm not going to be dictated to by any bloody woman!' On one occasion a woman was actually asked to leave one of these meetings on grounds that it was a caretakers' and not a full branch meeting. Fairly recently a paid official had to intervene to prevent a branch officer telling women that they were ineligible to attend the Annual General Meeting of their own branch. Until very recently the branch officers have refused to allow women to become shop stewards, on grounds of being part-time: two women were thus refused at the time of my field-work. In this way the branch separated the men and women, and excluded the women from normal business.

The views of the paid officials

The paid officials of the G & M were not so much critical of the women as sorry for them, sorry that they did not take unionism seriously, sorry that they could not go to meetings – in the evenings because they had to put the children to bed, and on Sunday mornings because they had to cook the dinner. The officials regarded these as unfortunate but inescapable facts of women's lives.

The attitude of NUPE's paid officials was different. They spoke of women, not in terms of secondary earners, but as labour grossly exploited by their employers – 'poor bloody women, and I say that with no disrespect'. Efforts were made to get women involved: officials said that when at meetings they came across a woman who showed any interest they would always stay behind and give her a word of encouragement. A few years previous to my research there had been a strike among hospital ancillary workers. An official spoke with great warmth and respect of the women who had come out over this dispute. Their support had been unshaking and contrasted to that of the men: 'My angels', he called them. A T & G official gave a similar bouquet to the steadfastness of women once they committed themselves to action. 'You ask a woman to stand there and picket and she will. She'll stay there until she's turned to a bloody icicle!' Women were thought of as different: 'they look different, they smell different and I like it that way!', in the words of one NUPE official. But this difference did not imply any lesser regard for women as union members. Sexism sometimes crept in as with the reference to one early woman official as a 'dolly bird'. But mostly it was kept well in check.

Crucial to the involvement of women is the implementation of the policy of securing and training more shop stewards. NUPE women shop stewards were encouraged by officials to attend the first evening course for women trade unionists put on in the city, and they were the only stewards to stay the course. And NUPE has begun putting on its own weekend bridging courses for women stewards or women interested in becoming stewards: a crèche is provided. One departure among school meals staff was to bring the union to the women. Three meetings were held, not in the city centre, but on the estates where a majority of the women live and work. Only one was well attended, but the union intended to persevere. NUPE's attitude towards its women members must stem from the fact that it is basically a women's union: its numbers and its subscriptions come from women, and its chief problem is low pay which is mainly a problem of women's jobs. There is a marked contrast to the G & M where only a third of the members were women.

The emergence of shop stewards: the effects of the 'Winter of Discontent'

Lastly I show how the dinner ladies' experiences in the 'Winter of

Discontent' led some of them to a new awareness of the significance of trade unionism to them and to their active involvement as shop stewards. The prevalent inflation was sharpening the awareness of all workers to the falling purchasing power of their earnings, but more so of women, who were more heavily involved with day-to-day catering and shopping. A pay claim for a wage of £60, as a basic minimum for a 35-hour week came into inevitable conflict with the Labour Government's plans to control inflation through a 5% limit on wages. The Government, as employer in the public sector, intended to enforce its policy. The lines were set for battle, and despite a slightly higher offer from the employers matters soon reached a stalemate. The unions decided to fight.

To make its own members, the Government and the general public aware of the issues and of its strength, NUPE decided to gather its forces together in a grand demonstration in London. A date was set for January. Except for the supervisor from NALGO and one woman with small children, all the women from the kitchen decided to go. Most of them had never before attended a meeting or gone on a demonstration. They left at 5.30 a.m. and returned in the small hours the next day. The experience had a number of important effects on the women.

It exposed them, perhaps for the first time, to the solidarity and comradeship of union members acting in concert with one another. It took the union out of the narrow confines of workplace and branch and showed it as a mass working-class movement. And it provided experience of common cause with people from diverse workplaces, both local and further afield.

The demonstration passed; the employers did not increase the offer. The union decided to take industrial action. They fought on two fronts, selected local authority strikes and a nation-wide health service strike which resulted in half the hospitals offering emergency cover only (BJIR, 1979). Locally, the action was virtually confined to the health service workers. Meanwhile the dinner ladies carried on working. They were upset about the bad press which the striking health service workers received; they thought they should have been asked to come out instead. They were eager to help. A strike committee was elected from the health service workers. When a support committee from local authority workers was later formed some of the women from the kitchen were present. One allowed her name to go forward as one of the two representatives of the dinner ladies. This led to her attending branch meetings and taking others from the kitchen with her; and it put her in a position where others were willing to listen to her point of view. It led her to contact with full-time officials, to her election as a shop steward in the branch and later to her attendance at a shop steward training course. She began to ask new questions of herself and of the women at work, questions about women's pay and conditions, the ideology of the family wage, the sexual division of labour and the dominance of men at branch meetings. These are questions which indicate a change of awareness on which trade union activity can be based and is now being built.

Three years later the two women who had been on the support committee were still shop stewards, and they had been joined by several others. But there had been even more remarkable changes to the NUPE branch. In 1978 the branch had been a general one catering for a variety of local authority workers. In 1980 at the instigation of the women it had been split into two, all education workers going into the new branch, whose secretary, main officers and stewards were, with one exception, all women. The branch itself grew between 1981 and 1982 from 170 to 700. Average attendance of women at branch meetings was between 10 and 15 in 1982. In 1978 it had been nil.

The formation of a branch run by women was a challenge to the erstwhile domination by men. The challenge to men's domination in this area was first taken up a year earlier by women in the G & M education branch where about 20 of the 200 men dominated a membership of some 2000 women. The efforts of the G & M women, who aimed to set up two new and separate branches, one for school meals staff and one for cleaners, failed. They met with opposition and delay from local branch officers and from paid officials. The original impetus cooled and the meetings failed because of lack of support. The gain made by the G & M women was that one woman, after more than a year of obstruction, became a shop steward and was allowed one day a month off to pursue her union activities.

The emergence of a female-controlled NUPE education branch following the failure of the G & M cleaners' branch illustrates the erratic advance of women in the union movement. The NUPE success marks a sudden change of consciousness on the part of the women, an extension of their awareness and of their confidence in their ability to help to shape their own working lives.

Conclusion

This kind of enquiry, which concentrates on particular cases and aims to trace relationships over a period of time, enlarges our understanding of social processes and social change. A survey can report the numbers of women activists and where they come from, but it cannot say how they came to be involved nor whether they represent a changing awareness, a vanguard of further involvement. In addition, research with this perspective makes it possible to seek connections between social movements in the wider society and the daily life of those who labour, in this case between the industrial unrest of the 'Winter of Discontent' and the changed awareness of the women in the school kitchen who came to perceive the union's struggle as their own.

Women's place
What comes clearly out of the study is the importance of the idea of woman's place, her primary identification with home and family, and the way this is supported by workplace culture, by low wages, by the broken work career and by the particular way women's earnings are integrated into the family. This means that family responsibilities tend to be given priority over responsibilities attached to work, and hence to union involvement (see also Cavendish, 1982; Hunt, 1980; Pollert, 1981). So important to women is this area of social life that it has been suggested that women's true trade union is the network of female kin that supports them in daily life and in crisis (Young and Willmott, 1957, p. 158, Oakley, 1981b, p. 272).

Yet even here there are signs of change or re-evaluation. The position of women in the working-class family has improved over the years. Remembering the authority their fathers exercised, the women in the kitchen congratulated themselves on their own emancipation. But they still felt that their men were and should be in final control. 'Just so far and no further' and 'then he puts his foot down', they said describing the limits of their freedom. They did not want it any different. There were other signs of change, splinters of awareness. 'On principle', said one 'I would not do all the housework.' Both went out to work and she insisted that both shared the household tasks. The women's movement had little direct influence on the lives of these women but the changed climate of public opinion, easily accessible birth control and the widely publicised, if somewhat ineffective, recent legislation regarding equal pay, did have an effect.

Growth of awareness
The evidence from the workplace shows as expected that most women lack interest in the local organisation of their unions. For most, the relevance of the union was confined to wage negotiations and to solving problems that individuals could not cope with on their own. Rates of pay for both occupations were negotiated nationally, so neither men nor women became involved in their unions through directly negotiating their own pay. For most women the union was service. It had little meaning as a framework for interpreting either their position in the labour force, or the day-to-day life of the workplace.

Yet practically all the women had a very sharp awareness of the structure of society. The dinner ladies knew very well that they were exploited, that as member of the working class they and their husbands were more likely than the middle and upper classes to suffer redundancy and unemployment. But, as shown in Purcell's research (1981), class relationships of this kind are usually accepted with fatalism: 'that's the way it always has been and that's the way it always will be'. Or they are deflected by means of scapegoating: in a city with only a small coloured population, the depression of the local economy could still be explained by 'immigrants taking away our jobs'. Yet such fatalism can also be understood, not as acceptance, but as a recognition that the odds are stacked against you, and it can and did coexist for some women with a determination to resist and to fight back.

The evidence of this research shows an increasing awareness on the part of individual women of the relevance of their union to their position as wage-earners and of the need for direct representation of themselves as women workers at their union. Changes in awareness were wrought by experience and through industrial dispute. Of great importance in cherishing this awareness was the institutional support given through union branches, full-time officials and shop steward training courses.

Notes

1. The research on which this article is based was financed by the SSRC.
2. The acronyms used are as follows: G & M, General and Municipal Workers' Union; NALGO, National Association of Local Government Officers; NUPE, National Union of Public Employees; T & G, Transport and General Workers' Union; TUC, Trades Union Congress.
3. The Winter of Discontent refers to the industrial unrest in late 1978 and early 1979 which occurred in response to a Labour government's attempt to impose a 5% limit on wage increases.
4. Early in the 1970s the school meals service was studied with a view to introducing a bonus system. Plans were dropped when it was discovered that the women were already working at a pace which would warrant payment at bonus rates (LAMSAC, 1972; NUPE, 1979).
5. In 1979 NUPE had the largest number, 1200, on day release courses. The T & G had the next largest, 821. Source: TUC Education Committee. In 1981 NUPE's latest reports from the branches gave the percentage of female stewards nationally as between 36% and 42%. Source: NUPE Head Office 1981.
6. The day of this interview, the caretaker was trying out a new uniform, an olive green boiler suit. He was considering both its utility and the kind of image it carried, and he asked my opinion of it. Concern with appearance and its effect on status, usually attributed to women, is here seen as an attribute of men. The women were more concerned with comfort.
   The attitude of the caretaker to some women was shown on another

occasion when they were discussing appropriate clothing for dinner ladies. They suggested it would be much better if women came dressed as bunny girls with long black stockings and little white tails. No one then would bother what the food tasted like.

7. There is evidence from this branch of the men using procedure to foil attempts at action by the women. When redundancies were announced in school cleaning staff, the cleaners led by a woman steward decided to strike. But though the strike motion was passed by meetings of the executive and of shop stewards, the officers insisted on a mass meeting. This meeting was controlled by men, paid officials and branch officers who spoke from the platform. The men strongly urged the women's projected action be abandoned and that instead the men should take action in the form of an administrative go-slow. They overwhelmed the meeting; the leading woman shop steward could not attend, and no other women were accustomed to public speaking. The men won the vote and control of action passed to them from the women. The men's plan may possibly have been more sensible; that is not the point. In a conflict between two groups, cleaners and caretakers, the men used procedure to overturn a decision which the women supported. In the event a change of control at the county council elections stopped the redundancies.

8. The 'last straw' which precipitated the women into forming their own branch was the retirement of the old branch secretary and the election in his place of a man, who though a member of and active in the union, was disabled and not employed at all. This was more than the school meals staff and cleaners were willing to accept.

9. On the surface, NUPE's success among the dinner ladies seems to be closely related to the support the union gives to women. More important, however, is the relation between sex segregated jobs and the particular structure and historical development of the union branch. The effect of job segregation at branch level may be to create pockets of male power and vested male interest and to inhibit women from entering the union at ground level and thus from moving upwards. In the G & M education branch, in 1979, women outnumbered men by ten to one. It had not always been so: in 1964 the number of men and women were more or less equal. But when women began to join the union in large numbers men were already tightly organised and in control of the branch. Men had made sizeable gains for themselves in working conditions, overtime pay and the control of promotion. Their situation was vastly superior to that of women. Moreover, because caretakers acted as managers and virtual employers of cleaners there was a wide area of possible conflict between the two groups (Fryer et al., 1978). The men had a strong

vested interest in maintaining their power and authority in the branch. In NUPE, on the other hand, a new branch with no pre-existing power structure was formed. In these circumstances, the segregation of jobs by sex was no threat to the women.

7 Women, Gender Relations and Wage Labour
Anna Pollert

Introduction

This paper is about the relationship between women workers' experience of both gender and wage labour. Its primary aim is to contribute towards a fuller understanding of the significance of gender for working-class consciousness.

Its empirical basis is a 'close up' case study of Churchmans, a declining branch of the Imperial Tobacco Company, betweeen 1971 and 1972. The factory employed 222 manual workers in 1972, out of whom two-thirds were women tobacco weighers and packers. While the male mechanics were employed in the capital-intensive and automated section of the firm, the women were concentrated in the labour-intensive departments. There was a clear division between male craftsmen and engineers, and semi-skilled and unskilled women workers. Photographs of nineteenth-century tobacco workers indicate that this sexual division of labour dates back to the beginnings of mass tobacco production; even before the introduction of machinery, the cigar and cigarette factories (as opposed to the earlier small workshops) were filled with rows of women workers. At Churchmans, considered an 'old fashioned' factory compared to the new, highly automated Wills of Hartcliffe, Bristol, most of the work involved machine weighing of loose tobacco. The operation for this was a 6 and 10-second cycle to complete under 'normal performance' – or a shorter cycle to earn more or to catch up after falling behind. Other work included separating the tobacco leaf from the stem – either hand 'stripping' or 'machine stripping'; hand packing of speciality tobacco; and spinning 'roll' tobacco for chewing.

My research was primarily focused on these women manual workers, including their shop stewards; foremen and managers were also both observed and interviewed. I was not myself employed in the factory and approached the situation openly as a researcher. I was not given interviewing facilities, or access to the personnel department documentary material, so most of my factory based information was gleaned on the shopfloor through informal tape recorded interviews and notes. Conversations were open-ended and allowed to flow; some were individual interviews, others group discussions. Incidents on the shopfloor and elsewhere were also recorded. There was, however, a basic scheme of problems which informed the research. This included the immediate experience of the job, and approaches to work; experience of and attitudes to marriage, the family and life outside the workplace; shopfloor life; experience of trade unionism; and broad political conceptions and social values.

The key focus of the study – that is, the relationship between gender and wage labour – was thus approached obliquely, from everyday events and topics, together with issues of intensive observation, with subsequent follow-up visits.

Theoretical perspectives
'Sexual oppression' is broadly used in this paper to denote the many ways in which women are socially and sexually subordinated because of their gender. While this is mediated and reproduced through gender relations between men and women (within the family, and the sexual division of labour, through state regulation and via a male dominated 'sexist' ideology), the ultimate source of this division, it is argued, is the exclusion of the family, the core of human reproduction, from social production and public life. This is a distillation of Engels' analysis of the connection between the rise of private property, privatised reproduction, monogamy, and women's oppression in class society (Engels, 1970). Engels, however, never confronted the issue of the persistence of women's oppression in the working-class family. His main mistake was to overestimate the independence of the family unit, and to underestimate the power and penetration of the state, in defining the family in terms of male dominance and control, and thereby perpetuating the economic dependence of women. Yet Engels himself, in his allusion to the difficult family 'role' of the proletarian woman, paradoxically hit on a process which actually began to offer another explanation for the problem he left unsolved:

> Only modern, large scale industry again threw open to her – and only to the proletarian woman at that – the avenue to social production, but in such a way that when she fulfils her duties in the private service of her family, she remains excluded from public production and cannot earn anything, and when she wishes to take part in public industry and earn her living independently, she is not in a position to fulfil her family duties (Engels, 1970, p. 501).

The weakness in the above is, of course, in the term 'duties'. The question of the possible socialisation of family functions, and therefore the disappearance of such 'duties' under capitalism was not explored by Marx and Engels. Most current theories point to the contradictory relationship between capitalism and the family, in that there are alternating and often simultaneous pressures both to socialise the family and keep it private. However, in the present historical period, it seems highy unlikely that capitalism could bear the cost of totally socialising human reproduction: that is, it cannot socialise the family entirely. In this situation, it remains the case that the responsibility for child-care and much household work is the private concern of the family. Why the burden should fall on *women* continues a problem, and returns us to where Engels left off.

Engels' basic point in the above quotation was that capitalism was *progressive* for women in that it threw them into wage labour, but progressive in a contradictory way, since it also intensified their oppression by creating the double burden of economic exploitation and domestic labour. A key to understanding this dialectical process, and also why it should continue to be *women* who shoulder this double burden is to look closely at the interaction of ideological *and* material processes involved in the sexual division of labour both inside and outside the family. So far, most of the analysis concerning the relationship between women's oppression and capitalism has failed to look at *consciousness*. Recent Marxist–feminist writing has become locked into a materialist mould – perhaps out of a well-founded aversion to idealist 'patriarchal' explanations – and has become prone to 'Marxist functionalism' – explaining all in terms of what 'capitalism wants'. Without falling again into another idealist trap – that is explaining women's oppression entirely through women's consciousness and the operation of ideological processes – it still remains necessary to bend the proverbial stick back again, to see the role of consciousness in material structure and processes, and vice versa.

The aim of this paper, then, is to try to draw out a picture of how women's perception and experience of female gender, as constructed by their role within the family, presents itself in a work setting. As it does so, we see that a vicious circle between gender oppression and working-class exploitation is set up which both perpetuates women's relegation into the domestic sphere and intensifies their exploitation as workers. This vicious circle is both material *and* ideological in the sense that the practices and ideas of employers and trade unionists in class terms, and of men and women in gender terms, create it. It is argued that such a dialectical approach to the relationship between women's oppression and exploitation is a vital dimension to the analysis of the perpetuation of women's oppression under capitalism, and a necessary complement to the more economic and structural arguments.

At the same time as attempting to explain working-class women's oppression as inextricably linked with their exploitation as workers, the other half of the picture is the contradictory progression out of this situation into emancipation. This was the main emphasis of Engels' analysis: wage labour brings economic independence to women, and by drawing them into *social* production brings them into the arena of class struggle at the point of production, through cooperation and organisation against capital. What needs to be drawn out here is the specific nature of these emancipatory processes for women, that is, not only how they share a common ground with all wage workers, but also (and what is concentrated on in this paper) how the experience of gender in wage labour can initiate struggles at distinctive starting points. Throughout this discussion the connection in women's consciousness between the family and the workplace is stressed, as is the interconnectedness between the struggles against sexual oppression and exploitation.

Oppression shapes exploitation

Introduction
The level at which absolute and relative surplus value are extracted from workers is the level of their exploitation. The degree to which workers place constraints on this process through organisation, sanctions and bargaining determines the level of class struggle, the balance of class forces. Various historical factors, both ideological and material, shape this capital–labour relationship. For example, vital preconditions for labour's control include the legality or illegality of trade unions, workers' rights to civil liberties, the extent to which existing trade unions are independent, or incorporated into the state, and the availability of and demand for labour.

The ways in which women's experience of gender affects their ability to organise obviously varies historically. Black women workers in Britain, migrant women workers in Europe, South East Asian women workers on the global assembly lines of the multinationals – all have distinctive situations and organisational problems in which the operation of gender oppression (along with other forms of oppression) can be analysed.

In the case of post Second World War Britain, where 40% of the workforce are women, two-thirds of whom are married, a key problem is the significance of domestic responsibility for women workers' labour market situation and their ability to impose controls over the sale of their labour power. My own approach to the significance of the family in this section is to analyse the way in which ideological and material processes of oppression merge into each other in the prospect and reality of marriage among women workers. The fact that all the workers at Churchmans worked full-time presented, in many ways, favourable conditions for workers' collective organisation: the hours were stable, the workforce was concentrated, and 90% of the workers were in one union, the Transport and General Workers' Union. The fragmentation typical of many women part-time workers and shift workers was not an issue here. Yet within these conditions, women's gender still imposed constraints on their experience of wage labour, which seriously undermined their commitment and ability to organise at work and shift towards themselves the frontiers of control.

Rational employers and men's beliefs
Out of eight 'job groups' in the Imperial Tobacco Ltd grading (job assessment) scheme for manual workers between 1974 and 1979, 77.4% of all women manual workers were in the *bottom three* groups, and 99.9% were in the *bottom four* groups. Against this, 21.6% of all men were in the bottom three groups, 46.1% were in the bottom four, and 53.9% in the *top four* groups (Pollert, 1981). Although 'women's work' had been officially abolished in 1972, women workers were effectively segregated in the lowest ranks of the occupational hierarchy, and, in spite of an equal pay policy since 1975, in 1978 women's average weekly earnings as a proportion of men's were still only 65%.

These figures for Imperial Tobacco Ltd as a whole illustrate the Pay and Proficiency Scheme used in all its branches, including the Churchmans factory. In 1978, after an official equal opportunity policy had been in existence for over six years, there was no redistribution in the sexual division of labour, and only a 5% improvement in the gap between men and women's average weekly earnings.

The official management explanation on the situation was that women were conservative and did not want men's jobs. Moreover, according to one training supervisor, they were: 'in a fool's paradise.... With the money coming in, they've never had it so good.' The idea that women workers seek little 'intrinsic' satisfaction from their work, are suitable for dull, repetitive work, are weak and lack leadership qualities has been found to permeate management thought (Hunt, 1975; Thorsell, 1967). So too are stereotypes of women as unstable and unreliable workers (Wild and Hill, 1970). Implicitly, these views are used to explain, if not to justify, the prevalence of women's subordination in the labour market. At Churchmans, where similar views were voiced, one personnel manager expressed the advantages and limitations of female labour for factory work: 'We want those who are not so bright that they will be bored by the repetitive work, and yet, bright enough to apply themselves to it and not risk injury on the machines.' Moreover, the patronisation was shared among all the men in the factory, not just managers.

John (shop steward): You tell me – if you're an employer and you pay exactly the same to a man or woman – which would you choose? Well it's obvious isn't it! A Man!

In effect a consensus existed among men that the world of 'work' was a man's world where women were only just tolerated – a sexual stereotype confirmed in other studies (Beynon and Blackburn, 1972; Nichols and Armstrong, 1976; Glucklich *et al.*, 1976). Predictably, 'women's place' was seen as 'in the home', and their responsibility for biological repro- duction justified sexual discrimination by employers.

Steven (chargehand): Look at it this way with this women's lib, equal pay, women are talking themselves out of work. Now, with a man, he's got a family to keep, he's more reliable. I mean men don't leave to have babies do they? But the women do! It's not fair! If a firm had any sense they wouldn't train a woman for a responsible job. Not unless she can't have any children – that's fair enough then.

This male ideology is an important factor in the process of female sub- ordination at work. However, too often in the past, the sociological explan- ations for the unequal division of labour in the workforce has been little more than an uncritical repetition of this ideology without any analysis of its operation in a social process. In reaction to such biased, and also such simplified idealist assumptions, more recent work has brought out social and economic changes in the capitalist labour process, together with employers' strategies of control, as underlying the development and perpetuation of 'women's work' (Braverman, 1974; Walby 1982) and as buttressing sexist ideology.

The difficult analytical task, is to draw together the ideological and material processes which actually take place in the maintainance of this gender differentiation, together with other factors relevant to the employer–worker relation. To put the question concretely: how and why did Imperial Tobacco Ltd, and Churchmans' management in our case, implement its grading system, its system of control in the workplace, and in particular, its use of female labour? At the same time, however, the question has to be asked: how, why, and to what extent did women workers *let* themselves be used in this way?

The material setting of the Churchmans' workers' situation, as defined by management policy, is a basic starting point. We are looking at the tobacco industry in post Second World War Britain. It had a well developed, centralised and bureaucratised system of collective bargaining. In the 1960s the employers' policies were largely influenced by the prevailing management concerns over productivity, wage drift, 'excessive' shop stewards' control and the need for flexibility and rationalisation (Pollert, 1981, Chapters 3–4). Imperial Tobacco, with a tradition of paternalism and employing women, had little shopfloor militancy and a strong tradition of labour process control with a workforce habituated to work study and time and motion study. Its particular concern in the late 1960s was to simplify the wage structure, and ease the way for productivity increases, greater automation and cutting the labour force. In this context, it adopted the prevailing management strategy of productivity deals, including the introduction of measured day work (a more stable payment system), job evaluation and grading, and flexibility and de-manning agreements with the trade unions.

For the workers, the immediate experience of this policy was very tight control by the setting of performance standards; that is, tight control by the payment system, the 'Pay and Proficiency Scheme', and for machine workers, direct control by the machines pace. For many older women, the productivity scheme was experienced as a distinct deterioration in conditions compared with the earlier period of simple piecework. For most younger women, the speed and monotony were disliked without any better reference point. Either way, the image of the 'satisfied' woman worker offers no model explanation for the apparent lack of resistance to the smooth running of the production system, and the seeming acquiescence to the grading system and prevailing allocation of 'women's work'. If we want to go beyond mechanistic explanations of employers' strategies, and take the observation that women workers are seen as trespassers on a man's territory as a *problem*, not an *explanation*, we have to take a deeper look at the consciousness of the women as actors in the social process.

Marriage, the temporary stay and the double burden
A fundamental point to be made about the experience of *women* workers is that they share the common ground of wage labour as experienced by *all* workers engaged in alienated work. To this extent, they face similar frustrations, disengagement and lack of control as all workers, and are drawn into the same organisations and forms of activity to defend and improve their situation. Likewise, their 'orientation' to work is 'instrumental':

> *Kate*: I grin and bear it. If you want money you have to work.
> *Jenny*: It's the money that keeps us here. That's all we're here for really.

Yet within this shared experience, differences between men and women emerge. There is the constant recurrence of the sexual division of labour, and attitudes towards it. And what is apparent is women's widespread acquiescence to the status quo, to the inferiority of women's work and to marriage and the family as 'careers' for women.

Kate: I can't imagine a man doing my work. It's too boring for a man. Women have much more patience.

Gale: Men'd go mad. It'd kill them with boredom. Girls are expected to do that kind of thing. Girls are thought to be the weaker sex.

Much of what was expressed by the women at Churchmans seemed to confirm the simplified explanation that women workers put up with boring work because they look towards marriage and the family as escapes. To this extent there appears to be collusion between male and management stereotypes and the women themselves that a woman's place is in the home. What is not so often clearly explained is that it is the nature of the work itself which pushes women further into the world of the family. As seen above, women factory workers suffer a sense of self-deprecation in their work. The boredom of the work itself, and continual patronisation by male co-workers and supervisors, exacerbate the already alienated nature of the work and make the world of wage labour alien to female gender identity. In some ways – as we shall see later – this can paradoxically precipitate challenge; in others, it pushes women further into the shelter of the isolated family.

Anna: What's it like here?

Jenny: Hateful. To tell you the truth, I can't stand it.

Anna: How much longer do you think you'll stay?

Jenny and *Jackie*: Till I get married.

Jenny: As soon as I gets married, I won't come back in here.

Anna: What'll you do?

Jackie: Stay home.

Anna: What'll you do at home?

Jackie: Have a couple of kids.

Val: Anything's better than working here. Well most women get married, don't they? Not all of them works all their lives like a man. Put it this way, I don't *want* to work when I'm married. I don't really believe in married women working. Well 'cos there's not much work anyway, and they ought to make room for people what've got to lead their own lives.

A number of points need to be made here. First, it is misleading to impute women's experience of wage labour to their 'orientation to work' in the 'action approach' tradition (Goldthorpe *et al.*, 1968), as though a 'family ideology' were imported from the outside. For it is the experience of a particular kind of work – low grade 'women's work' – which predisposes workers to seek alternatives outside. In other words, seeing wage labour as temporary, resorting to the identity of a dependant on someone else's wage labour, is a way of negotiating meaning in a hostile environment. This is also easily reinforced by the ideology of the male 'family wage' espoused by the trade union movement as a working-class advance (Humphries, 1977; Land, 1976).

At Churchmans the perception of wage labour as temporary persisted even among older women who had returned to factory work after a break to have children. Brenda, 26 years old with three children, still clung to the belief that she was 'not going to work for ever'. Ida, 45 years old with two children had worked at Churchmans for 22 years and pinpointed the nature of this mythology:

> When you're young you think you'll stop sometime and the years slip by; time flies when you get older. Things don't work out like that.

In a broad sense, this belief system was merely part of the day-to-day, almost hand-to-mouth, experience of alienated wage labour: each day is taken as it comes, and a lifetime can slip by before the totality is evaluated. But for the male breadwinner, there is no ideological escape – unless perhaps to set up 'a small business'. Either he is trapped, or he can try another job, or he must look to change. For women unskilled workers, all these alternatives exist, but the sense that wage labour is not really their world anyway can perpetuate the anachronistic picture of the single woman worker and the married woman at home. At Churchmans, this model had sufficient force to suppress the conscious assimilation of the fact that women's wage work was not a temporary phase, because the women were themselves or were surrounded by older, married women workers here in the factory itself and among acquaintances.

But the reproduction of this mythology can also be explained in terms of the material existence of the older woman, who theoretically should have been the ones to demystify the younger ones. They were experiencing the stress and strain of the 'double burden'. They sensed they were living an irreconcilable conflict. At one level (and in spite of the male family-wage model) they knew that two incomes were essential for survival:

> *Edy*: Let's face it, you can't live on one man's wage now. A woman's *got* to work if you want anything decent.

Yet the double load of work, when 'a rest' or going 'on the club' were only a means to catch up with the housework, created an extreme form of oppression:

> *Ida*: I mean, that time I had that rash, I thought it was coming on top of me then. I think you need a rest now and then, apart from your holidays. Because when you're working and you've a holiday, you sort of leave everything, your odd jobs that are piling up. Sometimes you have to get on the club to do your housework.

The sense of being trapped within this conflict – knowing on the one hand that she *had* to work and on the other that she could hardly go on – allowed the belief that work was 'only temporary' to operate as a psychological survival mechanism in an intolerable situation.

There is, then, a powerful ideological force which diverts women workers from coming to grips with the historical reality that the greater part of their lives will be spent as wage workers and essential earners. How this ambiguous self-perception as women and as workers, together with constant male social pressure, creates problems in trade union consciousness and organisation, is the subject of the next section.

Trade unionism and shopfloor control

Among the younger girls at Churchmans, the image of marriage as an escape became conflated with the generally casual approach observed among young, unskilled workers to their work and workplace. Predictably, it directed attention away from altering or improving working conditions through collective organisation.

> *Gale*: Most girls don't bother much about unions – that sort of thing. Well, it's not worth it, is it? Most of the younger girls, they plan to get married, they don't plan to stay long anyway.

With older women with more domestic responsibilities, lack of trade union involvement stemmed partially from not identifying closely with their activity as wage labourers, but also from lack of time and the double burden itself:

> *Vera*: You've got to go to the meetings, you've got to have plenty of time on your hands. You really want somebody single.
> *Pearl*: At night you just can't manage. You've got to go home, and do housework and cook meals; you don't feel up to it.

For most of the women at Churchmans, the family and trade unionism seemed mutually incompatible, both at a practical and at an ideological level. Pressures from husbands obviously reinforced the reluctance to 'cross boundaries' into what was seen as a male world.

> *Stella*: My husband'd say, well you do it, [union work], but your work in the home comes first – not messing around with things like that. Let somebody else do it.

Equally, sexism from other male workers and trade unionists alienated the women from their own union, exacerbating the usual schism between rank-and-file workers and the official trade union machine. At best, the male shop stewards at Churchmans were simply overworked and indifferent to women's problems.

Vera: He [shop steward] will just *tell* us what's going on. He never *asks*. And he hasn't got a lot of time.

At worst, they were patronising and contemptuous:

Aileen: I don't think much of the union men in here. Our shop steward – he don't talk to you. When he came in the stripping room for election he said, 'Will you vote for me? Thank you' – and went out without waiting for an answer. He's never around when you want him. A good shop steward would be there.

With the formalisation of bargaining associated with the productivity scheme, the language of trade unionism became more technical and incomprehensible to anyone not specially trained to understand it. And for women workers, who already claimed to 'feel soft in front of all those people', the discouragement from finding some voice in the negotiating process was multiplied.

Pearl: He was speaking in different terms to what we understood about the yardsticks. We didn't understand half what he was talking about.
Ida: Well, he wouldn't listen, he didn't want to know – we always get shouted down like. He never ever gave us a straight answer. He always went on to something else – bla, bla, bla.

The need for greater female participation in trade union affairs, especially for a woman shop steward, was clearly recognised by the women at Churchmans.

Stella: Really, we should do something, but we don't. Just let it slide and that's it. Think we can't do anything about it and don't bother.
Jenny: Yes, because, be fair, women can do as much as men now, but we don't get our way. Like a bloke's alright for a man's union, but I reckon it's different for girls.

Feeling that work and trade unions were men's affairs and lack of confidence perpetuated a vicious circle of non-involvement. And since both management and the union paid formal lip service to greater female participation in collective bargaining, most older women were apologetic about themselves.

Pearl: It's our own faults, 'cos none of us'll take it on.
Vera: Nobody'll take it on.
Pearl: That's what's wrong, see, we don't go to the meetings, none of the women. See, you've got the chance to go, like, but the majority of us is married, and we've got homes to go to.

These ideological and practical factors which prevented women from finding their own voice in shopfloor representation were the main reasons for their vulnerability to management control. But two other, linked processes must be briefly examined before we move to the more 'liberating' part of this paper.

The first process is the use of 'sexual politics' as a form of management control. This refers to the informal negotiation of situations and meanings between male supervisors and women workers at shopfloor level. At Churchmans, management-philosophy was imbued with the 'human-relations' school of motivating workers through good communication and informal groups. Supervisors were taught to be friendly and 'not to talk down'. At the same time, humour, laughs and pranks were one of the main forms of workers' accommodation with the work situation. There was a good deal of ragging and humorous flirtation between women and men, and within this context supervisors were frequently able to disguise discipline with sexual innuendo, jokes and flattery. While this often bordered on sexual harassment, most girls found it best to 'play the game', and turn a possible confrontation into a laugh. To do this they colluded both with sexist stereotypes of female sex objects – ('Hey gorgeous', 'It's your sexy looks get you into trouble') – and with management control. This is a form of individual social negotiation based on gender not usually available to male workers but very common for women workers who are most often subordinated to men. It is a process which both reinforces sexist stereotyping, and takes the edge off discipline and control issues at work. On the other hand, of course, the insidiousness of this relationship may itself be resented:

Val: You've got to be blue eyes in a factory, you know what I mean? Your face has got to fit, or else that's it.

The problem with mobilising resistance to such control, however, is that it works in a subtly divisive way: where some women find it an easier option to collude with sexist banter than to appear 'lacking in humour' and 'women's lib', those who experience victimisation for not cooperating in this shopfloor sexual politics receive little sympathy or support.

While this process has wide anecdotal confirmation, a second organis-ationally debilitating process took place at Churchmans, which has not been systematically studied in relation to the experience of women workers. This was the diversion of shopfloor issues away from the sphere of trade union negotiation, and into a management-run consultation body. The general process of worker incorporation through participation is well-documented, both in 'human relations' literature and in critiques of worker participation and industrial democracy schemes (Ramsey, 1980). At Churchmans there was suggestive evidence that women workers, even in a formally unionised workplace, might be more susceptible to this form of management incorporation, because of their inability to penetrate the male world of trade unionism. The pattern at Churchmans stemmed from the fact that women felt they could find a voice as 'welfare reps' – the Factory Council representatives – more easily than they would take on the role of shop steward. This was partly because it involved less time and commitment, but also because it was seen as a way of taking up 'domestic issues' – such as tea bays and overalls – without having to persuade un- interested and inactive shop stewards and union officials to act for them. The attraction of the Factory Council was that it seemed a short-cut to management and was accessible to women workers. And once women representatives were established, this led to a self-fulfilling process. Girls and women preferred to turn to a woman representative with a problem; they were not always sure what a 'union issue' should be about and what they could take to a (male) shop steward, and found a female fellow employee a more natural person to go to:

Anna: What do you do if there's a problem? Like reliefs (to take over the machines).
Val: They has meetings and that – Elma goes to them – the older woman. If we're not happy about something, we tells her, and she puts it to the committee.

Issues over timing, relief workers, relaxation allowances were then diverted to the Factory Council, a consultative body in which workers had no bargaining power. They were 'talking shops', where potentially controversial issues of workshop conditions or control were sunk into a welter of charity appeals, cheap tights 'for the girls', raffles and enter- taining projects. In this way, the development of conceptions of bargaining power or tactics was suppressed in a paternalistic relationship where one could only 'ask':

Pearl: Well, you can do nothing. Keep on asking them.

So, together with the fundamental sense of alienation and subordination in the world of wage labour and trade unionism, and with the operation of a subtle sexual disciplining process, this was yet another dimension, in which the employer's control indirectly drew on the male–female gender relationships in the workplace and reinforced women workers' sense of powerlessness – both as women and as workers.

Pearl: You can't cause a lot of trouble in here. We're not very big, see. And like with a small room like this, we don't stand much chance.

Gender, wage labour and contradictions

Having concentrated on a number of 'vicious circles' in which women's gender oppression undermines their consciousness as workers, we can move onto examining how the experience of wage labour can challenge sexual oppression, and how indeed the vicious circle can turn into its opposite as a source of movement and change.

The first essential and obvious point is the importance of collective experience for women workers. At Churchmans, group identity, 'mucking in', sharing experiences and laughs, ragging the men – all expressed a confidence and assertiveness drawn from shopfloor life, from working, from earning a wage and from being together. This is not to say that this necessarily posed any resistance to their situation; on the contrary, it could be argued that much of the support women gained from each other at work merely gave them the strength to return to domestic drudgery and survive the double burden. On the other hand, the confidence in face-to-face relationships and manner was, as the older women themselves argued, something they had learned, and an advance on their diffidence of twenty years ago.

Flowing from this concrete experience of wage labour is the fact that women workers' collusion with the male sexist ideology that their 'place is in the home', and that they are, or should be dependants on the male family wage, is only *partial*. Having analysed in the previous section the development of a mythology leading women away from grasping the permanence of wage labour in their lives, it is now necessary to emphasise the fractures and contradictions in that mythology, created by the actual concrete experience of working and having to work. At this level, there was a clear awareness that the male family wage was a myth – (although perhaps still a mythical *ideal*) – and that women were essential earners.

Pearl: If you want anything, *we* have to work for it.

Such comments denote a dignity and self-reliance in direct opposition to the dependence and submission of 'I expect to be supported by my husband if I'm married', or 'I think we'll have to give up our jobs – well, don't you think a man needs a job more?'

Another aspect of this common ground of wage labour is that it brings into consciousness some awareness that selling labour power creates profit and is part of an exploitative process.

Rene: Well, like, we're at the low end of the ladder, we're just working-class.
Anna: Could they pay more?
Rene: Yeah, I reckon they could, but it's their profits, that's why they won't.

This is not to say that this process was necessarily opposed; but to experience this first-hand sense of the employer–worker relationship takes women workers out of the syndrome of relying on working husbands for 'second-hand' experience of wage labour (Porter, 1978) and of course draws women into the same problems of the conditions under which that labour power is sold. So for the Churchmans women, in spite of their immediate alienation from their own union, and their immediate experience of gender subordination within it, at a *general* level, trade unionism was still seen as the essential defence of working-class interests. To this extent, they had a strong identity as workers and as working-class and supported the union:

Ida: Well, they've cut down the hours over the years. They've also given us a good wage.

Stella: It's a safeguard, isn't it? You've got something to fight for, if something goes wrong. Well, they're *supposed* to – whether they do or no, I don't know.

In a number of shopfloor conversations, the common ground of trade unionism between men and women became as apparent as the divisions. The clearest bond was the common experience of rank-and-file workers in the face of bureaucratic union leadership:

Pearl: My husband can't do nothing about the agreement, he says. It's up to the union. If they accept it, they got to put up with it. It's up to the union. We don't know. If they accept this present offer, we've had it.

Mitigating against this common working-class identity, was always women workers' ambiguity as dependants in the family, and as individuals selling their labour power at a price to reproduce themselves. This was expressed in the contradictory statements that wages at Churchmans were *good for a woman*, but inadequate in terms of consumption, or individual survival.

Emy: Wages is all right here – we can't grumble. We could have more, though – with higher rents and coal.

Sandra: You know I thought it was good wages in here. Well, it is, I suppose, except for the price of flats and food and bus fares.

It was always this contradictory consciousness, this collision between what a woman felt she deserved or expected as a worker and as a woman, which made her approach to the workplace inherently unstable. At one moment, gratitude for having a job, fear that equal pay would price women out of the market, resignation, apparent apathy, all the well-worn stereotypes of women as brakes on the labour movement, emerged. At the next, dissatisfaction, criticism, opposition might erupt. What was most noticeable at Churchmans, however, was the fact that it was women's sense of oppression at work – being treated like machines, and subordinates by men – which provoked most opposition, and led to other issues such as pay and control. Thus, while the prevailing sexual division of labour at home and at work might be generally accepted, in the concrete work situation the immediate deprivation of the labour process together with a clear perception of sexual discrimination on the shopfloor predominated.

Anna: Do you think you should get equal pay?
Jenny: Yes, because be fair, like, *we're* working. They're [the men] not doing anything. They're just standing around. And there's us, we nits, sat down working.

Patronisation fuelled the angriest revolt and – because most managers were men – 'factory' consciousness (Beynon, 1975, p. 98) coincided with feminist consciousness, and one brought about the other.

Anna: What do you think of the work?
Patti: It's boring. It drives you mad.
Anna: Some of the management here think that you're quite happy, that you're not bored.
Patti: *Not bored*! We tell them, every time we're there, we tell them.
Rene: They never listen, do they?
Patti: I'd like to see them here. I'd like to turn it upside down, see the Manager on a weighing machine for a week.
Mary: Not a week! An hour would be enough!

This type of explosion surfaced only occasionally; but it showed that the ideologies of 'the temporary stay' or 'the housewife in the factory' were only fragments in a contradictory consciousness. In a similar way, the debilitating effect of sexual oppression in the union was only partial, and could be punctuated by rapid leaps in learning. The fact that women workers have often suddenly taken the lead in class struggle and trade union tactics has been well observed, and at Churchmans, an uneventful, 'backward' factory, the same movement was observed.

One example of such a leap was the experience of redundancies in 1971. Bearing in mind the passivity of the union leadership and the complete lack of shopfloor organisation, a general attitude of resignation to the 'inevitable' among 'the women workers' was not surprising.

Ida: We didn't meet the union on that, did we Emy?
Anna: Did you think it was a union matter?
Ida: Well, I don't think they could have done anything. Because at the time, the trade wasn't very good.

A year later, one might expect only vague memories of this period. But this was not the case. There were very clear recollections of a short episode during which the Bristol Socialist Women Group distributed leaflets arguing for work-sharing with other factories belonging to the Imperial Tobacco Company. Most vivid was the memory of one woman steward from Wills, who spoke at an *ad hoc*, unofficial factory-gate meeting, which, a year later, was remembered as the women's *own* meeting:

Pearl: The union officer was very rude. In the canteen when he was on about the redundancies. He told the men to shut up when they said their opinions.

Anna: Did any of *you* say anything there?

Pearl: We had *our* meeting more out in the street. It was somebody from Wills, wasn't it, come to try to speak up.

Anna: What did you think of her?

Pearl: Very good, she was. *Very good.*

The point being made is that from complete apparant dormancy, a large number of women were prepared to hear new tactics and create their *own* activity and clearly remember this a year later. This openness about rank-and-file initiative sprang directly from their exclusion from male defined and bureaucratic trade unionism. Of course, this eagerness can be construed as double-edged: did the sense of the meeting being *their own* meeting as women suggest they felt the men were irrelevant? Was it feminist isolationism? In fact, information about several subsequent rank-and-file meetings held in a pub suggests that this was *not* the uppermost meaning of 'our meeting'; for there were men here too, and what began to develop was a unity between disaffected rank-and-file workers which began to bridge sexual divisions. It ended in failure, but nevertheless, the fact that any opposition was mobilised, that it was initiated and remembered by women, is the significant point.

There was another, minor episode which again illustrated the same evenness and volatility of consciousness. This was on an ordinary, uneventful day after a 'day off' for the first ever one-day strike in a small packing department. The superficial atmosphere was of indifference to the whole matter. The strike had been a 'non event'. And yet, as the first ever stoppage, it was rare, and at another level of awareness, exciting. I was surprised at the interest and excitement I caused as I mentioned that I had attended the strike meeting at Transport House. After a stream of questions, the girls, who throughout their previous interviews had claimed 'not to bother', had raised the problem of union leadership and representation. They claimed that had they been informed and encouraged, they would have become involved:

Jenny: What we need is *our own* shop steward. We're fed up being the last to know anything. And I'll tell you another thing.

We'll have an end to this grading. You just can't keep up
with it. If you're down one week, you have to make it up the
next. It's too much.

One strike, and the sense of exclusion from it, touched a nerve which
triggered a whole sequence of attacks on the status quo. But it was an
unstable flash of consciousness. The girls were well aware of their own
volatility, its potential for mobilisation, and its weakness;

Jenny: It's all right talking about it, but it's different doing it. What
we need is a spark to set it off. That's all we need, and then
we'll all join in. But there's no one to do it.

Conclusions

The aim of this paper has been to contribute towards an understanding of
the relationship between wage labour and gender at the level of working
women's experience. I have tried to analyse the familiar problems of the
connection between material existence and ideology, and develop some
insights into what is distinctive about the experience of wage labour for
women. The turn to women as actors and to consciousness is an attempt to
move towards a dialectical understanding of the relationship between
gender and class and more specifically of the position of women workers in
one area of the world capitalist system.

A major part of this paper has been devoted to examining the ideological
and material processes of gender oppression which converge on women
workers, weakening their resistance to capitalist control. This process was
referred to as 'oppression shaping women's exploitation'. This analysis,
however, is part of a wider, Marxist perspective which contends that wage
labour is nevertheless the key to women's emancipation, through a dialectical, contradictory movement. The 'double burden' of family responsibility and wage labour lies at the heart of this contradiction. The contradiction is also expressed at various levels of consciousness, in which
women 'negotiate' an ambiguous identity strung between two received
images of 'worlds': the male world of wage labour, the female world of
home and family. There is acceptance, even collusion, with male-
dominated sexist stereotyping – and rejection. More generally, received
ideologies are reproduced but also collide with concrete experience. This
fragmentary consciousness is an illustration of the working-class 'common
sense' of Gramsci's analysis:

Common sense is not a single unique conception, identical in time
and space. It is the 'folklore' of philosophy, and, like folklore, it takes
countless different forms. Its most fundamental characteristic is that
it is a conception which, even in the brain of one individual, is fragmentary, incoherent, and inconsequential, in conformity with the

social and cultural position of those masses whose philosophy it is. (Gramsci, 1971, p. 419).

Gramsci was concerned with the collision of bourgeois ideology and working-class experience. But because of the evident existence of a male-dominated system of ideas and images, working-class women collide not only with bourgeois ideology, but with 'sexist' ideology (where 'sexist' denotes female subordination to men). 'Making sense' of being both women and wage workers therefore involves the constant negotiation both of *gender* relations and *class* relations.

What is significant about this regarding women and wage labour is that parts of this 'common sense' are attempts to accommodate strains and conflicts. But other parts of these 'fragments' are more volatile: concrete experience can quite suddenly override apparently stable practices and conceptions, and trigger a 'domino effect' whereby whole layers of self-conceptions and traditions can be knocked down. Because of their gender oppression as well as their class exploitation, the trigger can start from either or both experiences together. It could be any number of situations: work discipline; relative deprivation in relation to men, or to other women workers; grievances building up from the inability to penetrate the union machine; grading or equal pay issues; the speed of work; job security. In each case, it becomes impossible to separate the feminist from the class issue involved because oppression and exploitation are so tightly bound together for women workers. So while oppression holds women down, it also provides many ignition fuses – which is, of course, the significance of oppression for all other oppressed groups.

In terms of action, working women's resistance to exploitation as workers cannot be separated from their resistance to oppression as women. The employer cannot be confronted effectively without organisation; organisation at work demands involvement in the union; organisation in the union is possible only by fighting female oppression there; recognition that this is necessary must be forced onto husbands. So the fight against exploitation at work becomes a fight against oppression in the family, and vice versa. But as Churchmans illustrated only too painfully, it is all uphill work.

8 'Getting On'. Gender Differences in Career Development: A Case Study in the Hairdressing Industry
Margaret Attwood and Frances Hatton

Although in recent years more attention has been paid to women and their work, studies are depressingly few and far between and Delamont's point (Delamont, 1980, p. 112) about the 'unexciting' working world of many women contrasts with the masculine world portrayed in many of the classics of industrial sociology. This paper sets out to look at the concept of 'getting on' in such an 'unexciting' occupation, hairdressing. We show how, even in an industry associated with women, both as a major source of income (i.e. as customers) and, as a major source of employees, relative success amongst female workers remains obscured by the men who occupy dominant positions within the industry.

Our interest in the hairdressing industry came about because of our concern with occupational suggestion and the ways in which certain occupations are defined as 'women's work'. We decided to examine how women are perceived within this industry and why they appear to be unlikely to 'succeed'.

Research techniques
During the first stage of the research project, representatives of key employers' organisations, trade unions, manufacturing bodies, training organisations and the larger, or more famous, hairdressing firms were interviewed. From this exploratory work we were able to build up a picture of the industry and of employment relationships within it.

We were able to gain access to a technical college in order to interview apprentices who had obtained day-release to attend the City and Guilds 760 course. Some were in the first year, others were in the second year. We interviewed them in 12 groups which ranged in size from 3 to 7. Each group discussion lasted about three-quarters of an hour. This method was chosen to avoid the possible intimidation of a one-to-one interview as well as to encourage full and frank discussion. Groups were chosen in consultation with teaching staff on the basis of friendship patterns. Interviews were tape-recorded and have been transcribed verbatim. We recognise that not all hairdressing apprentices obtain day-release and we will be interviewing groups of those who do not receive such training at a later stage of the research. At the same time we wrote to salons in the area listed in 'Yellow Pages' and received 15 replies. We consider this to be a satisfactory response in view of recent reports on low pay within the industry (ACAS, 1981; Crine, 1980). We had thought that this might make salon owners and managers reluctant to talk to us. One aspect of researching within an industry employing mainly women, but in which women are viewed in a particular way, is the difficulty we found interviewing individuals who see women as unambitious and unmotivated. Coupled with this is the problem of listening to other women describe their 'preference' for a subordinate role, which we found personally distasteful (Oakley, 1981a; Woodward and Chisholm, 1981).

Institutional arrangements

The hairdressing industry did not become a significant part of the tertiary sector of the British economy until after the Second World War. Prior to this, as a personal service for women, hairdressing had been performed either by domestic servants or not at all for the majority of women. The two world wars had a considerable impact on women for two main reasons. Firstly, married women became employed to provide the labour necessary for the 'war effort' (Oakley, 1974; Sharpe, 1976). This precipitated a change in approach to personal appearance. Hairstyles began to change; fewer women had long hair. Secondly, the numbers of domestic servants declined; work outside the home for working-class women became more varied and more easily accessible. Such women were reluctant to return to servitude after the war years. As Ewbank (1977) points out, hairdressing services became both a market for women to spend their earnings and a new career for predominantly working-class women. It may well be the case that the low pay afforded to hairdressing as an occupation today is a vestige of the days of the domestic servant. Low pay, reinforced by the status of 'service work', may explain why this is an industry staffed predominantly by working-class girls and women. Not only is there an association with service work but there is also the stigma of working largely with women as clients, which makes this an occupation acceptable to only a small section of the labour force! Moreover, it often seems that such women should be grateful for employment (Rowbotham, 1973).

During the 1950s, a period of comparative affluence, an industry developed, employing mainly women, to serve mainly female clients.

However, the names associated with hairdressing throughout the 1950s and 1960s were predominantly male. Raymonde, Vidal Sassoon and Xavier Wenger have become folk heroes. Today, there are about 110,000 people employed as hairdressers. Of these 77,600 are full-time employees of whom 86% are women (Department of Employment, 1981). In addition, there are large numbers of self-employed hairdressers who generally work in their own salons, are peripatetic or work full or part-time in their own homes. No figures of the numbers of self-employed in the industry have been published since the 1971 Census of Distribution when there were 36,047 self-employed people working full-time in the industry, of whom 55% were women (Census of Distribution, 1971). Occupational segregation increases as one moves up the hairdressing hierarchy. The recent Joint Training Council survey estimated that approximately 10% of men in the hairdressing industry are apprentices. The figure for women was 30%. In contrast a slightly earlier survey by the Advisory Conciliation and Arbitration Service revealed that, whilst 19% of men employed in the industry are managers or chargehand hairdressers, the figure for women is 4% (ACAS, 1981).

The occupational status of the hairdresser is rather ambiguous. The New Earnings Survey classifies hairdressing as manual work, although pay data is collected only for female employees (the numbers of men employed being too small for purposes of this survey). In view of the length and content of the apprenticeship, however, there must be some justification for the 'traditional' attribution of craft status to this occupation. Labelling as unskilled work may be a factor in the decline in the number of boys applying for apprenticeships whilst the number of female applicants continues to rise.

Minimum wages and conditions of employment are laid down by the Hairdressing Undertakings Wages Council. The Union of Shop Distributive and Allied Workers, the only union recognised for collective bargaining purposes anywhere in the industry, organises less than 5% of those who work as hairdressers. USDAW does not organise the workers' side of the Wages Council, having withdrawn in 1971 because of 'the unrealistic attitude by the independent members and employers' representatives concerning wage rates paid in the industry'.[2] Certainly wages are low (Attwood, 1981, p. 10).

There is no training board for the industry, the Hairdressing and Allied Services Industry Training Board having been wound up in 1972. The Joint Training Council for the Hairdressing Industry was set up in 1978. In addition, no single professional or trade body represents hairdressers. The National Hairdressers' Federation and the Guild of Hairdressers compete with each other for members and for professional recognition. Further, hairdressing is characterised by a lack of statutory rules governing entry to the craft. Also there is no licensing system other than voluntary registration through the Hairdressing Council.

The variation in the type and quality of training provided for hairdressers is a reflection of the enormous range of services provided to clients. In our preliminary discussions with institutional representatives it became apparent that the glamorous section of the industry has links with the fashion trade and is located mainly in the centre of cities and large towns. There are considerable differences between this type of hairdressing salon and that which predominantly serves the 'shampoo and set trade'[3] and is located in backstreets of cities, small towns or rural areas. Between the two extremes lie the 'middle of the road' salons serving a middle-class clientele and providing a range of hairdressing services including both blowdrying and the more traditional shampoo and setting.

A further dimension of differences within the industry is the contrasts that exist between large and small firms and between the efficient and the inefficient (Attwood, 1981). Our account supports the argument of Barron and Norris (1976, p. 49) that it is possible for a single industry to contain both primary and secondary labour markets. Our material on career success is further evidence of their contention that women tend to predominate in the secondary rather than the primary sector.

'Getting on' – the dominant model and the 'role' of women within this industry

With this product variation in the industry in mind, we attempted to define 'getting on' in industry-specific terms. We found it to be a difficult concept to define, linked as it is to measures of success. Conventional wisdom dictates that success, in career terms, is determined by upward movement in a hierarchy and is linked to achieving either higher status in office or greater power. Such a definition does not take into account 'success' in the individual's own terms. However, as the primary aim of the research is to examine the ways in which occupational segregation is maintained together with the reasons for the failure of most women to achieve 'success', we decided that we would take the industry's own definition of 'success'. We asked those occupying positions of power and influence in the industry to define 'getting on'.

'Getting on': the industry's view

We conducted 16 interviews with institutional representatives, 12 of whom were men and 4 women. From this data a model emerged of the successful hairdresser and of expected career development. A career for a hairdresser is viewed as following logically sequential stages, with great emphasis being placed on success in entrepreneurial terms. This individualism (Attwood, 1981. pp. 16–17) is institutionalised throughout the various stages. Apprentices are paid very low wages and expected to work hard in order to succeed. The payment of stylists encourages an additional individualist orientation – basic pay being relatively low but supplemented by commission and tips. Young people therefore follow a model of 'building your own clientele' which forms the basis of the drive to ownership of a salon. Whilst there appeared to be a logical progression from apprentice to stylist, further progress was seen as diverging in one of two ways: either into ownership of a salon or chain of salons, or into a more bureaucratic career in one of the larger organisations.

Hairdressing is seen by those within it as being a 'young industry' where opportunities for advancement are easily available to those who are prepared to work hard and take risks. There is seen to be an upper age limit beyond which success cannot be achieved. A male hairdressing teacher suggested:

> if you haven't made it by the time you're 25 then that's it really.

This divide between careers was explained again in terms of age:

> Because the industry is young and geared to fashion the impetus is to get on quickly . . .

Salon ownership was equated with the opportunity for considerable financial reward. There was recognition that wages are low but the rationale for this was that money could be made by opening one's own salon.

The 'role' of women
The majority of hairdressers are female and it therefore would seem logical that there should be significant numbers of 'successful' women in the industry. However, in our interviews it became apparent that the successful hairdreser is male. Many expressed concern at the declining numbers of young men applying for apprenticeships. One man said:

> It's a pity about the boys. After all they are tomorrow's managers and owners.

There was also a belief in the 'natural' role of women, whose career was seen to be marriage and motherhood. Women, therefore, were believed not to be ambitious:

> They [the girls] tend not to be as ambitious as the boys and have shorter-term goals.

Frequently, we were told:

> All these young girls can think of is marriage . . .

There is, however, evidence from the first stage of our research to suggest that many women do aim to own their own salons. Of the 15 salon owners interviewed so far, 10 were women. Later stages of our research are beginning to show much the same pattern. There is no statistical information on salon ownership broken down by gender but we would suggest that, for many women hairdressers, salon ownership is a career goal which is achieved. Such women are, however, invisible within the industry. On close examination, it became apparent that there is an additional dimension. A 'successful' individual not only opens his or her own salon but does so in the fashionable and glamorous area of the industry. Our research so far has indicated that women tend to open salons catering for the less glamorous 'shampoo and set trade'. Glamour and, to a lesser extent, youth are the important components of success in this industry and are related to a particular view of women. Both as hairdressers and as clients women are viewed as passive and malleable for as long as they remain young and therefore attractive. Male managers in fashionable salons talked of their job and their relationship with the client as 'helping a woman to look good', 'creating an image for a woman'. They seemed to believe that many women prefer male stylists and saw this as enabling them to promote their business interests based on their beliefs about the significance of client preferences. It was apparent that they knew that this was a major factor in their own success and one which is very much linked to the failure of female hairdressers.

This attitude of controlling the appearance of women permeates the entire industry, with the notable exception of the 'shampoo and set' section. However, it should be noted that male hairdressers only relate to younger, fashionable or rich clients in this way. By implication older women, who are less inclined to follow fashion changes and are, therefore, less malleable, are seen as unattractive, both as hairdressers and as customers.

'Getting on', therefore, means operating within a particular section of this industry – and if, as we have found so far, women tend to own salons in the less glamorous areas, it is hardly surprising that they remain invisible.

Apprenticeship and beyond
Most of the girls we interviewed seemed to have a very positive approach to the occupation and were looking forward to the day when their training was completed. The job gave them both technical and social satisfaction. Satisfaction with the techniques of hair care seemed to derive from the malleability of the medium and the opportunities which it gave for creativity. One girl said:

If you are prepared to try almost anything, some customers will let you do more or less anything, so you can play away with the hair for hours.

Apprentices appeared to value the perceived independence of their occupational role. The chance to develop new skills was welcomed and a sense of achievement appeared to be linked to the opportunity to produce a unique finished product.

Many compared their jobs with alternative occupations, in particular factory work, and explicitly rejected the latter for its perceived monotony. Clearly they did not see hairdressers as occupying roles 'at the bottom of the labour market, both in class and in sexual terms' (Pollert, 1981). It may be for this reason that they appeared to view marriage not as a 'career' as did the girls working at Churchmans, but as a fairly inevitable event which would occur at some, as yet unknown, time in the future.

Elaboration of this is necessary for the work undertaken during apprenticeship, and during the first year in particular, was viewed with some contempt. Apprentices frequently described themselves as 'dogsbodies' who undertook 'skivvying jobs'. The apprenticeship was clearly something to be 'gone through' so far as many of these young people were concerned and the characteristics of a 'rite of passage' were emphasised by the seeming tendency to increase the hardship suffered by apprentices. In some salons this seemed to be achieved by increasing the 'distance' between stylists and apprentices. Apprentices described what happened when the salon was quiet:

> We have to find something to do which is harder work. The stylists go sit down. The apprentices can't.

Pressure of work also appeared to create problems in relationships with clients, for apprentices seemed to have to mediate on occasions between overworked stylists and customers wanting a quicker service:

> If someone's under the dryer and they want to come out and the stylist isn't ready for them, the person you've put under the dryer will keep looking at you as if it's your fault and the stylist will say, 'Just leave them for another five minutes so I can get this lady out' which happens when you're really busy.

A major topic of conversation in our discussion groups was the nature of the tasks carried out by apprentices. Much of this appeared to fall into the category of 'dirty work' – cleaning floors, toilets, blinds, mirrors, windows, rubbish bins, combs, brushes, rollers, etc., washing towels. Other tasks were less dirty but required few skills. Making coffee and tea and shampooing clients fell into this category. There were some graphic descriptions of these 'back-stage' facets of hairdressing:

> Cleaning the toilets, emptying the bin, scrubbing the floor. Hair smells. If people come in for dry haircutting, if that's kept up there for a couple of days, that doesn't half whiff . . . smells all mouldy . . .

Apprentices complained about the results of the kind of work which they were required to do. Some had dermatitis from constantly shampooing clients' hair, others had sore feet and backache from being on their feet all day. Others complained of their broken nails and feared the onset of varicose veins in later life. One boy said simply, 'You get hair all over your body.'

The hours of work and pay were also sources of vociferous complaint:

> The pay is terrible, for the hours you work.

> Money. It's just not enough to survive on. You have to rely on your tips but then again you don't get many of those either.

The clash between work and social life because of the length and distribution of the working week is clear from this exchange between three female apprentices:

> In our shop we have three late nights which goes on after we shut. . . . I mean on Tuesday sometimes I'm there till half past eight clearing up, and we have one till seven and one till six and Saturday we stay open till four so they're long hours and we don't really get no lunch breaks.

> I don't like working Saturdays. I never liked working Saturdays. . . .

> Neither do I cos I like to go out Saturday. . . .

However, most of the apprentices had a fairly clear understanding of these unsalutary features before entering the industry. For most of this had been gained by working as 'Saturday girls' in hairdressing salons. Some had also been told of the less desirable aspects of the occupation of hairdressing by teachers and others involved in the provision of careers advice to young people. Others had been warned by friends or relatives who were hairdressers about the negative aspects of the job. A few commented that the reality had turned out to be somewhat worse than the image with which they were presented.

However, there was a quite clear acceptance of the legitimacy of even the most distasteful aspects of the job and of the lowly position of the apprentice:

> You've got to start from the bottom.

> The rotten jobs are what apprentices are for.

It appeared that the end of the apprenticeship became a highly valued goal because of the evils which then became part of the past.

It's much nicer when you don't have to take all the rubbish out and keep passing rollers and shampooing.

You don't have to be careful about sitting down all day. 'Can you do this?' 'Can you do that?' That's what you'll get away from.

Ordering other people around seemed to be a legitimate mode of behaviour in the industry. The boredom and drudgery of the apprenticeship is alleviated by beginning to be able to do to others that which thus far has been done to oneself:

It's better when someone else starts. Then you can order them around.

Can it be said that apprentices have some notion of a 'career'? They seem to have developed an expected rate of movement from one role to another by means of a training programme, however formally or informally defined. Hairdressing as a highly labour-intensive service occupation is not subject to rapid or extensive technological change. Most hairdressers begin their working lives as apprentices and progress to the job of stylist over a period of three to five years. Some become salon owners or managers or artistic or style directors, often at a relatively early age. In different parts of the industry the career paths may differ. For example, there is some evidence to indicate that some of the larger chains of salons have developed internal labour markets. Here identification with the organisation is encouraged and individuals, who are recognised as particularly able, may progress from apprentice to stylist to senior stylist to salon manager or style director in less than a decade of work in a single company. However, these salons are not the norm. It would appear that career paths for the majority of apprentices are more restricted. Most, once qualified, will spend the rest of their lives working in salons similar to those in which they have trained. A few will become salon owners or managers in this section of the industry.

Many of the female apprentices, especially those who had not done well at school, saw their future selves primarily as working wives and mothers. Like the girls studied by Sharpe (1976) they recognised the need to work after marriage and expected to stay at home when children are very small. However, they said that they intended to return to work when their children were old enough. Most stopped short, however, of wanting to do anything involving the commitment they saw as characteristic of a full-time career. Many clearly had given thought to combining work with motherhood and saw working from home as a solution:

You can do it from home. Loads of people do that.

Several of them used the term 'doing it on the side' and, realising the sexual imagery they had used, became embarrassed – this seemed to be a response to a tension between job aspirations and gender role stereo-typing. Some explained that, whilst they saw themselves as working, they nonetheless subscribed to the traditional family role division and saw their work as primarily a way of supplementing family income and contributing a 'second wage'. Some saw their work as secondary to their husband's careers and saw hairdressing as 'women's work'. This was confirmed by their view of male hairdressers as homosexual and in this way 'lesser men'.

For other girls hairdressing as an occupation appeared to fall into Hughes' category of 'adventure' (Hughes, 1974). Many of these girls had aspirations to work in hairdressing salons on cruise liners. For them 'going on the liners' was a way of combining a desire to travel and an association with the glamour of the industry. Others saw working in London as a desirable end, although interestingly, it was not the work which was seen as being significantly different, but rather the customers:

> It's the people isn't it. Rich and that, wanting different styles all the time. Not like the ladies here. They're boring. No. London is posh and working in a West End salon is posh 'cos of the clients.

For others, hairdressing was a 'gateway' to achievement and responsibility in another occupation. For this minority hairdressing presented a means to another end and a way of combining different ambitions. Beauty therapy was the most frequently mentioned of these other occupations.

As we indicated earlier, the number of male apprentices in the industry is relatively small. However, our work shows that there are significant differences between boys and girls so far as careers are concerned. For boys the notion of 'getting on' as a hairdresser seems to coincide more closely with the definition of success of institutional representatives discussed earlier. Even where the next stage was the same, for example 'going on the liners', the reasons given for wanting to do this were quite different. Where girls saw such jobs as an 'adventure', boys seemed to view it as just another opportunity to make money in a situation where both pay and tips were thought to be better. Similarly, for girls it seemed that ownership of salons was seen as a means of attaining independence, whereas for boys it was again a means of becoming wealthy.

These gender differences extended into apprentices' perceptions of a successful hairdresser. There was a high degree of unanimity among the apprentices that the most important relationship for the hairdresser is that with the client. Most seemed to feel that successful hairdressers are those who are able to develop good relationships with clients and who also, though less importantly, have the necessary artistic skills. The girls were just as certain as the boys about the way to become successful but much less certain about their ability to achieve this. One girl summed up the dominant view on the interaction between male stylists and female clients.

> They can get away with murder. 'Let's give you a new style', they say. Because if the bloke turns round to the woman and says, 'Oh, that looks nice', she's getting a man's point of view and when she gets home she'll think, 'Well if that bloke liked it, my husband will think the same.'

Many of the girls appeared to feel that male stylists tended to trade on the preference of many younger women, in particular, to be attended by a male stylist. They described male stylists they knew as 'charming' their female clients, 'getting away with more' and, thus, exploiting the client relationship to their own advantage. This resulted in male stylists being in greater demand by clients and, probably, reaping greater material rewards for less effort.

The relationship with a male client is more fleeting than with a female client since fewer hairdressing services are generally required. Just as the girls doubted their ability to manipulate the client relationship to their own advantage, so too many doubted their ability to develop the necessary creative and imaginative skills to become famous. One girl was very pessimistic in this context:

> I don't think I'd ever be able to create different styles. I wouldn't be able to do anything like that. I wouldn't have enough ability. You know like when you see 'designed by so-and-so', I wouldn't be able to do that.

The boys generally seemed more determined to get on and this appeared to give them the motivation to survive in an occupation which is labelled as 'women's work'. This may have been the reason why the apprenticeship appeared to be a more stringent trial for the boys than for the girls. Hairdressing lacks the 'essentially masculine ethos' of work regarded as essential by working-class boys (Willis, 1978). In their terms it is 'cissy' work which, at least at the apprentice stage, requires subservience both to clients and stylists and where low pay characterises the early years. The male apprentices to whom we spoke seemed to see apprenticeship as a state to be endured.

> You put up with it 'cos if you work hard you can get on.

This, on occasions, seemed to have resulted in the turning of the employment relationship to their advantage, *vis-à-vis* the girls. For example some planned to negotiate more advantageous commission rates once they were qualified stylists, arguing that women rarely do this.

The ideology of work held by these boys seemed to contain something of the protestant ethic in the recognition of a connection between hard work and success, combined with elements of machismo, which were similar to the perceptions of 'real work' expressed by Willis's 'lads' (1978, p. 96). This latter view seemed implicit in the career plans of the boy who told us:

> [I want to] make a lot of money and own my own shops and pay other people chicken feed wages.

It seems to us that there are clear differences in the views of work, both present and future, expressed by male and female apprentices. Many of the girls appear to have chosen hairdressing because they had failed to gain formal qualifications at school, and therefore found many careers closed to them. Hairdressing as an accepted area of 'women's work' was felt to be an area where they might be successful. However, many girls again branded themselves as failures, both in relation to their clients and in the development of artistic skills.

The unsuccessful/successful woman
We have already suggested that within the industry the successful young hairdresser operates in the glamorous or fashionable sector. Not only is success visible here in terms of industry wide fame, but it is also assumed that this primary sector is more profitable. The older female client who predominates in the 'shampoo and set trade' is not seen as contributing towards success. As a result of this process women salon owners become invisible in industry-wide terms, since most of their businesses appear to be located in this secondary sector. Further, many female hairdressers leave the industry within a few years of becoming qualified and there was little recognition in our interviews that those who leave may re-enter the labour market later. In this way such women become invisible, or their businesses are seen to be unimportant, as the assumption is that any income earned by these women is 'pin money'. In interview women salon owners were consistently described in ways denoting a lack of seriousness. Marriage was clearly seen as ending potential careers. The women were seen as 'occupying time', 'earning a little extra', but not as making a positive contribution toward the industry.

Women salon owners we interviewed suggested that the relationship between client and stylist involves issues other than hair care, but this was found to be ignored by those who work in the more glamorous parts of the industry, who see the need to build up a large clientele purely in functional and financial terms.

With only one exception all the women interviewed had returned to hairdressing after the birth of their children. Nearly all of them talked of the isolation they experienced as full-time mothers. The majority said they felt a need for independence and had returned to hairdressing as a way of achieving this. We found that these women expressed feelings of empathy with their female clients and were conscious of the social aspects of their role. One spoke of women's needs in the following ways:

> ... they can come here to relax, away from home, kids and house-work, and it's nice to have someone else do your hair, makes you feel and look better. Also, we chat. They know that they can tell me things and that I'll listen and be sympathetic. For a while you can get away totally, and that's important.

In many of the salons there was a feeling of a 'community of women' in which men, customers and hairdressers alike, were excluded. Indeed one spoke most disparagingly of male colleagues:

> I don't think much of the men in this industry. They'll say anything, flatter chat and you know that the woman is uncomfortable and what's more that the style just doesn't suit her. I call that dishonest and I'm afraid that many of them are just that ... dishonest.

Associated with this perception of women as clients was a recognition of the needs of employees. Part-time staff were often employed and on terms that were mutually convenient. Additionally, women salon owners were able to determine their own hours of work, and manage their work and home lives in this way.

As with Hunt's (1980, pp. 169–70) working wives in Silverdale, it appeared that our small sample of 'unsuccessful–successful' hairdressers saw their salons as a place where domestic experiences could be carried over into the work context and where there was greater scope for the development of relationships with other women – both clients and staff – than had been possible in the relative isolation of their own homes. In these ways, we found these women termed themselves as successful.

However, success has ambivalent properties for women and we would argue that many of these women have reinterpreted the industry definition of 'getting on'. Several suggested that their primary aim was not to make large amounts of money but to achieve independence through work, which was for them both enjoyable and convenient. Failing to expand was couched in terms of 'too much responsibility' or 'just not worth it'. There was a strong desire not to exploit either customers or staff.

There was a tacit recognition of industry definitions of success, although in the long term this was regarded as unimportant for the women:

> Regretfully, it's the men who've made this industry what it is today. Not that that's all good mind you, but that says a lot about the women working in it.

It seems that for these female salon owners acceptance of their role as working wives and mothers was associated with a perception of themselves as relatively insignificant hairdressers. However, there was a quite positive desire not to be seen to exploit other women, whether they be clients or employees. There was recognition that the development of their existing businesses to serve a more sophisticated clientele was not a desirable goal. We argue that acceptance of their occupational roles in the secondary labour market in this industry is not accidental, but a response to, and a deliberate rejection of, the values and occupational ideology of owners and managers of businesses in the primary labour market. They perceive the possible exploitation of women at their own stage in the life-cycle. This leads to an implicit rejection of the youth culture (with its tendency to label women as beautiful objects) and of the glamorous high fashion sector of the industry. Associated with this is a tacit reinterpretation of the industry and definition of 'getting on' put forward by institutional representatives and an emphasis on concepts such as independence and caring for women as clients.

Conclusions

From our research we have found that the expected average 'life' of the female hairdresser is around five years. After this it is expected that young women will leave employment in order to raise a family. This, it was suggested, marks the end of a career for the female hairdresser. However, we found that not only did many of the female apprentices have ambitions to open their own salons, but also that many salon owners are women. It would appear that many women in this industry have two distinct career stages, which are often separated by a gap of several years. As a result of this gap, and the tendency to own salons in the 'shampoo and set' market segment, women appeared to have become invisible in the eyes of institutional representatives. As a result we found that there was a split in perception of potential along gender lines, young boys being seen according to their career potential whilst young girls are viewed according to their 'natural' sex roles.

'What happens to the young women who leave the industry in their early twenties?' was a question which intrigued us. There is no statistical data to answer this question but time and time again in our interviews it emerged that many do *not* leave the occupation, but become a largely invisible 'reserve army' of low paid home hairdressers. Much of this work undoubtedly is part of the so-called 'black economy'. We found that because of the poor incomes received, many apprentices also provide this service to their family and friends, often with the cooperation and knowledge of their employers. In this way the low pay of the apprentice is legitimated. However, employers continuously expressed concern about the practice of home hairdressing, arguing that home hairdressers, most of whom are said to be married women, undermine the economic viability of hairdressing businesses. Recently it has been suggested to us in interviews that the clients of most home hairdressers are elderly women or young mothers with small children, who find it difficult to visit a salon. If this is so then home hairdressers may not be a threat to business interests. No research has yet been done in this area, but it may be that the damage reportedly done by home hairdressing is a myth.

What is relevant here is the expectation of young female hairdressers that they will leave formal employment for a period of time. Such young women seem to value their work and their independence and many appear to wish to maintain their skills in order to return to work in a salon at a later stage of their lives. So, whilst home hairdressing may be seen as an economic threat by some people in the industry, the reality for women who undertake such work is substantially different. However, home hairdressers, in the main, do charge low prices for their services. Some apprentices recognised this commenting that the client will negotiate the price she pays for the service and that, particularly where the hairdresser is working in the client's home, the power balance swings in the client's favour. The concern of the home hairdresser for the client's welfare, together with her own poor self-image, leads her to charge a price which barely meets the costs which she meets in providing this service.

The tendency to label female hairdressers as failures rebounds back on the industry in the belief that the home hairdresser undermines profitability in the salon. Our work to date leads us to suggest that only when the industry revalues women's contribution to its success will hairdressing cease to be a low status, low pay occupation.

Notes

1. Hairdressers normally enter the occupation as apprentices (though some are trained in private schools). After training two years are spent in a role known as 'operative hairdresser' after which the individual is recognised as a fully fledged stylist. Under the 1964 Hairdresser's (Registration) Act the Hairdressing Council is charged with the duty of maintaining a register of hairdressers. Registered hairdressers are required to have satisfactorily completed either a three-year indentured apprenticeship with provision for attendance at day-release classes or a two-year full-time course. In either case the course of study must have been located in a local education authority college and examinations must be approved (i.e. City and Guilds 760 or equivalent). At present less than 10% of hairdressers are registered. This situation is radically different from that which exists in the United States and most of Western Europe where by law only master craftsmen may open salons and only qualified craftsmen may practise

as hairdressers.
2. Personal communication from M. Gordon, National Officer, Union of Shop Distributive and Allied Workers, October 1980.
3. 'Shampoo and set trade' is a term frequently used in this paper to denote a particular part of the hairdressing industry, i.e. a salon that serves a neighbourhood of a city, town or rural area and whose clients predominantly require this sort of business.

9 Feminisation and Unionisation: A Case Study from Banking
John Heritage

Introduction

An important by-product of the women's movement has been a growing awareness within sociology of the sexual division of labour at the workplace (Beechey, 1978; Barron and Norris, 1976; Brown, 1976; Crompton and Jones, 1982; Ellis, 1981; Gardiner, 1975a; Garnsey, 1978; McNally, 1979; Purcell, 1979; Wainwright, 1978; West, 1978, 1982). As the dates of these citations suggest, this awareness is a comparatively recent phenomenon and, with a few notable exceptions (particularly Caplow, 1964; Myrdal and Klein, 1968), the pre-1970 student of the general sociological literature on occupations could be forgiven for acquiring only a subliminal recognition that women made up a substantial proportion of the labour forces of most developed industrial societies.

The sexual division of labour has been an important focus in a series of studies of the British banking industry (Blackburn, 1967; Mumford and Banks, 1967; Graham and Llewellyn, 1976; Heritage, 1977; Egan, 1982) and the present paper considers the impact of the sexual division of labour on unionisation within the industry. It will be proposed that the progressive feminisation of routine office work in banking was a significant factor in the growth and recognition of the National Union of Bank Employees (NUBE, now the Banking, Insurance and Finance Union, BIFU) within the industry during the late 1960s. By extension, it will be suggested that accounts of white-collar unionism cannot continue to ignore the phenomenon of sexual divisions within the white-collar labour force. The arguments of this paper will be developed by reference to events in banking during the period 1960–70 – a period of rapid white-collar union growth in the United Kingdom (Price and Bain, 1976), during which NUBE became the first white-collar union in this century to gain recognition as a negotiating body by means of unaided industrial action.

Historical background: the creation of a feminised office proletariat in banking

At the end of the Second World War, banking was a predominantly masculine occupation in which men constituted a little over 70% of employees in the London Clearing Banks.

As the figures summarised in Table 9.1 indicate, women were less than a third of the banks' labour force in 1948, but constituted a majority of employees by 1970. This progressive feminisation of the labour force in banking occurred against a background of more general growth of employment in the industry and, while the male labour force grew by approximately 40% between 1948 and 1970, the female labour force grew by some 270% during the same period.

The men who entered banking in the early 1950s, as today, were expected to follow a career which would pass through a number of recognisable steps. First there would be a period of routine office clerical work with ledgers, standing orders and so on, progressing through work on the counter – the 'shop window' of banking – to more senior and specialised functions such as dealing with securities, foreign transactions and the like. During this period, male staff were expected to equip themselves for promotion by studying for qualifications administered by the Institute of Bankers. Subject to success in the Institute's examinations, promotion beyond the routine clerical level involved two recognisable jumps. The first was to posts involving special technical competence or responsibility – accountant, senior clerk, senior securities clerk, etc. – which were normally 'appointed' posts, so called because such promotions required ratification by the General Manager of the bank. The second step was to executive, managerial and sub-managerial posts – termed 'board appointments' since they required formal ratification by the directors of the bank. These latter jumps involved a measure of competition among male staff. A young man who would take the trouble to compute his chances of achieving a board appointment would, basing himself on 1948 statistics and fail-

Table 9.1   The growth of male and female employment in the London Clearing Banks, 1948–70

	% Men	% Women	Total employees
1948	71.1	39.9	84,869
1955	64.5	35.5	93,833
1960	57.4	42.6	114,618
1965	52.4	47.6	144,775
1970	47.0	53.0	176,875

Source: Figures released by the Committee of London Clearing Bankers, 1971

ing to anticipate the growth of female employment in the industry, conclude that he had a roughly one in four chance of achieving his objective and rather more chance of reaching an 'appointed' post.

By contrast, the young women who increasingly entered banking during the 1950s and 1960s did not expect, and were not expected, to make a career in banking. On average, they remained in bank employment for about four years (NBPI, 1969, p.5) and, by and large, they took no steps to gain the qualifications necessary for 'career' promotion beyond the routine clerical posts.[1] Thus of the 76,000 women employed in the London Clearing Banks in 1967, 98.7% were routine clerical staff. Of the 10,245 managerial posts in the London Clearing Banks, 99.65% were occupied by men and the latter occupied 93.65% of the 13,515 'appointed' posts (NBPI, 1969, Appendix G, p.24). These figures can be set into relief by noting that, during this same year, men constituted almost exactly 50% of the banks' labour force. A similarly extreme pattern can be derived from figures for the United States' banks. There the number of female bank clerks ('bank tellers') doubled between 1960 and 1970 (from 93,000 to 215,000) and had doubled again (to 410,000) by 1978. During the same period, male bank clerks actually declined numerically (from 39,000 to 38,000).[2] Estimates from the middle of this period indicate that while women occupied 73% of clerical posts, they occupied only 15% of 'official/managerial' posts (Alexander and Sapery, 1973, p.3; for a more recent case study, see Cabral *et al.* 1981).

Although many of the women who entered banking during the 1960s may not have expected or wished to make a career in banking (Mumford and Banks, 1967; Blackburn, 1967; Myrdal and Klein, 1968; Graham and Llewellyn, 1976; Heritage, 1977), the recruiting policies followed by the banks reinforced this assumption and, more generally, reflected the view that while men would pursue careers in the industry, short-term female employees would continue to perform the bulk of routine clerical work. Thus during the 1960s the differential recruitment of men and women followed a pattern in which women were recruited in direct proportion to the rapidly rising volume of routine work, while men were employed in proportion to the much slower growth in the numbers of bank branches which they would eventually command (Heritage, 1977, pp.144–5). The banks' assumptions about the occupational roles of men and women permeate the National Board for Prices and Incomes reports of the period (NBPI, 1965, 1967, 1969) and the Wilde Report (1973) on career qualifications within the industry. These same assumptions were reflected also in the minutiae of employment policy. Thus throughout the 1960s age-incremental salary scales for women embodied progressively narrowing incremental steps after the age of 24 and thus provided a material and symbolic disincentive to remain in bank employment. For men over 24, by contrast, the incremental steps widened (NBPI, 1965). During the same period, the banks did not hesitate to dilute the educational qualifications required for female entrants while, if anything, adopting a more restrictive policy towards men. As late as 1975, on application forms for the Midland Bank, only male entrants were asked: 'Do you undertake to study for and make every effort to pass the Diploma Examinations of the Institute of Bankers?'

In sum, the late 1950s and early 1960s witnessed the progressive feminisation of routine clerical work in banking. While routine clerical staff had previously comprised some female employees together with a proportion of men who were slowly 'working their way through the system' and a residue of 'non-promotable' men, this pattern was changing by the early 1960s. The increasing proportion of female routine clerical staff led to accelerated, and more certain, promotion for men with the result that, during a period of 'over-full' employment, the banks could compete more effectively in the labour market for well qualified male 'career' entrants. Moreover, by employing young women (75% of whom were under 23 in 1965 according to NBPI, 1969) with generally low and short-run expectations of work and on age-related salary scales, a comparatively docile clerical labour force could be maintained while keeping average labour costs to a minimum.

Overall, it can be suggested that by the mid 1960s routine office work was predominantly undertaken by 'non-career' female employees. These workers constituted an 'office proletariat' in every sense. But they had a turnover rate of 25% per annum for women under 24 and of 21% per annum overall (NBPI, 1969). The 'office proletariat' renewed itself, on average, every four and a half years. It is to the paradoxical impact of this emerging feminised office proletariat on trade unionism in banking that we now turn.

Trade unionism in banking and the 'recognition problem'
Throughout the past 60 years collective organisation in banking has been characterised by competition between 'internal' staff associations organising employees on a 'bank by bank' basis and a single national union, the National Union of Bank Employees (now BIFU). Although the former achieved recognition for negotiating purposes from their inception in the 1920s, they generally remained unaggressive and ineffective 'staff side' representatives throughout the post-war period until 1960 and were largely perceived as such by bank employees (Blackburn, 1967). By contrast, the more militant and aggressive NUBE encountered sustained opposition from the bank employers from its inception (Allen and Williams, 1960; Blackburn, 1967; Bain, 1970), and its lack of recognition during the period 1920–60 seriously impaired its effectiveness as a collec-

Table 9.2   Percentages of staff organised by NUBE and the combined bank
staff associations

	Staff Associations	NUBE
1950	44.9	26
1955	52.5	39.1
1960	52.3	35

tive organisation and its appeal to bank staffs. Throughout the period the bank employers displayed a clear preference for the recognised staff associations and membership of the latter was widely understood to be appropriate for 'career' staff. NUBE membership – although considerable – was, by contrast, more generally associated with 'youth' and 'immaturity' and (permanent or transitory) 'disgruntlement'. Throughout the 1950s the recognised, but ineffective, staff associations maintained a considerable membership advantage over the aggressive, but unrecognised, NUBE, as Table 9.2 shows.

During this period, the staff associations enjoyed the benefits of recognition in the form of institutionalised access to staff and the 'credit effects' (Bain and Elsheikh, 1976) of claims to success in the context of pay awards. Although the latter were announced as negotiated on a separate 'bank by bank' basis with the individual staff associations, the reality of the matter was that, in conditions of increasing oligopoly in the banking industry, bank salaries were determined through a process of tacit collusion in which an initial pay settlement in one bank would rapidly become the 'norm' for the remainder (Cameron Report, 1963; Heritage, 1977). In this context NUBE, which advocated overt national pay negotiations, could offer only a focus for the expression of staff frustration. During the mid 1950s for example, when pay settlements were low, large numbers of bank workers expressed their dissatisfaction by transferring from staff association to union membership. Throughout this period, neither the union nor the staff associations made systematic attempts to cater to the needs and aspirations of the growing numbers of female bank employees and indeed, throughout the decade, the female memberships of both organisations declined relative to male membership.

During the period 1920–60, two major attempts were made to secure recognition for NUBE within the context of a national negotiating framework for banking (see Blackburn, 1967, pp.156–61, pp.167–9 for details). These efforts broke down under a combination of factors. On the one hand, the resistance of individual bank employers or staff associations was sufficient to undermine attempts at constituting national negotiating machinery on an industry-wide basis. On the other hand, when union membership was comparatively low its officers tended to abate their demands for inclusion in national machinery for fear of being consistently outvoted in 'staff-side' decision-making constitutionally based on proportional representation. While both of these factors were rooted in the long history of competition and distrust between the union and the staff associations, the ability of these organisations to form a unified staff side was further hindered by the manipulation of these factors by the bank employers. For example, it was not difficult for individual banks to persuade the officers of their staff associations of the dire consequences of being 'swamped' by the union. Moreover, during periods of union growth and corresponding pressure for inclusion within national negotiating machinery, larger than usual salary increases could be awarded and credited to staff association negotiations. In turn, membership would return to the staff associations and union officers would, once again, become reluctant to press for national negotiating machinery. The failure of NUBE to achieve recognition was thus based on a complex of dynamically interrelated factors. These persistently combined over a period of 50 years in a stalemate situation which the union was powerless to break by force. The union's inability to compel the employers and the staff associations to recognise it may be traced back to the nature of bank employment itself.

Bank employment: patterns of loyalty and alignment

For the past 70 years the individual clearing banks have successfully sought to create and maintain a 'unitary' ideology (Fox, 1966) among successive generations of their employees. The latter are expected to view the enterprise as a 'team' under legitimate managerial leadership to whom loyalty is owed as of right. By and large, bank employees have viewed the individual banks in this way (Allen and Williams, 1960; Blackburn, 1967; Heritage, 1977).

The success of this unitary ideology among bank staffs is not difficult to explain. The majority of bank employees work in small 'High Street' branches, 75% of which – in 1965 – had a staff of fewer than 14 (NBPI, 1967, Table 9.1). A rigid division of labour is absent from such branches (even after mechanisation). Flexibility and mutual cooperation among staff are essential for the smooth running of the branch. The atmosphere of secrecy, and in modern times danger, which attends large financial transactions promotes a sense of teamwork and solidarity. Moreover the banks have continuously operated an open system of internal promotion through which clerks may, in principle, aspire to the highest positions within the bank and expect too that these positions will not be filled by 'outsiders'. Correlatively, the managers at all levels will have been promoted from within and do not believe, nor expect others to believe, that they have differing or conflicting aims from their subordinates even though they represent the bank directorate to the average bank clerk and exercise a measure of influence over his prospects. The career structure and the manner of its operation in banking thus operate to promote a sense of identification, justice and belonging within a particular bank.

Additionally, for the most part of the period 1920–70, it was impossible for clerks to move from the employ of one bank to another. By the age of 30, a bank clerk is equipped with a set of non-transferable job skills and pension rights.[3] He is 'locked into' the structure. For the 'career man', the only way forward is 'up' and, in recent years especially, his chances of upward progression have been considerable. In this context, the average male 'career oriented' clerk will perceive two avenues to economic advancement: individual promotion and collective negotiation. The former will have considerably greater anticipated pay-off than the latter, though the rational clerk will pursue both. However, in pursuit of the latter, the clerk will on the whole seek to avoid joining organisations or adopting positions that he perceives as jeopardising his promotion chances. Faced with a choice between a recognised staff association which 'speaks for him' and is approved by the management which he aspires to join, and an unrecognised union which although adopting militant postures is broadly ineffective and membership of which is perceived as incompatible with managerial status, our clerk will display a tendency to join the former, a tendency which steadily increases as he becomes more senior (Blackburn, 1967). Thus while a pool of 'non-promotable' men may remain with the union, even the below average 'career man' may show a disproportionate tendency to eschew union membership in favour of the local staff association. And, of course, the chief consideration which holds him to this choice is hope of advancement.

But what then of those who have neither the hope nor the expectation of advancement, the ever increasing proportion of 'non-career' female bank workers? The key to their dispositions lies in the short-term nature of their anticipated employment with the bank. As we have seen, the majority of female bank employees during the period 1955–70 were aged 17–23. For them, bank employment is a 'job of work' which yields sufficient income which, since most live at home with their parents and have few family responsibilities, will be spent on 'soft' consumer items (Heritage, 1977, pp.249–332). For most, bank work is not unpleasant, the employers are reasonable if not overgenerous, and marriage is the 'light' at the end of a none too arduous 'tunnel' (Heritage, 1977; see also Myrdal and Klein, 1968; Mumford and Banks, 1967; Graham and Llewellyn, 1976). In this context, trade union membership is routinely perceived in 'cost-effective' terms (Heritage, 1977, pp.333–416) and the unrecognised (and comparatively 'expensive') NUBE was not regarded as a good 'buy'.

Moreover the union was doubly unavailable to women workers. Firstly, lacking recognition, the union could not avail itself of the 'institution-alised access' to employees at the workplace which was freely provided to the recognised staff associations. Secondly, in the small branches with their prevailing 'unitary' ideological atmosphere, branch norms (Black-burn, 1967) established by the longer serving men favoured the staff associations. Since, up to 1960 at least, union policies held out no specific attractions for women, the latter lacked any incentive to join it, for although their mouths were scarcely stuffed with gold, discontent over salaries was episodic and the really disgruntled had a further choice which was unavailable to their male counterparts, namely to take their skills else-where. These considerations go some substantial distance towards accounting for the fact that when white collar unions (including NUBE) are unrecognised and male membership is low, female membership is usually still lower (for further discussion of this phenomenon and its con-verse, that when white collar unions are recognised and male membership is high, female membership is often higher, see Heritage, 1977, pp.56–69).

In sum, the growth of a feminised 'office proletariat' in banking pre-sented, and continues to present, a paradoxical aspect. For on the one hand it is truly a proletariat locked into low level wage employment, and indeed carrying out the 'functions of labour' (Carchedi, 1977), with no hope of 'career' advancement and no strong ties of identification (whether antici-patory or otherwise) with management. But, on the other, it was, and to some considerable extent remains, a short-term proletariat with its most cherished goals and interests lying outside and beyond the world of work, with little interest in the latter and, by extension, in trade union represent-ation. Thus the creation of a feminised office proletariat did little to ruffle the surface of existing industrial relations patterns in banking up till 1965. However in its independence from the will and behest of the employers, it did generate a *potential* for future disturbance of the existing, male domin-ated pattern, and this potential was to increase *pari passu* with the growth of the office proletariat itself.

Drawing these points together, we can now see the full range of factors underlying the stability of the industrial relations pattern in banking. On the one hand, we have two classes of clerical employee having different, exogenously generated, expectations of employment which are strongly reinforced within the workplace. On the other, we have two types of collective organisation locked into bitter competition for membership. In this context, the bank employers were able to adjust the balance of competition between the collective organisations so as to forestall the emergence of a stronger staff side negotiating body, while simultaneously satisfying the employment demands of male and female employees at rela-tively low costs. At the same time, the expanding and potentially destabilising female clerical proletariat remained inarticulate and voiceless. Women bank employees had been conditioned during the 1950s and 1960s by patriarchal attitudes which were readily transferred from the family to the workplace (Oppenheimer, 1973) and which readily justified female subservience within the industry. They therefore made few demands of their employers or their staff bodies. The latter, locked in competition for male 'career' membership, lacked the incentives and the inclination to work hard at organising the transient female labour force which could, in any case, only be achieved by diverting resources from the 'real' membership race – that for men.

Yet, during the late 1950s and early 1960s the female proletariat in banking continued to grow, and at an accelerating pace. And while it remained quiescent during the early part of the 1960s, its progressive growth provided both the challenge and the incentives for collective organisations to develop policies that catered to its interests and aspirations. This task NUBE achieved with explosive results.

The growth of trade unionism in banking: 1960–70
In banking the 1960s were to be a contrast to the industrial relations torpidity of the late 1950s. In part, this change was expressed in the increased aggression with which the bank staff associations began to pursue pay claims (Robinson, 1969). More importantly, however, this was the period in which the union began to orient its policy statements towards its growing female constituency. Thus while the union's (1919) founding constitutional statement had included the objective 'Equal pay for men and women, no sex distinction', this philosophy had remained unactivated throughout the 1940s and 1950s. The union now increasingly stressed its declared policy of equal pay for women which was reaffirmed at every Annual Delegate Conference from 1962 onwards. In keeping with its revised orientation, the union also set aside special women's seats on its NEC (a progressive move in the early 1960s) and simultaneously began to give increasing prominence to a further policy objective – first established in 1956 – of a five-day working week for bank employees. As it turned out, this issue has, and continues to have, a special salience for women workers.

During this same period, by contrast, the bank staff associations developed no comparable initiatives. Summarising the attitude of the bank staff associations in 1963, at a point at which women represented some 46% of the banks' labour force, the Chairman of the Central Council of Bank Staff Associations expressed the following view of women workers in banking:

> The turnover of young women is terrific and they are not an integral part of banking; they are just the labour force. They are not worth their membership as they are mainly birds of passage. I am negotiat-

ing for the senior man; the person who is making his career in banking. (*New Society*, 11 April 1963).

Nor were these words empty rhetoric. The bank staff associations failed to design policy objectives that would cater to the goals of women workers. And, in their pay negotiations, now being pursued with increased vigour, the staff associations consistently sought higher settlements for the 'senior man'. The pay awards of 1962, 1963 and 1964 each contained additional payments over the basic increase for 'appointed' and 'overscale' staff (the latter comprising men over 31 or younger men no longer within the basic clerical grades). As we shall see, this indifference to nearly half the banks' labour force represented a serious miscalculation which would subsequently cost the staff associations tens of thousands of members and, ultimately, their monopoly of recognition in the industry.

However, notwithstanding the steady growth of the female labour force within the industry during this period and the progressive divergence between the union and the staff associations on policy stances attractive to women, the early 1960s witnessed no simple trend towards union membership among women workers. In fact, if anything, the reverse was the case, as Table 9.3 shows.

From Table 9.3, it can be seen that, while both the union and the staff associations had difficulty in maintaining their female memberships during the early 1960s, it was the union which more substantially failed to maintain membership levels. Indeed the union began the period organising 7000 fewer women than the staff associations and ended it organising 11,000 fewer. This superficially surprising result was the product of a number of factors.

Firstly, as we have seen, women bank workers during this period had a high rate of turnover and all the collective organisations had to work hard, against this background, simply to maintain existing levels of membership. In this context, the union suffered a double handicap as a result of its

Table 9.3 *Membership densities of NUBE and the combined staff associations in the London Clearing Banks, 1960–65, by sex*

| Year | Combined Staff Associations | | | NUBE | | |
	Male	Female	All	Male	Female	All
1960	60.7	41.1	52.3	41.1	26.6	35.0
1961	59.4	39.7	50.8	41.2	28.4	35.6
1962	58.7	36.3	48.6	41.0	28.7	35.4
1963	58.0	37.9	48.8	40.4	28.7	35.0
1964	59.8	38.4	49.8	36.6	22.5	30.0
1965	59.9	39.1	50.0	36.5	23.3	30.2

lack of recognition. Firstly, it lacked the ease of institutional access to bank staffs which was afforded to the staff associations (in the form, for example, of lists of new entrants to banking from the banks' personnel offices) and the union's recruitment of the continuously expanding, high turnover, female labour force was correspondingly hampered. Secondly and more significantly, the union's lack of recognition undermined its perceived effectiveness to women workers whose short-run approach to bank employment was paralleled by an equivalent desire for immediate results from union membership. Thus NUBE density increases among women between 1960 and 1963 coincided with a major campaign for recognition which culminated in an appeal to the ILO which was backed by the TUC. This argued that staff associations were under the domination of the bank employers and that their existence constituted a means by which the bank employers sought to exclude the union as a negotiating body representative of bank employees (Cameron Report, 1963). During this period, the recognition of NUBE appeared imminent and its increased credibility was readily converted into increased membership. The subsequent collapse in the union's membership (in 1964/65) reflected the failure of this campaign for recognition and was, in part, the effect of real negotiating successes, achieved by recourse to arbitration, by the bank staff associations during this latter period (Robinson, 1969; the impact of these successes on the several memberships of the staff associations is considered in detail in Heritage, 1977, pp.433–6 and 536–550). Finally, it is worth recalling the influence of branch norms which, especially in the smaller and more numerous branches, favoured the staff associations and may have served to blunt the impact, and the appeal, of the new union policies to women workers.

However, if Table 9.3 shows that policies geared to the female labour force may have no visible pay-off in membership terms, Table 9.4 shows the reverse. It points out the real value of persisting with such policies.

Table 9.4 Membership densities of NUBE and the combined staff associations in the London Clearing Banks, 1965–70, by sex

Year	Combined Staff Associations			NUBE		
	Male	Female	All	Male	Female	All
1965	59.9	39.1	50.0	36.5	23.3	30.2
1966	59.6	37.7	49.1	34.8	22.4	28.8
1967	57.7	33.3	45.6	41.7	33.9	37.9
1968	55.8	30.3	42.7	43.5	36.5	40.0
1969	53.8	26.5	39.5	42.8	36.2	39.4
1970	54.3	24.8	38.7	–	–	38.9

As Table 9.4 shows, after a further fall in membership during 1966, the density of NUBE membership rose in 1967 by 9.1% overall and by 11.5% among women. In aggregate terms, NUBE membership grew by 17,000 in 1967 alone of whom nearly 10,000 were women. By the end of the decade, women bank workers had transferred their predominant allegiance from the staff associations to the union and, as a result, by 1970 the union organised more workers overall than the staff associations for the first time in over 40 years. These developments arose centrally out of the union's successful struggle for recognition in 1967 and it is to the details of this struggle that we now turn.

The events of 1967: the issues, the strikes and their consequences

The growth of NUBE during 1967 and the union's successful use of the strike weapon against the clearing banks constitute a pattern of events in which women bank workers played a major part. The events and their impact on women workers are most usefully viewed against a background in which three major issues converged: (i) the question of union recognition; (ii) the development of the 1967 pay claim; and (iii) the vexed question of the five-day week in banking.

One outcome of the union's complaint to the ILO mentioned earlier, and the resulting Cameron Inquiry, was the latter's recommendation 'beyond the immediate purview of the inquiry' that a joint initiative be established by the clearing banks, staff associations and the union to establish Joint National Negotiating Machinery for the industry in which an employees' side would contain representatives of both NUBE and the staff associations. This was indeed initiated in 1964, but the resulting working party proceeded without the support of the Midland and National Provincial Bank Staff Associations and the managements of these two banks also took no part in these negotiations 'out of deference to the wishes of their associations'. Despite these difficulties, the 'rump' working party succeeded after 14 sessions in producing a draft constitution for national negotiating machinery which was submitted to all parties in March 1967. The proposals thus laboriously hammered out were rejected outright by two of the banks' managements (National Provincial and Westminster) and ignored by the management of the Midland Bank. A similar pattern of rejection emerged from the staff associations of these banks. Of all the institutions involved in the negotiations only the National Bank, NUBE, Barclays Bank Staff Association and the District Bank Staff Association were unreservedly in favour of the proposals. The remainder of the bank employers (Barclays, Lloyds, Martins, District, Glyn Mills and Williams Deacons) and the staff associations (Glyn Mills, Lloyds and Martins) withdrew from the arrangements because of the lack of support from the larger clearing banks. As a result, in July 1967 the Committee of London Clearing Bankers announced the collapse of the machinery.

Matters were no more satisfactory on the pay front. In the context of the Labour Government's incomes policy pay awards in banking had been frozen since 1965. Early in 1967, a pay award of $2\frac{1}{2}\%$ was negotiated to take effect from July 1967. This pay increase, which followed a $2\frac{1}{4}$ year 'pay pause' for bank staffs, proved unpopular among bank employees who had seen a steady decline in the real value of their earnings during the previous two years and in a context which their representatives seemed powerless to alter. Once again, as in the mid 1950s, NUBE stood to reap a harvest of the disgruntled and disaffected.

Overshadowing both these issues, however, was the question of the five-day week in banking. Critical to the union's proposals on this issue was the elimination of Saturday opening in banks which had been canvassed since 1956. By 1963 the United Kingdom remained the only major industrialised country in the world where banks continued to open on Saturdays, and in February 1964, the Committee of London Clearing Bankers created a special committee to investigate the question of banking hours. In June 1965, the CLCB announced that legislation was being sought to make Saturday a non-business day and in July 1966 a Private Member's Bill to permit Saturday closing was promoted. In the same month, the issue was referred to the Prices and Incomes Board which had been requested to investigate the structure and levels of bank charges.

The clearing banks now began to retreat once more from the issue and to canvass support for a shift system which would simultaneously maintain Saturday opening yet provide a five-day week for bank staffs – a proposal which was rejected by the union's 1966 Annual Delegate Conference. When the report from the NBPI was published in February 1967, it contained no specific recommendations and, in October 1967, the CLCB published proposals which, far from providing for Saturday closing, allowed only half-day closing of banks on local early closing days with an extra evening shift from 5 to 7 p.m. on the local late night shopping evening. As a concession to staff opinion on the Saturday closing issue, the banks proposed to introduce a five-day accounting week to enable more staff to take Saturday as a rest day.

While it is clear that, in making these proposals, the bank employers sought both to follow the recommendations of the NBPI and to appease their frustrated staff, there can be little doubt that their proposals were wholly inadequate in the developed climate of frustration which then existed among bank employees. Moreover the issue was clearly a 'national' one in which the CLCB made decisions in a concerted fashion and in which there was no possibility of presenting the proposals as the outcome of 'bank by bank' deliberations with the staff associations. The response to

Table 9.5   'New' and 'struck off' members of NUBE distributed on a
monthly basis for 1967

			New members		Struck off members
		January	828 ————		——— 1453
		February	880		1381
2½% pay	→	March	850		577
award		April	840		1187
		May	1166		954
				8850 8271	
		June	1016		1117
Failure of	→	July	569		373
recognition		August	1040		510
		September	1656 ————		—— 719
Hours					
announcement	→	October	6119 ———		⌐— 576
		November	7050 18782		1710 534
		December	5618 ———⌐		⌐— 600

these proposals by bank workers was profoundly negative and, as during the previous upsurge of discontent in 1955, bank staff began to join NUBE in large numbers.

Thus in 1967, the three major issues outlined above came to a head. Since decisions on the three issues were announced at separate points in the year, their several impacts on NUBE membership can be assessed by reference to Table 9.5.

Table 9.5 clearly demonstrates that, despite the low pay awards announced in March and April of 1967 and the breakdown in negotiations over national negotiating machinery in July, union recruitment during the first nine months of the year was barely sufficient to maintain NUBE membership at 1966 levels. During the last three months of the year, by contrast, when the 'hours' issue was paramount, the union achieved a net gain of over 17,000 new members, 58% of whom were women. Indeed during this three month period, aggregate female membership of the union rose by an astonishing 60%.

In this context, the union which had unsuccessfully canvassed the idea of strike action over the 'hours' issue during 1966 now began to integrate the issues of pay, hours, recognition and equal pay as a package of demands backed by strike action. In the event, strikes took place in South Wales during 24 and 25 November and were continued in the North and Midlands on 8 and 9 December. These strikes affected 480 branches and involved 4500 staff. A majority of the latter were women who, with little to fear from the bank employers, were prominent in picketing and related strike activities.

Although the strikes scarcely crippled the banks, their psychological impact was very considerable. Almost immediately they prompted a referendum among Yorkshire Bank staff over the question of staff representation which resulted in the dissolution of the Yorkshire Bank Staff Association. By the end of November one of the smaller clearing banks, Williams Deacons, had offered to recognise the union and the Central Council of Bank Staff Associations had initiated proceedings to recast its constitution so as to fit itself for participation on a joint 'staff side' in national negotiation machinery. By December, 9 of the 11 clearing banks (the dissenters being Coutts Bank and the Midland Bank) had indicated their willingness to recognise NUBE under the terms of the national negotiating machinery which had been rejected earlier in the year. The union however, which was planning further industrial action for 29 and 30 December, now held out for further concessions on the scope of the issues to be dealt with under the joint machinery. Finally at an 'eleventh hour' meeting on 28 December, the 9 banks and their staff associations acceded to these demands, and the union had won its 50 year struggle for national recognition. In the subsequent year, the Midland Bank bowed to the inevitable and accorded recognition. The year also witnessed an abrupt concession by the banks to the demand for Saturday closing. The 1968 pay negotiations incorporated substantial movement towards equal pay for women, a goal which was finally achieved in 1971.

In reviewing the events of 1967, it is tempting to conclude that the 'hours' issue alone was sufficient to galvanise the female labour force into strike action. But, although married women workers may have deeply desired more time to carry out their domestic roles and their unmarried counterparts may have desired more leisure in which to dispose of their income, this interpretation remains too narrow. While it is undeniable that the 'hours' issue ignited the dispute, it is also the case that the more bank staffs joined the union in response to this issue, the more 'winnable', and hence salient, the 'pay' and 'recognition' issues became. Ultimately, it appears the collection of issues became fused, as a collection, in the minds of angry bank employees. And, although women workers led the way in this regard, their anger also spread across the board to their male colleagues.

Turning now to the concession of recognition by the bank employers, it is abundantly clear that this was not the product of sheer 'industrial muscle'. Not only did the Midland Bank resist recognition for an extended period after the strikes had taken place, but the remainder of the banks could undoubtedly have withstood a campaign of strikes far more severe than the 'token' actions which took place. On the other hand the strikes received a favourable press reaction and undoubtedly damaged the public image of British banking. While the banks were prepared to frustrate the growth of trade unionism in an unpublicised war of attrition, they were less prepared to resist publically the recognition of a trade union which, by this point, was organising nearly 40% of their employees. Moreover the banks could, by the end of 1967, correctly forecast the content of the Donovan Commission report which endorsed Bain's (1967) recommendation of legislation on trade union recognition and anticipate the implementation of this recommendation regardless of the outcome of the 1970 General Election. In this context, further resistance to the recognition of NUBE may well have been construed as fruitless, if not positively counter-productive.

Discussion

The central proposal of this paper is that the feminisation of routine clerical work in banking and the association of a separate female 'office proletariat', was the crucial factor lying behind the growth and recognition of NUBE during the period 1965–70. This proposal may be regarded as somewhat heretical by those who follow Bain (1970) in asserting that the sexual composition of the labour force has no influence on trade union growth or density or, alternatively, by those who cite the generally lower density levels of female white-collar union membership to assert that a large female labour force will generally exert an inhibiting effect on union growth.

Such 'aggregative' arguments however tend to give insufficient weight to structurings of interests which are 'local' to specific industries at particular historical moments. In the case of banking, the proposal is that the creation of a separate clerical class – concretised in the sexual division of labour in the industry – served to exert a potentially destabilising influence on the balance of forces underlying the earlier industrial relations equilibrium in banking. Conjoined with an appropriate issue, this potential was actualised resulting in the first strike in the London Clearing Banks this century. The logic of this proposal, pared down to its essentials, is as follows.

1. While, as we have noted, a range of factors contributed to the bank employers' decision to recognise the union in December 1967, these factors were also present during other periods (1940–42, 1955–6, 1963, and 1964–7) when union recognition was being actively sought. The factor that was present during the last quarter of 1967, but was absent during all these other periods, was the union's capacity and determination to engage in strike action. During these earlier periods, including the first half of 1967, the banks could proceed to stonewall through periods of pressure for union recognition in the expectation that this pressure would

either subside or be defused by some concession to staff demands.

2. If we now ask why the union was unable to mount strike action before this period, the reply must focus on the predominance of male 'career oriented' bank employees who viewed their major prospects in terms of individual promotion rather than collective negotiation. With the progressive feminisation of routine clerical work, a separate clerical class was gradually created in banking which had no stake in a 'career' in the industry and, correspondingly, no powerful allegiance to the banks. While initially indisposed to join the union because of its perceived inefficacy, this feminine clerical class required only a single, salient issue to galvanise its support for the union and this turned out to be the five-day week issue of 1967. Such an issue would not have engendered support for strike action among a predominantly male labour force. Indeed, if the history of the union is a reliable guide, it is dubious whether any issue could have resulted in such an action in the absence of a separate clerical class. It is therefore concluded that the feminisation of the clerical labour force was a necessary, though not a sufficient, condition for the growth and recognition of NUBE during this period.

Conclusion

In so far as the sexual division of labour characteristic in banking is widespread in other white-collar occupations, it will prove valuable for students of white-collar unions to bear such divisions – and their interactions with other parameters of the 'white-collar situation' – in mind in interpreting trends in union membership and policy. While the events of the present case study are perhaps atypical, the relevancies of the study are not confined to banking.

Aggregative data on sexual divisions within the British occupational structure exhibits a similar patterning to that found, in microcosm, in banking. Thus, while 1.5 million men joined the British white-collar labour force between 1951 and 1971, there was no increase in the numbers of men in routine white-collar sectors. By contrast, of the 1.8 million women who were likewise super-added to white-collar occupations, nearly 1.2 million women were employed in the routine clerical and sales sectors (Goldthorpe and Llewellyn, 1977, p.279, Table 3). Thus, despite the much canvassed claim that occupational mobility is alive and well within British social structure and the associated claim that one of its mechanisms is 'work-life' mobility, it is clear that, in aggregate terms at least, male occupational mobility has been purchased by the feminisation of routine white-collar occupations. Moreover, since 'work-life' mobility is, through the operation of many factors, denied to women, it is not difficult to see that, as in the case of banking, enhanced male 'work-life' mobility has been achieved through this denial.

This state of affairs presents challenges to white-collar unions which, for a variety of reasons (Ellis, 1981), they have been slow to take up. Moreover, it may be speculated that the extension of continuous female participation in the labour force will accentuate this challenge by undermining the influence of patriarchal attitudes within the family and at the workplace. The present study suggests that where white-collar unions take steps to address and articulate the goals and aspirations of their female memberships, the latter will not be found wanting in the determination to achieve their objectives.

Notes

1. Thus in Heritage's sample, interviewed in 1972/3, 92% of the men had either completed or were studying for the Institute of Bankers professional qualifications, while only 8% of the female sample had done so (Heritage, 1977, p. 263).

2. Sources: for 1960 and 1970, US Census Bureau, *1970 Census of the Population, Characteristics of the Population*, Vol. 1, Part 1, Table 221: Detailed Occupation of the Experienced Labor Force and Employed Persons by Sex: 1970 and 1960. For 1978, US Department of Labor, Bureau of Labor Statistics, *Employment and Earnings During 1978: An Analysis*, Special Labor Force Report 218, Table 23: Employed Persons by detailed occupation, sex and race.

3. Pension rights are now transferable and moves were initiated by the Wilde Committee (1973) to make banking qualifications more transferable also.

10 Patriarchal Structures: the Case of Unemployment
Sylvia Walby

Introduction
The exclusion of women from forms of work that carry good pay and status is a form of sexual inequality which has important effects on many other aspects of sexual divisions. This paper will examine this exclusion as revealed by the higher rates of unemployment suffered by women than men. Given the importance of paid work for a person's position in our society the structures that exclude certain categories of people from it are of particular importance. The connections between gender differences in unemployment rates and systematically structured sexual inequality will be explored here. Such forms of sexual inequality cannot be regarded as deriving from capitalism alone, and a concept of patriarchy is required for them to be adequately understood.

There are two main approaches to explaining the pattern of women's unemployment. Firstly, there is the position that women's situation in the family explains the ease with which employers are able to shed female rather than male workers at times of declining demand for labour (Mincer, 1962, 1966; Beechey, 1977, 1978). Women are seen to be able to leave paid work and 'return' to the home at little cost to themselves or anyone else. Secondly, there is the argument that the structure of the labour market is very important and that it is to the nature of the jobs which women hold that we should turn for an explanation of women's rates of unemployment (Milkman, 1976; Bergmann, 1980; Bruegel, 1979; Barron and Norris, 1976).

The family and unemployment
Both Mincer (1962, 1966) and Beechey (1977, 1978) argue that married women withdraw from the labour force during times of recession and declining demand for labour because their position within the family enables this to happen with far fewer problems than for men.

Mincer, a neoclassical economist, sees women's participation in paid work as 'flexible' because of the alternative forms of work which are open to them in the household. It is the availability of these alternative forms of productive activity which is held to be the explanation of why married women spend only part of their time in paid work. Those periods of paid work are, apparently, chosen to fit in with the upturn of the business cycle when the best pay and conditions are available. Periods out of the labour market are thus seen as chosen and not constituting involuntary unemployment.

Mincer's model assumes a three-way choice between paid work, leisure and unpaid housework, but has no conceptual space for married women's unemployment. It would appear that a woman's work is never done, and that she can always do some unpaid housework if there is no paid work available. This is a highly unsatisfactory conceptual schema in its denial of the possibility of married women's unemployment.

Beechey draws on Marx's analysis of the reserve army as a mechanism which is necessary to suppress wage demands, especially during periods of expansion when otherwise scarce labourers might be able to force up the level of wages.

Beechey sees married women as a source of the industrial reserve army for capital because of their relation to their husbands. Married women may be paid low wages and be easily dismissed because they are partially supported by their husbands' wages and do not bear all the costs of the reproduction of their labour power. They may be dismissed more readily than men because they can fall back on the financial support of their husbands, and also have somewhere to go and something to do. Married women are thus seen as a reserve army of labour ready to be drawn out of the family into paid employment in a manner similar to the agricultural workers in Marx's analysis.

However, a central problem in Beechey's analysis is her inability to explain why, if women are so cheap, capital does not continually employ them in preference to men. She argues that capital employs women during economic upturns because they are cheaper than men; that is, unlike men, they can be paid less than the value of their labour power. There would appear to be no reason, within the logic of capitalism, why they should not be employed all of the time. Beechey suggests that capital wishes to maintain the family and that this puts limits on women's paid employment. However, no suggestion is made that the use made of women workers during economic booms undermines the family, so Beechey is still in need of an explanation as to why it should be so at other times.

I would argue that both Mincer's and Beechey's accounts are defective in that they fail to look at patriarchal relations in the labour market and household. Mincer, like most neoclassical economists, assumes that the labour market works smoothly and competitively. Inequalities in wages and participation rates are conceptualised as reflecting the inequalities in human capital which people bring to the labour market. Consequently, Mincer can have no explanation of such central features of the labour market as the segregation of the sexes and ethnic groups into occupations with unequal wages and conditions of job security. Both Mincer and Beechey need to analyse systematically the role of male dominated unions in protecting male jobs at women's expense (cf. Hartmann, 1976; Home Office, 1929; Cockburn, 1981; Braybon, 1981) and the role of other male organisations (Oakley, 1976) sometimes with the support of a male dominated legislature or parliament (Andrews, 1918; Scarf, 1980; Braybon, 1981). We need to investigate the causes and consequences of the occupational segregation of the sexes (Bergmann, 1980a; Milkman, 1976; OECD, 1976).

Another major problem with Beechey's and indeed Mincer's argument is the lack of empirical evidence to substantiate these claims. Several writers (Milkman, 1976; OECD, 1976; Bruegel, 1979) have argued that women have not withdrawn from the economy during recessions in the way in which the theory predicts. They argue that labour market structures are more important in explaining women's continued position in paid work.

Occupational segregation and the reserve army thesis
The OECD examined the 1974–5 recession among OECD member countries and Milkman the 1930s depression of the USA. They each reached the conclusion that women are protected from the worst of these recessions by occupational segregation. In each instance women were to be found concentrated in the service sector which was less affected by unemployment during the recession than the manufacturing sector where men were concentrated. The sex-typing of occupation was, it is argued, too rigid to allow for the substitution of one sex by the other, so women were not removed from their jobs and replaced by men. Occupational segregation which usually operates to the detriment of women in excluding them from many well paying and high status jobs was believed in this instance to have acted to protect women from greater expulsion from paid work than men.

However, Milkman does not have unequivocal evidence to support the drawing of these conclusions. The data she presents from the 1930 US Census shows that women's unemployment rates were lower than men's in almost all occupations, not just in the service sector. The general rates of unemployment were lower in the service sector, but since women's rates were lower than men's in most occupations, occupational segregation is not needed to explain the direction of the difference of men's and women's rates, only for the amount. Comparisons with other sources suggest that

Censuses significantly understate the amount of women's unemployment, however. So it might be the case that women's rates would have been higher than men's, but for women's concentration in the service sector. However, we do not have adequate data from the 1930s to give a reliable answer.

Bruegel (1979) looked at the question of whether the concentration of women in the service sector protected women from becoming an unemployed reserve army during the recession of the mid 1970s in Britain. She suggests that at the level of the entire economy women's concentration in services did protect women's employment as a whole from higher rates of unemployment. However, she suggests that a different and more complex picture emerges if the figures are further disaggregated. She argues that individually women are more vulnerable to redundancy than are men in similar circumstances. Thus in manufacturing women lost their jobs proportionately more than men in a manner which fits the reserve army thesis. She suggests it is useful to differentiate between full-time and part-time women workers. It is predominantly part-time workers who have lost their jobs rather than full-timers, and part-time workers are usually married women. It is then part-time married women workers whose employment fluctuations most fit the reserve army model.

The existence of occupational segregation provides a further problem for the thesis that women constitute a reserve of labour. If the labour market is so rigidly segregated then it is not clear that women can constitute competition for workers in other sub-markets. If Milkman is correct that substitution of male for female workers does not occur because of rigid sex-typing of occupations then women do not constitute a reserve army for male-typed occupations. Women, in this situation, would only be a reserve army for female-typed occupations (see also Connelly, 1978).

Braverman's (1974) work provides a different explanation of the changing sexual composition of the labour force. Rather than a static conception of available jobs Braverman has a dynamic conception of the construction and destruction of jobs. The jobs that are being created at this point in the development of monopoly capitalism are unskilled jobs in the service sector which are being filled largely by women, while the ones which are being destroyed are the skilled jobs in manufacturing which were filled largely by men. The destruction of the household economy by the production more cheaply by capital of the goods and services it once produced provides the growing reserve of female labour to fill these jobs. This is a conception of women as an ever-growing reserve army because of long-term changes in capitalism and its impact on the family rather than Beechey's conception of fluctuations in women's paid employment and a static conception of the family. Braverman's analysis is supported by more empirical evidence of post-war changes in the sexual division of labour than is that of Beechey.

However Braverman, like Beechey, neglects to consider the role of patriarchal relations in the labour market. It is now a standard criticism of Braverman that he did not take account of worker organisation (Friedman, 1977; Rubery, 1978), and the neglect of patriarchal forms of worker organisation may be considered part of this. A simultaneous resistance to deskilling and to the entry of women into certain areas of paid work is a far from uncommon historical event (Andrews, 1918; Braybon, 1981; Cockburn, 1981). The success of skilled male workers on some of these occasions in resisting both deskilling and the entry of women into an area of work is evidence that Braverman is mistaken to ignore the importance of the organisation of male workers in shaping the labour process.

Labour market structures

Having cast serious doubt on the proposition that women's movements out of employment and their unemployment can be explained solely by reference to their position within the family it is appropriate to examine those writers who focus on labour market structures for such an explanation.

Bergmann (1980a, 1980b) has argued that sex segregation in employment is the cause of consistently higher rates of unemployment among women than men in the post-war period in the US. Bergmann argues that women are more likely to be unemployed than men because they are crowded into a small number of occupations which do not provide sufficient employment for the number of women who seek it. Men, on the other hand, are able to enter a greater number of occupations proportionate to their number and hence do not suffer such high unemployment as women. Women are confined in this way by the discriminatory hiring practices of employers. While the number of women seeking paid employment in the post-war period has substantially increased relative to men, the number of occupations to which women are allowed entry has not increased. The implication is that women's higher rate of unemployment has been exacerbated during, if not confined to, the post-war development of the economy. Bergmann thus argues that it is the sex-segregated structure of employment which is the root of women's higher unemployment rather than the problems arising from their position within the family.

Bergmann's analysis is an attempt to explain the different levels of unemployment among men and women within the neoclassical economic framework. The main explanatory element in Bergmann's analysis is that of employers' discrimination against women in certain occupations. We are left with the question of why employers discriminate against women, and Bergmann cannot answer this satisfactorily.

The dual labour market approach of Barron and Norris (1976) focuses on the institutional structure of the labour market in order to explain patterns of employment. Barron and Norris contribute to the understanding of sex differences in unemployment through their analysis of how women come to be found occupying jobs which are themselves unstable and which lead to high turnover. Instability of jobs and a high rate of turnover are important contributors to unemployment.

Barron and Norris suggest that women are more likely to be in jobs which are unstable and lead to a high turnover of workers because of the way women fit into the secondary sector of the dual labour market. Their analysis is in two parts: firstly, an explanation of why the labour market is segmented into primary and secondary jobs, and secondly, why it is women who tend to fill the secondary slots. Instability rather than stability of jobs is one of four characteristics which, according to Barron and Norris, differentiate primary and secondary jobs. Unstable jobs are also characterised by low pay, while stable jobs typically have high pay. There is little mobility across the boundary between these two sectors, and, finally, primary sector jobs are generally tied into long promotional ladders unlike secondary jobs (Barron and Norris, 1976, p.49).

Barron and Norris suggest that the structure of the labour market is a consequence of firstly, attempts by employers to retain workers whose skills they need, and secondly, an attempt by employers to buy off the best organised workers. So on the one hand it is a consequence of dirctly econ-omic factors which make employers seek to retain those key workers that have skills that the employer would find hard to replace; and on the other hand a result of political and organisational factors which make the employer seek to structure the workforce in a hierarchical manner in order to control the workforce.

Barron and Norris argue that if pay is taken as evidence of a job's second-ary status then such jobs are primarily occupied by women. Barron and Norris suggest that women are primarily secondary workers because of five characteristics: dispensability, clearly visible social differences, little interest in acquiring training, low economism and lack of solidarity. They argue that it is often incorrectly supposed that a person's labour market attri-butes are a consequence solely of themselves rather than merely the slots they have occupied in the labour market. It would appear that employers hold unsubstantiated beliefs that women possess these five characteristics of secondary workers. Employers perceive women as conventionally set apart from men and with less commitment to advancement at work be-cause of women's orientation to their domestic situation and their socialisation. Women are seen as reluctant to struggle to obtain, or even seek, high monetary rewards. Thus the characteristics of women at work are seen to fit with those required from secondary rather than primary workers.

A major problem with Barron and Norris's analysis is, ironically, their lack of appreciation of, and analysis of, patriarchal structures in the labour market. Despite their emphasis on the importance of the labour market much of their article is taken up with what is merely a description of the characteristics that women bring, or are believed by employers to bring, to the labour market. They describe the structuring of the labour market into two sectors in non gender-specific terms. They do not see the structure of the market as being determined or even shaped in any way by sexual divisions. It is seen as a consequence of the employers' needs both to retain skilled labour and to buy off the better organised workers (who are referred to in a non gender-specific manner). Sexual differentiation is seen as largely determined outside the labour market in the sexual division of labour in the household.

There are two ways in which they approach the problem of patriarchal structures, but fail to complete their analysis. The more important is the discussion of women's supposed lack of solidarism. This is always seen in terms of women not managing to organise, never in terms of men being organised against women in the labour market. The nearest they get to men being an opposing force is to suggest that male trade unionists do not assist women trade unionists to the point of being obstructive. They never mention men actively organising against women, although there is now a lot of evidence to support this (e.g. Hartmann, 1976; Andrews, 1918; Oakley, 1976; Scharf, 1980).

They do refer to general attitudes hostile to women working and women working in particular jobs, but this is seen as relatively diffuse rather than as politically organised. In fact much of their article is about attitudes; it refers to ideological intervention in the labour market more than political and organisational interventions. I think they are mistaken to see patriarchal intervention in the labour market as so confined to the level of ideology.

There is a further problem with Barron and Norris's work in that it is not clear that 'dualism' is the best way to characterise the structures of the labour market. Hakim (1979), for example, suggests that the horizontal and vertical occupational segregation of the sexes constitutes a particularly important form of labour market organisation. Horizontal occupational segregation occurs when men and women work in different types of occupations, and vertical segregation when men are working in higher grade occupations than women.

Other writers have also suggested the need to take into account more divisions than one of primary and secondary and have characterised the labour market as 'segmented' rather than 'dualistic' (Edwards, Gordon and Reich, 1975) or as composed of a 'vertical mosaic' (Kreckel, 1980). One major division between labour market theories is whether the divisions are seen to be based on skill, such as employers' attempts to keep workers who have learned valuable firm specific skills (e.g. Doeringer and Piore, 1971) and those who see the segmentation based on power struggles between different groups (e.g. Gordon, 1972; Rubery, 1978; Edwards, Gordon and Reich, 1975). The latter group of radical labour market theorists can be divided again on the issue of gender divisions by whether these divisions are seen as byproducts of struggles between capital and labour (e.g. Humphries, 1977, 1981) or whether they are seen as a central feature of analysis (e.g. Hartmann, 1976) or whether indeed they are effectively ignored altogether (e.g. Kreckel, 1980).

Hartmann argues that the attempts to exclude women from certain occupations were a deliberate attempt by male workers to better their own position at the expense of female workers. She argues that a patriarchal division of labour existed long before the advent of capitalism. This division of labour was, however, perpetuated by male workers in industrial capitalism and exploited by capitalist employers for their own benefit. The most important aspect of this process for Hartmann was the active organisation of male workers seeking to exclude women workers from their trades.

Comparative empirical evidence

Much of the material covered so far has been rather abstract and lacking in empirical substantiation. The widely varying accounts of the extent of women's unemployment relative to men's and of how this changes over time need reliable empirical data if they are to be evaluated. Most of the accounts that did utilise empirical material were restricted to one historical period in one country. Yet questions of the relative importance of different social structures are often particularly illuminating by comparative analysis. In order to advance my argument that patterns of women's unemployment are not reducible to either capital or the family, but that patriarchal labour market structures are of crucial importance it is necessary to find some supporting empirical evidence.

There are serious methodological difficulties in conducting such an exercise because of the grossly inadequate ways in which the measurement of women's unemployment has frequently been attempted. For instance in the UK the official rate of unemployment until recently was obtained from counting those who register as unemployed. Since the major reason for registering was to collect benefit and many married women are ineligible to claim benefit the count seriously underestimated the number of unemployed women. The new count is now based solely on those collecting benefit and thus is an even more serious understatement. Many women are ineligible to claim unemployment benefit because of an interrupted National Insurance record, and married women cannot claim social security in their own right. Hence we cannot use registration rates to investigate gender rates of unemployment. Survey methods of measuring unemployment do not have this problem of omitting women because of the patriarchal benefits system, and it is to these that we must turn. However, the distinction between unemployment and economic inactivity for married women is a problem for surveys which only casually ask for employment status and present no definition of these statuses. Consequently, the UK Census, for example, seriously underestimates the number of unemployed married women and may not be used for comparative purposes. The UK Census shows even fewer married women to be unemployed than the underestimate produced by the registration rate (UK Census, 1961).

It is likely that the person who fills in the Census form, usually the male 'head of household', prefers to describe his wife who is without paid work as a housewife rather than as unemployed since this has higher status for him. There are no probe questions which would lead to any check on this. The loss of the Census as a source of data is particularly unfortunate because of its wide coverage of the population and over time.

The remaining sources of measures of gender rates of unemployment are the sample surveys. In the UK the first such regular survey to ask ques-

Table 10.1 Unemployment rates in the EEC in 1979, extended concept,[a] 14 + years

	D	F	I	NL	B	L	UK	IRL	DK	Total EEC %
Total	3.0	6.9	7.9	6.7	7.3	2.4	5.2	9.8	6.9	5.8
Male	2.3	4.6	5.3	4.8	4.1	1.7	4.6	8.2	4.8	4.2
Female	4.2	10.2	13.3	11.1	13.5	4.2	6.0	13.6	9.6	8.3
F/M[b]	1.8	2.2	2.5	2.3	3.2	2.5	1.3	1.7	2.0	2.0

Key
D = W. Germany
F = France
I = Italy
NL = Netherlands
B = Belgium
L = Luxembourg
UK = United Kingdom
IRL = Ireland
DK = Denmark

Source: Eurostat, *Labour Force Sample Survey 1979*, Office for Official Publications of the European Communities, 1981, Table 18.

Notes: [a]Persons with a main occupation, unemployed persons and non-active persons with an occasional occupation or seeking paid employment, by reference to the population of same age and sex.
[b]Author's calculation.

tions about unemployment is the General Household Survey which began in 1971. There is no reliable way of comparing UK gender rates of unemployment before this date (cf. Sorrentino, 1979). Given slight variations in definitions in unemployment between countries the best source of data comparative with the UK is the EEC Labour Force Sample Survey (LFS). This survey has been carried out biennially in the nine EEC countries since 1973 and provides reliable comparative data on the labour force.

The EEC LFS shows very great variations in the unemployment ratios in the nine countries of the EEC (see Table 10.1). This might be considered quite remarkable given the apparently similar social structure of these Western industrialised nations. Particularly variable is the male to female unemployment rates. This varies from the female rate being 1.3 times the male rate in the UK in 1979 to being 3.2 times the male rate in Belgium in the same year. In the period 1973 to 1979 the UK consistently has the lowest or next to lowest ratio of female to male unemployment (Eurostat, 1980). The considerable difference in these figures is inconsistent with assumptions that models including only the family and capital can explain the relation between male and female rates of unemployment.

Rather than build explanatory models or gender rates of unemployment based on one country's experience we should be asking why the UK ratio of women's to men's unemployment is the lowest in the EEC. Can this be explained by the UK being the least patriarchal country, that women have better employment prospects relative to men than any other EEC nation? This delightful proposition would not however seem to be the case. On the contrary, I would argue that women's lesser unemployment relative to men is due to their worse employment conditions relative to men in the UK as compared to other EEC countries. As a consequence employers are relatively more keen to employ women.

One of the most important labour market structures in this respect is the division between full-time and part-time jobs. While both men and women have full-time jobs the part-time jobs are almost exclusively held by women.

The variation in the percentage of women with part-time jobs in the EEC is enormous from 10.6% in Italy to 46.3% in Denmark in 1979. The UK has the second highest percentage at 39.0%, a figure which is consistently greater than most other countries (see Table 10.2). The conditions of employment in terms of rates of pay and job security for part-timers are, on average, considerably worse than those for full-timers. This is not only due to custom and practice and the activities of trade unions but also because much employment protection legislation does not apply to part-time workers. In a time of redundancy it is common practice for part-timers to be dismissed before full-timers and this is often actively followed trade union policy. The protection, against arbitrary dismissal afforded by the Employment Protection Act of 1975, is only extended to those working more than 16 hours a week. Bruegel (1979) has shown that the numbers of part-time workers shows much greater fluctuations than do those of full-time workers. In the UK a further advantage is afforded employers of part-time workers in the possibility of nil or reduced National Insurance payments because of the threshold beneath which payments need not be made. They are also exempt from the provisions of the Industrial Relations, Redundancy Payments and Contracts of Employment Acts. This extreme differentiation of part-time and full-time workers for the provision of these state actions is unique to the UK. In other EEC countries social security contributions are made either irrespective of the number of hours worked, for instance in Germany and the Netherlands, or else the

Table 10.2 Part-time women as a percentage of women with an occupation in the EEC, 1979

	D	F	I	NL	B	L	UK	IRL	DK	Total EEC
Male	1.5	2.5	3.0	2.8	1.0	1.0	1.9	2.1	5.2	2.2
Female	27.6	17.0	10.6	31.6	16.5	18.1	39.0	13.0	46.3	25.6

Source: Eurostat, *Labour Force Sample Survey 1979*, Office for Official Publications of the European Communities, 1981, Table 20

Table 10.3 Proportion of women in higher level occupations in the EEC, 1970–71

Country	All professionals[b]	% of women among Managers and Administrators[a]	All professionals, managers and administrators	Census year[b]
Belgium	44	10	34	1970
Denmark	55	17	50	1970
France	43	12	37	1968
W. Germany	34	14	31	1970
Ireland	49	5	42	1971
Italy	46	6	43	1971
Luxembourg	33	8	30	1970
Netherlands	34	6	30	1971
United Kingdom	38	8	31	1971

Notes: [a] International Standard Classification of Occupations (ISCO) categories 'professional, technical and related workers" includes for example scientists, engineers, accountants, jurists, teachers, artists, writers and athletes.
[b] In some cases data refer to most recent labour force survey.

Source: Calculated from International Labour Office *Yearbook of Statistics*, 1977

theshold on earnings is extremely low, for instance in France (Manley and Sawbridge, 1980).

As a consequence of this differentiation of part-time and full-time work women in the UK suffer particularly bad employment conditions as compared to men, while part-time workers are particularly attractive to employers. Women part-time workers are thus attractive because of the poor conditions under which they can be employed in the UK.

Women in the UK are concentrated in worse jobs than in most other EEC countries. Despite the high participation rate of women in the UK only a low percentage of them are to be found in professional, managerial and administrative jobs as compared to other EEC countries (see Table 10.3).

These poor employment conditions for women in the UK can be seen as contributing to the relatively low unemployment rate of women as compared to men in the UK and to the high participation rates of women in paid work in the UK in comparison with the rest of the EEC. The UK had 44.3% of women over 14 in paid employment in 1979 – one of the highest proportions in the EEC (see Table 10.4).

It can be argued that employment rates are as important to consider as unemployment rates when looking at the exclusion of people from paid work. Unemployment is notoriously hard to measure, partly because of the fuzzy edges to the concept, while employment is easier because of the use of payment as the criterion (cf. Shiskin, 1976). For men of working age the exclusion from paid work usually means that the person's status is unemployed whereas women who may also be housewives may be defined as economically inactive as an alternative to unemployed. The difficulties in identifying the boundary between economically inactive and unemployment make the measurement of changes in employment rather than unemployment particularly attractive. The use of employment figures gives

Table 10.4 Percentage of women over 14 either in or seeking paid employment in the EEC in 1979

Germany	37.6
France	44.8
Italy	30.3
Netherlands	29.0
Belgium	33.2
Luxembourg	28.3
United Kingdom	44.3
Ireland	31.6
Denmark	55.2
Eur 9	38.6

Source: Eurostat, *Labour Force Sample Survey, 1979* Office for Official Publications of the European Communities, 1981, Table 16

Table 10.5 *Activity ratios by age groups and sex in the EEC, 1979 [a] (%)*

Age groups	D	F	I	NL	B	L	UK	IRL	DK	All EEC
14–19 Female	27.2	19.3	20.1	17.9	14.3	33.8	35.1	36.4	34.1	25.2
20–24 Female	70.9	72.1	53.9	66.1	66.5	71.3	71.1	73.8	84.7	67.5
25–29 Female	62.8	71.9	52.7	45.6	69.1	54.2	55.3	46.2	88.1	60.7
30–34 Female	55.4	68.0	45.6	34.4	60.3	39.2	54.5	29.4	84.0	55.0
35–39 Female	54.2	65.0	41.4	35.4	51.6	33.6	64.1	25.3	80.8	54.3
40–44 Female	53.4	62.2	38.6	35.9	44.2	29.7	70.4	27.6	78.8	53.7
45–49 Female	51.9	60.3	36.6	32.1	37.0	37.0	24.9	67.8	27.7	51.6
50–54 Female	46.0	54.7	32.5	26.0	28.9	18.9	65.2	27.3	65.9	47.0
55–59 Female	40.1	47.3	22.8	19.1	19.5	17.9	54.8	24.9	52.9	39.2
60–64 Female	16.5	24.6	10.9	11.0	6.8	(8.6)	25.4	17.8	30.2	18.5
65–69 Female	5.5	9.0	6.0	7.9	2.1	—	7.5	9.8	15.7	6.9
70+ Female	2.1	2.6	2.3	(0.7)	0.9	—	1.7	3.5	2.0	2.0
Total	52.5	57.1	48.5	48.1	48.9	48.0	58.4	53.9	64.2	53.7
14+ Male	69.5	70.6	68.2	67.6	65.5	69.1	73.7	76.0	73.7	70.3
Female	37.6	44.8	30.3	29.0	33.2	28.3	44.3	31.6	55.2	38.6

Note: [a] Persons with a main occupation, unemployed persons and non-active persons with an occasional occupation or seeking paid employment, by reference to the population of same age and sex.
Source: Eurostat, *Labour Force Sample Survey, 1979*, Office for Official Publications of the European Communities, 1981, Table 16

the same picture of the attractiveness of female labour to employers, with the high participation rate of women in the UK, and of poor conditions of employment.

A more detailed comparison of participation rates across the EEC reveals substantial differences in the age participation rates. Most writers on women's paid employment assume that the biggest barrier for women is child-care. The figures for the UK that show the highest participation rates for the ages before and after the years of child-care would appear to support this. However, the UK is almost unique in the EEC with such a pattern. In most EEC countries the highest participation rates are found during the twenties and early thirties which are the child-bearing years. Child-care is thus not the reason why women have lower participation rates than men. The family and children cannot be used as a simple explanation of women's labour force participation behaviour (see Table 10.5).

Having argued that the UK has more patriarchal labour market structures than other EEC countries which is a major reason for the lower ratio of male–female unemployment rates in the UK it is pertinent to look for reasons for this. We have seen that worker organisation is particularly important in structuring the labour market (cf. Rubery, 1978). Since trade unions are a major form of worker organisation it is appropriate to look at differences in trade unions between the UK and the rest of the EEC. There are problems here in the availability of the relevant information. Most comparative trade union histories (Clegg, 1976; Kendall, 1975; Stearns, 1975) have nothing to say about divisions between men and women trade unionists. Trade union histories that do look at women (Lewenhak, 1977; Soldon, 1978) do not take a comparative perspective. The only exceptions do not compare EEC countries (e.g. Jacoby, 1976). However, it is possible to make a speculative comparison based on knowledge as to how different types of union organisation within one country affect gender issues and then apply this knowledge to the greater or lesser preponderance of such types of unions in other EEC countries.

We know that in Britain and America the unions that were particularly hostile to women were the skilled craft unions. The general unions for the semi and unskilled workers were less prone to exclusionary practices against women. The skilled craft unions base their privileged position in the labour market not only on the possession of sought after skills, but on militant union ability. They engage in exclusionary practices against other workers. This closure has operated not only against unskilled workers however, but also specifically against women. Their exclusion of non-apprenticed labour from their areas of work acts to protect their occupational privileges, but their historical refusal to allow women to become apprentices is a specifically patriarchal practice. Most analyses of the exclusionary practices of these male dominated craft unions have concentrated on major social confrontations of these unions and relatively unskilled female workers. This is a situation where their struggle against their employers for the retention of their privileges is co-extensive with their struggle against women. For instance, Andrews (1918) and Braybon (1981) look at the actions of the Amalgamated Society of Engineers during the First World War at a point when they were both fighting deskilling of their work by the introduction of less skilled women by the employers.

Britain has a greater representation of such skilled craft unions than other EEC countries. This is largely because of the greater tendency of unions to be organised around occupations than industries in the UK. This might be a reason why women are better treated by continental than British trade unions, and their conditions of work not so differentiated from and worse than those of men. However, these suggestions need much further exploration into comparative trade union activities around issues of gender than I have done here.

Patriarchal relations in the labour market

So far I have suggested that there are two structures in the labour market which are of particular importance for differentiating men's and women's chances of unemployment. Firstly, there is the division between full-time and part-time work where the latter has considerably worse conditions of employment and rates of pay than the former and which is taken almost exclusively by married women. Part-time workers are much more vulnerable to becoming unemployed than full-timers. Secondly, there is the segregation of men and women into different and far from equal occupations. This has varying effects: it might protect women from unemployment if they are concentrated in a sector less hit by recession or it may confine women to jobs that are unstable, thus increasing the likelihood of unemployment. To these I want to add a third item: the existence of systematic practices, the effect of which is often to dismiss women before men in redundancy situations. These include the practices of 'last-in, first-out', dismissing part-timers before full-timers and dismissing (in some places and times) married women first.

An important issue is how to conceptualise these three within a wider social theory. Can they all be usefully conceptualised as patriarchal structures? All three could be regarded as fulfilling the general criterion of a structure of being a property of the social system not of individual actors (cf. Giddens, 1979). These practices exist outside of the particular individual who might be carrying them out at any one moment. However, the first two – the division between full and part-timers, and occupational segregation – could be considered more deeply 'sedimented' than the third set of practices – customary practices of who gets dismissed first. The first two have a much more uniformly stable existence in British history than the latter which is subject to much more variation. For instance, while the practice of sacking married women first is often cited of situations before 1975 (e.g. Scharf (1980) of the 1930s in the U.S.A.; Mackay *et al.* (1971) of British employers 1959–66), it is less mentioned now, presumably partly because it is illegal. The practice of sacking part-timers before full-timers, currently a common, though far from universal, practice, is now being challenged as being contrary to the Sex Discrimination Act and cases are being brought to Industrial Tribunals. Consequently, while the first two might be usefully conceptualised as labour market structures, the third might be more usefully described by a term which implies less enduring qualities such as 'a set of practices'.

A second issue in the characterisation of these structures and set of practices is whether they should be described as 'patriarchal'. First, it is necessary to establish the definition of the term 'patriarchal'. There are two issues here: firstly, whether the term should include a notion of generational inequality; and secondly, of how systematic and autonomous gender inequality must be to count as patriarchy. I conclude elsewhere (Walby, 1982) that the inclusion of generational inequality unnecessarily complicates the issues and that the term 'patriarchy' is better restricted to gender inequality only.

The second issue in the conceptualisation of patriarchy is that of how systematic and autonomous sexual inequality must be for patriarchy to be the appropriate term. Writers such as Beechey (1979) and Barrett (1980) are wary of the term patriarchy to describe sexual inequality because they see capitalism as the major structuring principle in contemporary society. To use the term patriarchy presumes that sexual inequality is systematic and analytically autonomous from other structures such as capitalism (cf. Delphy, 1977; Firestone, 1971). The argument in this paper is that such a concept of patriarchy is useful and indeed necessary in the analysis of contemporary society.

The question now is whether the two labour structures and set of practices which were identified earlier as having a significant impact on gender differences in unemployment rates should be described as patriarchal. These structures and set of practices are of major importance in explaining why women's rates of unemployment are generally higher than men's but less so in the UK than in other EEC countries. It is important to decide whether the term 'patriarchal' is to be applied on the basis of the effects of the structure or set of practices, on the basis of the motivation of the individuals concerned, on the basis of the gender of those involved, on the basis of the power relations embodied in the structure, or some other basis.

Taking the gender of those involved as the basis for applying the term patriarchal is not a reliable index since it is possible for women as well as men to participate in structures which adversely affect women and vice versa. However, the gender composition might sometimes be taken as an indicator and the power relations embodied in the structure. If these are patriarchal relations then the structure might be usefully referred to as patriarchal. To take the motivation of the individuals concerned as the basis would confuse the analysis in situations where the adverse effects on women are an unintended consequence of individuals' actions, although this will often be in line with the effects of the power relations embodied in the structure. For instance, the 'last-in, first-out' rule may not be consciously intended to declare women reduntant before men, while at the same time having that consequence. It is not necessary to know what male members of the engineering union thought they were doing when they were trying to exclude unskilled women from skilled work during and after the First World War to know that this had patriarchal effects. One important basis of the description of a structure as 'patriarchal' may be done by reference to its effects. If a structure or set of practices is patriarchal in its effects, then it is useful to describe it as a patriarchal structure or set of patriarchal practices. On these criteria the structures and set of practices identified in this paper should be described as patriarchal.

There is a tendency in many writings on patriarchy for it to be conceptualised as a rather monolithic overarching structure. There is often seen to be one base from which all other aspects of patriarchy derive. For instance, Firestone (1971) sees reproduction as the basis of patriarchy, while Delphy (1977) traces it back to the domestic mode of production. This might be seen as a consequence of the need felt by those writers to establish patriarchy as a structure independent of capitalism in a particularly stark way. Hartmann (1976; 1979) is one of the few exceptions to this. Further developments on the analysis of patriarchy need to differentiate between forms and structures of patriarchy in order to avoid the problems of a static analysis which stem from a monolithic conception of patriarchy.

This paper has tried to do this by differentiating the patriarchal structures and practices which affect the distribution of unemployment. It has been argued that patriarchal labour market structures and sets of patriarchal labour market practices are particularly important in determining the pattern of women's unemployment and employment in relation to men's, and that many writers on this area have overstated the importance of the family (Beechey, 1977, 1978; Mincer, 1962, 1966). The comparative analysis of different patriarchal structures and practices has revealed wide variations and shows the importance of differentiating between patriarchal structures.

Acknowledgement
I would like to thank the following for discussions and comments on earlier drafts of this paper: the Lancaster Regionalism Group (in particular John Urry), David Morgan, and contributors to the session at the conference.

Notes on Contributors

Margaret E. Attwood Senior Lecturer in Personnel Management and Industrial Relations, Anglian Regional Management Centre, North East London Polytechnic. Author of 'The Employment Relationship in the Hairdressing Industry – a Preliminary Analysis' in *Service Industries Review* (November 1981).

Nicky Britten Research Associate with the Medical Research Council's National Survey of Health and Development at the Department of Community Health, Bristol University. Previously worked on the Child Health and Education Study, also based in Bristol. Degrees in mathematics and management science and has conducted research on social mobility, class imagery and the conditions of service of contract research staff.

Tony Chapman First degree at University of Lancaster and now working at Plymouth Polytechnic on the Scottish Mobility Study data on an SSRC linked Studentship, with special emphasis on women's social mobility.

Sheila Cunnison Author of *Wages and Work Allocation* (1966). Recently and currently engaged in a variety of research projects in the Humberside Region.

Frances M. Hatton Visiting Research Fellow, Anglian Regional Management Centre, North East London Polytechnic. Presently completing a Ph.D. on women working in the catering industry and working on a project on girls in non-traditional areas of employment.

Anthony Heath University Lecturer in Sociology, Department of Social and Administrative Studies, University of Oxford. Current research on men and women in the class structure and a comparison of their attainments at school and work.

John Heritage Lecturer in Sociology at the University of Warwick. Current research on the televised presentation of public figures.

Judy Lown First degree in Sociology from University of Essex. Has been teaching in adult and higher education and currently working as a Project Officer on the Women's Studies course at the Open University, completing her doctorate and pursuing her interests in feminist history and theory.

Chris Middleton Studied at LSE 1965–71. Currently lecturing in Political Sociology and on Gender Relations at Sheffield University. Author of various articles on Marxism and feminism and the social history of women's labour.

David H.J. Morgan Senior Lecturer, Sociology, University of Manchester. Author of *Social Theory and the Family* (1975) and a paper on masculinity and social research in *Doing Feminist Research* (Ed. by H. Roberts 1981).

Geoff Payne Has taught at several universities and polytechnics in Britain and North America and is former Director of the Scottish Mobility Study. Currently Dean of Social Science at Plymouth Polytechnic.

Judy Payne Taught Research Methods at Newcastle Polytechnic for several years before joining the MRC Medical Sociology Unit at the University of Aberdeen as a research officer in 1974. Since 1978 she has worked on Statistics and Systems Analysis at Plymouth Polytechnic.

Anna Pollert Has taught Sociology and Industrial Relations at Bristol Polytechnic and Women's Studies at Bristol University Extra-Mural Department. She has researched a study of women factory workers employed by Imperial Tobacco Ltd on which she based her book, *Girls, Wives, Factory Lives* (1981).

Daphne Taylorson Lecturer in the Sociology of Education, Department of Education, University of Manchester. Current research on women in higher education.

Sylvia Walby Studied Sociology at Reading and Essex Universities. Currently Lecturer in Sociology at Lancaster University and Convenor of the Women's Studies Minor.

Bibliography

Acker, J. (1972) 'Women in social stratification: a case of intellectual sexism', *American Journal of Sociology*, **78** (4).

Advisory Conciliation and Arbitration Service (ACAS) (1981) *Earnings of Employees in Hairdressing*.

Alexander, R. and Sapery, E. (1973) *The Shortchanged: Minorities and Women in Banking*, Dunellen.

Alexander, S. (1976), 'Women's work in 19th century London: a study of the years 1820–50', in J. Mitchell and A. Oakley (eds.), *The Rights and Wrongs of Women*, Penguin.

Allen, V.L. and Williams, S. (1960) 'The growth of trade unionism in banking', *The Manchester School*, **28**, 299–318.

Anderson, M. (1971) *Family Structure in Nineteenth Century Lancashire*, Cambridge University Press.

Andrews, I.O. (1918) *Economic Effects of the War Upon Women and Children in Great Britain*, Assisted by Margaret A. Hobbs, Carnegie Economic Studies of the War, New York, Oxford University Press.

Anthias, F. (1980), 'Women and the reserve army of labour', *Capital and Class*, **10**, Spring.

Ashton, T.S. (1954) 'The treatment of capitalism by the historians', in F.A. Hayek (ed.) *Capitalism and the Historians*, Routledge and Kegan Paul.

Attwood, M.E. (1981) 'The employment relationship in the hairdressing industry – a preliminary analysis', *Service Industries Review*, **1** (3) November.

Bain, G.S. (1967) *Trade Union Growth and Recognition*, Royal Commission on Trade Unions and Employers' Associations: Research Paper no.6, HMSO.

Bain, G.S. (1970) *The Growth of White Collar Unionism*, Oxford University Press.

Bain, G.S. and Elsheikh, F. (1976) *Union Growth and the Business Cycle*, Blackwell.

Barker, D. Leonard and Allen, S. (1976) *Sexual Divisions and Society: Process and Change*, Tavistock.

Barrett, M. and McIntoch, M. (1979) 'Christine Delpy: towards materialist feminism', *Feminist Review*, **1**, 95–105.

Barrett, M. (1980) *Women's Oppression Today: Problems in Marxist Feminist Analysis*, Verso.

Barron, R.D. and Norris, G.M. (1976) 'Sexual divisions and the dual labour market', in Diana Leonard Barker and Sheila Allen (eds.) *Dependence and Exploitation in Work and Marriage*, Longmans.

Barry, K. (1979) *Female Sexual Slavery*, New York, Avon Books.

Beechey, V. (1977) 'Some notes on female wage labour in capitalist production', *Capital and Class*, **3**, Autumn, 45–66.

Beechey, V. (1978) 'Women and production: a critical analysis of some sociological theories of women's work', in Annette Kuhn and Ann Marie Wolpe (eds.) *Feminism and Materialism: Women and Modes of Production*, Routledge and Kegan Paul.

Beechey, V. (1979) 'On patriarchy', *Feminist Review*, **3**.

Bergmann, B.R. (1980a) 'Occupational segregation: wages and profits when employers discriminate by race or sex', in Alice H. Amsden (ed.) *The Economics of Women and Work*, Penguin.

Bergmann, B.R. (1980b) 'Curing high unemployment rates among blacks and women', in A.H. Amsden (ed.) *The Economics of Women and Work*, Penguin.

Berkner, L. (1975) 'The use and abuse of Census data for the historical analysis of family structure', *Journal of Inter-displinary History*, 5.

Beynon, H (1975) *Working for Ford*, Penguin

Beynon, H. and Blackburn, R.M. (1972) *Perceptions of Work: Variations Within a Factory*, Cambridge University Press.

Blackburn, R.M. (1967) *Union Character and Social Class*, Batsford.

Block, R. (1978) 'Untangling the roots of modern sex roles: a survey of four centuries of change', *Signs*, 4(2) winter, 237–252.

Braverman, H. (1974) *Labor and Monopoly Capital: The Degradation of Work in the Twentieth Century*, New York, Monthly Review Press.

Braybon, G. (1981) *Women Workers in the First World War: The British Experience*, Croom Helm.

British Journal of Industrial Relations (1979) 13(2), London School of Economics.

Brown, R.K. (1976) 'Women as employees: some comments on research in industrial sociology', in D.L. Barker and S. Allen (eds.), *Dependence and Exploitation in Work and Marriage*, Longmans.

Brown, R. (1978) 'Work', in P. Abrams (ed.) *Work, Urbanism and Inequality*, Weidenfeld and Nicolson.

Browning, H. and Singleman, J. (1978) 'The transformation of the US labour force', *Politics and Society*, III (3–4).

Brownmiller, S. (1975) *Against Our Will*, Penguin.

Bruegel, I. (1979) 'Women as a reserve army of labour: a note on recent British experience', *Feminist Review*, 3.

Bruegel, I. (1982) 'Do mothers count?' BSA Conference, Manchester University, April (mimeo).

Burman, S. (ed.) (1979) *Fit Work for Women*, Croom Helm.

Burnham, J. (1941) *The Managerial Revolution*, Penguin.

Cabral, R., Ferber, M.A., Green, C.A. (1981) 'Men and Women in fiduciary institutions: a case study of sex differences in career development', *Review of Economics & Statistics*, LXIII (4).

Calder, A. (1971) *The Peoples War*, Panther.

Cameron Report. Report of the Inquiry by the Honourable Lord Cameron into the Complaint made by the National Union of Bank Employees on 12 March 1962 to the Committee on Freedom of Association of the International Labour Organisation (1963), Cmnd 2202, HMSO.

Campbell, M. (1942) *The English Yeoman Under Elizabeth and the Early Stuarts*, New Haven, Yale University Press.

Caplow, T. (1964) *The Sociology of Work*, New York, McGraw-Hill.

Carchedi, G. (1977), *On the Economic Identification of Social Classes*, Routledge and Kegan Paul.

Cavendish, R. (1982) *Women on the Line* Routledge and Kegan Paul.

Census of Distribution (1971) HMSO.

CFL (1916) *Courtauld Family Letters 1782–1900*, ed. by S.A. Courtauld, 7 volumes, Cambridge University Press.

Chamberlain, R., Chamberlain, G., Howlett, B. and Claireaux, A. (1975) *British Births 1970, Volume 1. The First Week of Life*, Heinemann.

Chamberlain, G. Philipp, E., Howlett, B. and Masters, K. (1978) *British Births 1970, Volume 2: Obstetric Care*, Heinemann.

Chambers, J.D. (1974) *The Workshop of the World: British Economic History from 1820 to 1880*, Oxford University Press.

Chaytor, M. (1980) 'Household and kinship: Ryton in the late 16th and early 17th centuries, *History Workshop Journal*, 10.

Chaytor, M. and Lewis, J. (1982) Introduction to A. Clark, *Working Life of Women in the 17th Century,* Routledge and Kegan Paul.

Clark, A. (1919 reprinted 1968 and 1982) *Working Life of Women in the Seventeenth Century,* Frank Cass & Co (1982 edition: Routledge and Kegan Paul).

Clark, C. (1957) *The Conditions of Economic Progress,* 3rd edn., Macmillan.

Clark, L.M.G. and Lange, L. (eds.) (1979) *The Sexism of Social and Political Theory, Women and Reproduction from Plato to Nietzsche,* Toronto.

Clawson, M.A. (1980) 'Early modern fraternalism and the patriarchal family', *Feminist Studies,* **6**(2).

Clegg, H.A. (1976) *Trade Unionism Under Collective Bargaining,* Blackwell.

Cockburn, C. (1981) 'The material of male power', *Feminist Review,* **9,** Autumn, 41–58

Coleman, D.C. (1969) *Courtaulds – An Economic and Social History,* Vol.1, Clarendon Press.

Coleman, D.C. (1975) *Industry in Tudor and Stuart England,* Macmillan.

Connelly, P. (1978) *Last Hired, First Fired, Women and the Canadian Work Force,* Toronto, The Women's Press.

Coote, A. and Kellner, P. (1981) 'Hear this, brother: women workers and union power', *New Statesman Report 1,* London.

Coussins, J. and Coote, A. (1981) *The Family in the Firing Line,* London, NCCL/CPAG.

Crewe, T., Robertson, D. and Sarlvik, B. (1981) 'A description of surveys conducted by the BES research project', Technical Paper 1981:1, Department of Government, University of Essex.

Crine, S. (1980) 'The unkindest cut', Submission to the Hairdressing Undertakings Wages Council, *Low Pay Paper,* London, Low Pay Unit.

Crompton, R. (1980) 'Class mobility in modern Britain', *Sociology,* **14**(1).

Crompton, R. and Jones, G. (1982) 'Clerical "proletarianisation": myth or reality?', in G. Day *et al.* (eds.), *Diversity and Decomposition in the Labour Market,* Gower.

Dahrendorf, R. (1959) *Class and Class Conflict in an Industrial Society,* Routledge and Kegan Paul.

Dalla Costa, M. (1972) *Women and the Subversion of the Community,* Falling Wall Press.

Davidoff, L. (1973) *The Best Circles,* Croom Helm.

Davidoff, L. (1974) 'Mastered for life: servant and wife in Victorian and Edwardian England', *Journal of Social History,* **7**(4).

Davidoff, L. (1979) 'Class and gender in Victorian England: the diaries of Arthur J. Munby and Hannah Cullwick', *Feminist Studies,* Spring.

Davies, N.Z. (1982) 'Women in the crafts in 16th century Lyon', *Feminist Studies,* **8**(1).

Delamont, S. (1980) The Sociology of Women, George Allen & Unwin.

Delphy, C. (1976) 'Continuities and discontinuities in marriage and divorce', in D.L. Barker and S. Allen (eds.), *Sexual Divisions and Society: Process and Change,* Tavistock.

Delphy, C. (1977) *The Main Enemy: A Materialist Analysis of Women's Oppression,* London, WRRC publication: Explorations in Feminism, **3**.

Delphy, C. (1979) 'Sharing the same table: consumption and the family' (trans. by D. Leonard), in C.C. Harris (ed.), *The Sociology of the Family: New Directions for Britain,* Sociological Review Mono. 28, Keele University Press.

Delphy, C. (1980) 'A materialist feminism is possible', trans. by D. Leonard, *Feminist Review,* **4**.

Delphy, C. (1981) 'Women in stratification studies', in H. Roberts (ed.), *Doing Feminist Research,* Routledge and Kegan Paul.

Department of Employment (1981) *New Earnings Survey.*

Dobb, M. (1963) *Studies in the Development of Capitalism,* Routledge and Kegan Paul.

Doeringer, P.B. and Piore, M.J. (1971) *Internal Labour Markets and Manpower Analysis,* Lexington, Mass., Lexington Books.

Duncan, R. and Perrucci, C. (1976) 'Dual occupation families and migration', *American Sociological Review,* **41,** April.

Dworkin, A. (1981) *Pornography: Men Possessing Women*, The Women's Press.

Edholm, F., Harris, O. and Young, K. (1977) 'Conceptualising Women', *Critique of Anthropology*, **3** (9/10).

Edwards, R. (1982) 'Underneath they're all redundant', *New Statesman* 19 February.

Edwards, R.C., Reich, M. and Gordon, D.M. (1975) *Labour Market Segmentation*, Lexington Books.

Egan, A. (1982) 'Woman in banking: a study in inequality', *Industrial Relations Journal*, **13**(3), 20–31.

Eisenstein, Z. (1979) 'Developing a theory of capitalist patriarchy', in Z. Eisenstein (ed.), *Capitalism, Patriarchy The Case for Socialist Feminism*, New York.

Ellis, V. (1981) *The Role of Trade Unions in the Promotion of Equal Opportunities*, Research Review Commissioned by the EOC/SSRC Joint Panel on Equal Opportunities.

Emmison, F.G. (1976) *Elizabethan Life: Home, Work and Land*, Chelmsford, Essex Records Committee, Essex Records Office Publications no.69.

Engels, F. (1970) 1884 'The origin of the family, private property and the state', in Marx and Engels (1970), *Selected Works in One Volume*, Lawrence and Wishart.

Eurostat (1980) *Labour Force Sample Survey, 1973, 1975, 1977*, Luxembourg, Office for Official Publications of the European Communities.

Everitt, A. (1967) 'Farm labourers', in J. Thirsk (ed.), *Agrarian History*, 396–465.

Ewbank, J.R.N. (1977) *A Social and Economic Survey of Hairdressing*, MA Thesis, University of Sheffield, Department of Social and Economic History.

Finer Report (1974) *Report of the Committee on One Parent Families*, DHSS, London, HMSO.

Firestone, Shulamith (1971) *The Dialectic of Sex*, Paladin.

Flandarin, J.L. (1979) *Families in Former Times: Kinship, Household and Sexuality*, Cambridge University Press.

Floud, J. and Halsey, A. (1961) 'Introduction', in A. Halsey, J. Floud and C. Anderson, *Education, Economy and Society*, Collier-Macmillan.

Fogarty, M.P., Rapoport, R. and Rapoport, R. (1971a) *Sex, Career and Family*, George Allen and Unwin, P.E.P.

Fogarty, M.P., Allen, A.J., Allen, I.A. and Walters, P. (1971b) *Women in Top Jobs*, George Allen and Unwin, P.E.P.

Fox, A. (1966) *Industrial Sociology and Industrial Relations*, Royal Commission on Trade Unions and Employers' Associations, Research Paper no.3, HMSO.

Fox, B. (1980) 'Women's double work day: twentieth-century changes in the reproduction of daily life', in B. Fox (ed.), *Hidden in the Household*, Ontario, The Women's Press.

Fox-Genovese, E. (1977) 'Property and patriarchy in classical bourgeois political theory', *Radical History Review IV*, 2–3, spring–summer.

Fox-Genovese, E. (1982) 'Placing women's history in history, *New Left Review*, **133**, May–June.

Friedman, A. (1977) 'Responsible autonomy versus direct control over the labour process', *Capital and Class*, **1**, 43–57.

Friedman, S. (1982a) 'Heterosexuality, couples and parenthood: a "natural" cycle?', in S. Friedman and E. Sarah (eds.), *On the Problem of Men*, The Women's Press.

Friedman, S. (1982b) 'The Marxist paradigm: radical feminist theorists compared', BSA Conference Paper, April 1982.

Friedman, S. and Sarah, E. (eds.) (1982) *On the Problem of Men*, The Women's Press.

Fryer, R.H., Fairclough, A.H. and Manson, T.B. (1978) 'Facilities for female shop stewards: the Employment Protection Act and collective agreements', *British Journal of Industrial Relations*, **16**(3), London School of Economics.

Gardiner, J. (1975a) 'Women in the labour process and class structure', in A. Hunt (ed.), *Class and Class Structure*, Lawrence and Wishart.

Gardiner, J. (1975b) 'Women's domestic labour', *New Left Review*, **89**, January–February, 47–58.

Gardiner, J. (1976) 'Political economy of domestic labour in capitalist society', in D.L. Barker and S. Allen, (eds.), *Dependence and Exploitation in Work and Marriage*, Longman.

Garnsey, E. (1978) 'Women's work and theories of class stratification', *Sociology*, 12(2), 223–243.

General Household Survey London, HMSO.

Gershuny, J. (1978) *After Industrial Society?*, Macmillan.

Giddens, A. (1979) *Central Problems in Social Theory: Action, Structure and Contradictions in Social Analysis*, Macmillan.

Glass, D. (ed.) (1954) *Social Mobility in Britain*, Routledge and Kegan Paul.

Glucklich, P., Hall. C.R.J., Povall, M. and Snell, M.W. (1976) 'Equal pay experience in twenty-five firms', *Department of Employment Gazette*, December.

Glyn, S. and Oxborrow, J. (1976) *Inter War Britain*, Allen and Unwin.

Goldthorpe, J. (1980a) *Social Mobility and Class Structure in Modern Britain*, Oxford University Press.

Goldthorpe, J. (1980b) 'Reply to Crompton', *Sociology*, 14(1).

Goldthorpe, J.H. and Hope, K. (1974) *The Social Grading of Occupations*, Clarendon Press.

Goldthorpe, J.H. and Llewellyn, C. (1977) 'Class mobility in modern Britain: three theses examined', *Sociology*, 11, 257–288.

Goldthorpe, J.H., Lockwood, D., Bechhofer, F. and Platt, J. (1968) *The Affluent Worker*, Cambridge University Press.

Goody, J., Thirsk, J. and Thompson, E.P. (1976) *Family and Inheritance*, Cambridge University Press.

Gordon, D.M. (1972) *Theories of Poverty and Underemployment: Orthodox, Radical, and Dual Labor Market Perspectives*, Lexington, Mass., Lexington Books.

Graham, S. and Llewellyn, C. (1976) 'Women in the occupational structure: a case study of banking', unpublished paper, Nuffield College, Oxford.

Gramsci, A. (1971) *Selection from the Prison Note Books*, Lawrence and Wishart.

Hakim, Catherine (1979) *Occupational Segregation: a comparative study of the degree and patterns of the differentiation between men and women's work in Britain, the United States and other countries*, Department of Employment Research Paper no. 9, Department of Employment.

Hall, C. (1979) 'The early formation of Victorian domestic ideology', in S. Burman (ed.), *Fit Work for Women*, Croom Helm.

Hamilton, R. (1978) *The Liberation of Women*, George Allen and Unwin.

Hareven, T. (1982) *Family Time and Industrial Time*, Cambridge University Press.

Harris, O. (1981) 'Households as natural units', in K. Young, C. Wolkowitz, and R. McCullagh, *Of Marriage and the Market*, CSE Books.

Harrison, J. (1974) 'The political economy of housework', *Bulletin of the Conference of Socialist Economists*, III, 35–52.

Hartmann, H. (1976) 'Capitalism, patriarchy and job segregation by sex', *Signs*, 1(3), spring.

Hartmann, H. (1979) 'The unhappy marriage of Marxism and feminism: towards a more progressive union', *Capital and Class*, 8.

Harvie, C. (1977) *Scotland and Nationalism*, Allen and Unwin.

Heath, A. (1981a) *Social Mobility*, Fontana.

Heath, A. (1981b) 'Women who get on in the world – up to a point', *New Society*, 44 (952), 12 February.

Heritage, J.C. (1977) *The Growth of Trade Unionism in the London Clearing Banks, 1960–70: A Sociological Interpretation*, unpublished PhD dissertation, University of Leeds.

Hill, C. (1967) 'Pottage for freeborn Englishmen: attidues to wage labour in the sixteenth and seventeenth centuries', in C.H. Feinstein (ed.), *Socialism, Capitalism and Economic Growth*, Cambridge University Press.

Hilton, R. (1975) *The English Peasantry in the later Middle Ages*, Clarendon Press.

Hilton, R. (1976) (ed.) *The Transition from Feudalism to Capitalism*, New Left Books.

Hilton, R. (1978) 'Reasons for inequality among medieval peasants', *Journal of Peasant Studies*, **5**(3), 271–284.

HMSO (1968) *Standard Industrial Classification*, HMSO.

HMSO (1971) *British Labour Statistics Historical Abstract, 1868–1968*, Department of Employment.

Hobsbawm, E. (1969) *Industry and Empire*, Penguin.

Hogrefe, P. (1975) *Tudor Women: Commoners and Queens*, Ames, Iowa, Iowa State University Press.

Holt, R.V. (1938) *The Unitarian Contribution to Social Progress*, Lindsey Press.

Home Office (1929) *A study of the factors which have operated in the past and those which are operating now to determine the distribution of women in industry*, Cmd 3508, HMSO.

Hope K. and Goldthorpe, J. (1974) *The Social Grading of Occupations*, Oxford University Press.

Hoskins, W.G. (1957) *The Midland Peasant*, Macmillan.

Hufton, O. (1975) 'Women and the family economy in 18th century France', *French Historical Studies*, **9**.

Hughes, E.C. (1974) *Men and their Work*, Glencoe, Illinois, Free Press of Glencoe.

Humphries, J. (1977) 'Class struggle and the persistence of the working class family', *Cambridge Journal of Economics*, September.

Humphries, J. (1981) 'Protective legislation, the capitalist state and working class men: the case of the 1842 Mines Regulation Act', *Feminist Review*, **7**, 1–33, spring.

Hunt, A. (1975) *Management Attitudes and Practices towards Women at Work*, Office of Population Censuses and Surveys, HMSO.

Hunt, P. (1980) *Gender and Class Consciousness*, Macmillan.

Hutton, D. (forthcoming) 'Women in fourteenth-century Shrewsbury', in L. Charles and L. Duffin (eds.), *Women's Work in Pre-Industrial Britain*, Croom Helm.

Jack, S.M. (1977) *Trade and Industry in Tudor and Stuart England*, Historical Problems: Studies and Documents no.27, George Allen and Unwin.

Jacoby, R.M. (1976) 'Feminism and class consciousness in the British and American women's trade union leagues, 1890–1925', in Berenice A. Carroll (ed.), *Liberating Women's History: Theoretical and Critical Essays*, Urbana, University of Illinois Press.

Johnson, T. (1972) *Professions and Power*, Macmillan.

Joint Training Council for the Hairdressing Industry (1981a) *Policy for Training*.

Joint Training Council for the Hairdressing Industry (1981b) *Survey of Manpower and Training Needs in the Hairdressing Industry*.

Joyce, P. (1980) *Work, Society and Politics: The Culture of the Factory in later Victorian England*, Harvester Press.

Keeling, A. (1980) 'Women and mobility', Seminar paper, Department of Social and Political Studies, Plymouth Polytechnic (unpublished).

Kelly, J. (1979) 'The doubled vision of feminist theory: a postscript to the "Women and Power Conference" ', *Feminist Studies*, **3**, spring.

Kelly-Cadol, (1975) 'History and the social relation of the sexes', paper presented to the Barnard College Women's Centre Conference 'The Scholar and the Feminist II: Toward New Criteria of Relevance', April.

Kelsall, R.K. (1938) *Wage Regulation under the Statute of Artificers*, Methuen.

Kendall, W. (1975) *The Labour Movement in Europe*, Allen Lane.

Kreckel, R. (1980) 'Unequal opportunity structure and labour market segmentation', *Sociology* **14**, 525–549.

Kussmaul, A. (1978) *Servants in Husbandry in Early Modern England*, Cambridge University Press.

Lacey, K. (1981) *Women and Work in the Medieval Town*, Unpublished paper delivered to the Urban History Conference.

Land, H. (1975) 'The myth of the male breadwinner', *New Society*, October, 71–73.

Land, H. (1976) 'Women: supporters or supported?', in D.L. Barker and S. Allen (eds.),

Sexual Divisions and Society: Process and Change, Tavistock.

Land, H. (1980) 'The family wage', *Feminist Review*, **6**.

Lazonick, W. (1978) 'Historical origins of the sex-based division of labour under capitalism', *Harvard Institute of Economic Research*, discussion paper.

Lee, D. (1981) 'Skill, craft and class', *Sociology*, **15**(1).

Leghorn, L. and Parker, K. (1981) *Women's Worth: Sexual Economics and the World of Women*, Routledge and Kegan Paul.

Lewenhak, S. (1977) *Women and Trade Unions*, Ernest Benn.

Local Authorities Management Services and Computer Committee (1972) *A Study into the Feasibility of Introducing a National Bonus Scheme for School Meals Staff.* Quoted in *NUPE* (1979), (1), 14–15.

Lockwood, D. (1958) *The Blackcoated Worker*, Allen and Unwin.

McClendon, M.J. (1976) 'The occupational status attainment processes of males and females', *American Sociological Review*, **41**(1).

McDonoagh, R. and Harrison, R. (1978) 'Patriarchy and relations of production', in A. Kuhn and A.M. Wolpe (eds.), *Feminism and Materialism*, Routledge and Kegan Paul.

MacFarlane, A. (1970) *The Family Life of Ralph Josselin*, Cambridge University Press.

MacFarlane, A. (1978) *The Origins of English Individualism*, Blackwell.

McIntosh, M. (1979) 'The welfare state and the needs of the dependent family', in S. Burman (ed.), *Fit Work for Women*, Croom Helm.

MacKay, D.I., Boddy, D., Brack, J., Mack, J.A. & Jones, N. (1971) *Labour Markets Under Different Employment Conditions*, George Allen and Unwin.

McNally, F. (1979) *Women for Hire: A Study of the Female Office Worker*, Macmillan.

Maher, V. (1981) 'Work, consumption and authority within the household: A Moroccan case', in K. Young *et al.* (eds.) *Of Marriage and the Market*, CSE Books.

Mandel, E. (1975) *Late Capitalism*, Verso.

Manley, P. and Sawbridge, D. (1980) 'Women at work', in *Lloyds Bank Review*, 29–40.

Marx, Karl (1954) *Capital* Vol. 1 (reprinted 1961, Lawrence and Wishart).

Merrington, J. (1976) 'Town and country in the transition to capitalism', in R. Hilton (ed.), *The Transition from Feudalism to Capitalism*, New Left Books.

Middleton, C. (1979) 'The sexual division of labour in feudal England', *New Left Review*, 113–114, January–April, 147–168.

Middleton, C. (1981) 'Peasants, patriarchy and the feudal mode of production in England: a Marxist appraisal, parts 1 and 2', *Sociological Review*, **29**(1) New Series: 105–154.

Middleton, C. (forthcoming), 'Women's labour and the transition to pre-industrial capitalism', in L. Charles and L. Duffin (eds.), *Women's Work in Pre-Industrial Britain*, Croom Helm.

Milkman, R. (1976) 'Women's work and the economic crisis: some lessons of the Great Depression', *Review of Radical Political Economy*, **8**(1), spring.

Millett, K. (1969) *Sexual Politics*, New York, Abacus.

Mincer, J. (1962) 'Labour force participation of married women: a study of labor supply', in National Bureau of Economic Research *Aspects of Labor Economics: A Conference of the Universities – National Bureau Committee for Economic Research*, Princeton, US, Princeton University Press.

Mincer, J. (1966) 'Labour force participation and unemployment: a review of recent evidence', in Robert A. Gordon and Margaret S. Gordon (eds.), *Prosperity and Unemployment*, New York, John Wiley & Sons.

Molyneux, M. (1979) 'Beyond the domestic labour debate', *New Left Review*, **116**, 3–28.

Monk, D. (1970) *Social Grading on the National Readership Survey*, London, JICNRS.

Mumford, E. and Banks, O. (1967) *The Computer and the Clerk*, Routledge and Kegan Paul.

Myrdal, A. and Klein, V. (1968) *Women's Two Roles*, 2nd edn., Routledge and Kegan Paul.

National Board for Prices and Incomes (NBPI) (1965) *Salaries of Midland Bank Staff*, Report no.6, Cmnd 2839, HMSO.

National Board for Prices and Incomes (NBPI) (1967) *Bank Charges*, Report no.34, Cmnd 3292, HMSO.

National Board for Prices and Incomes (NBPI) (1969) *Pay in the London Clearing Banks*, Report no.106, Cmnd 3943, HMSO.

Nef, J.U. (1932) *The Rise of the British Coal Industry*, Routledge and Kegan Paul.

Nef, J.U. (1934–5) 'The progress of technology, and the growth of large-scale industry, 1540–1640', *Economic History Review*, original series V(1), 3–24.

Nelson, J. (1979) 'Women in trade unions: the use of special women's officers, committees or groups: their existence in unions and effectiveness', Unpublished, London: Women's Research and Resources Centre.

Newby, H. (1975) 'The deferential dialectic', *Comparative Studies in Sociology*, 17(2), April.

Nichols, T. and Armstrong, P. (1976) *Workers Divided*, Fontana

NUPE (1974) *Organization and Change in the National Union of Public Employees*, NUPE.

NUPE (1979a) *Recipe of Action: NUPE's Report on Staffing and Conditions in the School Meals Service*, NUPE.

NUPE (1979b) *Journal of National Union of Public Employees*, no.1, NUPE.

Oakley, A. (1974) *Housewife*, Allen Lane.

Oakley, A. (1976) 'Wise women and medicine man: changes in the management of childbirth', in Juliet Mitchell and Ann Oakley (eds.), *The Rights and Wrongs of Women*, Penguin.

Oakley, A. (1981a) Interviewing women: a contradiction in terms', in H. Roberts (ed.), *Doing Feminist Research*, Routledge and Kegan Paul.

Oakley, A. (1981b) *Subject Women*, Martin Robertson.

O'Brien, M. (1981) *The Politics of Reproduction*, Routledge and Kegan Paul.

Office of Population Censuses and Surveys (1970) *Classification of Occupations 1970*, HMSO.

Oppenheimer, V.K. (1973) 'Demographic influence on female employment and the status of women', *American Journal of Sociology*, 78, 946–961.

Oppenheimer, V.K. (1977) 'the sociology of women's economic role in the family', *American Sociological Review*, 42(3).

Oren, L. (1973) 'The welfare of women in labouring families: England 1850–1950', *Feminist Studies*, Winter.

Organisation for Economic Cooperation and Development (1976) *The 1974–5 Recession and the Employment of Women*, Paris, Organisation for Economic Cooperation and Development.

Osborn, A.F. and Morris, A.C. (1979) 'The rationale for a composite index of social class and its evaluation', *British Journal of Sociology*, 30, 39–60.

Osborn, A.F. and Morris, A.C. (1982) 'Fathers and child care', *Early Child Development and Care*, 8, 279–307.

Pahl, J. (1980) 'Patterns of money management in marriage', *Journal of Social Policy*, 9(Pt III).

Parkin, F. (1971) *Class Inequality and the Political Order*, Paladin.

Payne, G. (1977) 'Occupational transition in advanced industrial societies', *Sociological Review*, 25(1).

Payne, G., Ford, G. and Robertson, C. (1977) 'A reappraisal of "Social Mobility in Britain" ', *Sociology*, 11(2).

Payne, G., Ford, G. and Ulas, M. (1979a) 'Occupational change and social mobility in Scotland since the First World War', British Association for the Advancement of Science, Sections F and N, Edinburgh, September (mimeo). Reprinted with minor changes as Payne *et al*., 'Social mobility and occupational change', in M. Gaskin (ed.) *The Political Economy of Tolerable Survival*, Croom Helm.

Payne, G., Ford, G. and Ulas, M. (1979b) *Education and Social Mobility* Edinburgh, SIP Occasional Papers no.8, SIP.

Payne, G. and Payne, J. (1981) 'Social mobility and the labour market', BSA Annual

Conference, Aberystwyth, April. Reprinted in extended form as 'Occupational and industrial transition in social mobility', *British Journal of Sociology*, forthcoming.

Pinchbeck I. (1981) *Women Workers and the Industrial Revolution*, Virago.

Pleck, E. (1976) 'Two worlds in one: work and family', *Journal of Social History*, **10**(2).

Pollert, A. (1981) *Girls, Wives, Factory Lives*, Macmillan.

Porter, M. (1978) 'Consciousness and second-hand experience: wives and husbands in industrial action', *Sociological Review*, **26**(2) May.

Power, E. (1975) *Medieval Women*, (ed. by M.M. Postan), Cambridge University Press.

Price, R. and Bain, G.S. (1976) 'Union growth revisited: 1948–1974 in perspective', *British Journal of Industrial Relations*, **14**, 339–355.

Purcell, K. (1979) 'Militancy and acquiescence amongst women workers', in S. Burman (ed.), *Fitwork for Women*, Croom Helm.

Purcell, K. (1981) 'Female manual workers, fatalism and reinforcement of inequalities', paper presented to the BSA Annual Conference, April.

Ramsey, H. (1980) 'Participation: the pattern and its significance', in T. Nichols (ed.), *Capital and Labour: A Marxist Primer*, Fontana.

Rapoport, R. and Rapoport, R. (1971) *Dual Career Families*, PEP, Penguin.

Rapoport, R. and Rapoport, R. (1976) *Dual Career Families Re-examined: New Interpretations of Work and Family*, Martin Robertson.

Reid, I. (1977) *Social Class Differences in Britain*, Open Books.

Rich, A. (1977) *Of Woman Born*, Virago.

Rimmer, L. and Wicks, M. (1981) 'The family today', *Journal of the Modern Studies Association*, **27**, autumn.

Ritter, K. and Hargen, L. (1975) 'Occupational positions and class identifications of married working women', *American Journal of Sociology*, **80**(4).

Roberts, D. (1979) *Paternalism in Early Victorian England*, Croom Helm.

Robinson, O. (1969) 'Representation of the White Collar Worker: The Bank Staff Associations in Britain', *British Journal of Industrial Relations*, **7**, 19–41.

Rosaldo, M.Z. (1980) 'The use and abuse of anthropology: reflections on feminism and cross-cultural understanding', *Signs*, **5**(3).

Rosenfeld, R. (1978) 'Women's intergenerational occupational mobility', *American Sociological Review*, **48**.

Rowbotham, S. (1973) *Women's Consciousness, Man's World*, Penguin.

Rubery, J. (1978) 'Structured labour markets, worker organisation and low pay', *Cambridge Journal of Economics*, **2**.

Rubin, G. (1975) 'The traffic in women', in R. Reiter (ed.), *Toward an Anthropology of Women*, New York, Monthly Review Press.

Runciman, G. (1966) *Relative Deprivation and Social Justice*, Routledge and Kegan Paul.

Rupp, R., Ross, E. and Bridenthal, R. (1980) 'Examining family history', *Feminist Studies*, **5**(1).

Ryan, M. (1981) *Cradle of the Middle Class*, Cambridge University Press.

Saville, J. (1969) 'Primitive accumulation and early industrialisation in Britain', *Socialist Register, 1969*, 247–271.

Scharf, L. (1980) *To Work and To Wed: Female Employment, Feminism, and the Great Depression*, Contributions in Women's Studies no.15, Westport, Connecticut, Greenwood Press.

Scott, R.J. (1973) *Women in the Stuart Economy*, unpublished M.Phil thesis, London University.

Sewell, W.H., Hauser, R.M. and Wolf, W.E. (1980) 'Sex schooling and occupational status', *American Journal of Sociology*, **86**(3).

Shanley, M.L. (1979) 'Marriage contract and social contract in seventeenth century English political thought', *Western Political Quarterly*, **32**, March.

Sharpe, S. (1976) *Just Like a Girl*, Penguin.

Shiskin, J. (1976) 'Employment and unemployment: the doughnut or the hole?', *Monthly*

Labor Review, February.

Signs (1980) Special issue, *Women – Sex and Sexuality*, **5**(4).

Soldon, N.C. (1978) *Women in British Trade Unions: 1874–1976*, Dublin, Gill and MacMillan.

Sorrentino, C. (1979) *International Comparisons of Unemployment*, US Bureau of Labour Statistics Bulletin, Washington, DC, US Bureau of Labour Statistics.

Stacey, M. (1981) 'The division of labour revisited or overcoming the two Adams', in P. Abrams, R. Deem, J. Finch, and P. Rock, *Practice and Progress: British Sociology 1950–1980*, George Allen and Unwin.

Stageman, J. (1980) *Women in Trade Unions*, Industrial Studies Unit, University of Hull.

Stearns, P. (1979) *Paths to Authority: The Middle Class and the Industrial Labour Force in France, 1820–1848*, Illinois, Champaign.

Stearns, P.N. (1975) *Lives of Labour: Work in a Maturing Industrial Society*, Croom Helm.

Stevenson, J. (1977) *Social Conditions in Britain Between the Wars*, Penguin.

Stewart, A., Prandy, K. and Blackburn, R.M. (1980) *Social Stratification and Occupations*, Macmillan.

Stone, L. (1977) *The Family, Sex and Marriage in England 1500–1800*, Weidenfeld and Nicolson.

Summers, A. (1979) 'A home from home – women's philanthropic work in the 19th century', in S. Burman, (ed.), *Fit Work for Women*, Croom Helm.

Tawney, A.J. and Tawney, R.H. (1934–5) 'An occupational census of the seventeenth century', *Economic History Review*, Original Series V, 25–64.

Taylor, B. (1979) 'The men are as bad as their masters . . . ': socialism, feminism and sexual antagonism in the London tailoring trade in the early 1830s', *Feminist Studies*, **5**(1), spring.

Thirsk, J. (1961) 'Industries in the countryside', in F.J. Fisher, (ed.), *Essays in the Economic and Social History of Tudor and Stuart England*, Cambridge University Press.

Thirsk, J. (ed.) (1967) *The Agrarian History of England and Wales, Vol IV, 1500–1640*, Cambridge University Press.

Thirsk, J. (1978) *Economic Policy and Projects*, Clarendon Press.

Thomas, K. (1959) 'The Double Standard', *Journal of the History of Ideas*, April.

Thorn, B. and Yalom, M. (eds.) (1982) *Rethinking the Family: Some Feminist Questions*, Longmans.

Thorsell, S. (1967) 'Employer attitudes to female employees', in L. Dahlstrom, (ed.), *The Changing Roles of Men and Women*, Duckworth.

Thrupp, S. (1948) *The Merchant Class of Medieval London*, Chicago, University Press.

Tomes, N. (1977–78) 'A "torrent of abuse": crimes of violence between working-class men and women in London, 1840–1875', *Journal of Social History*, **2**.

Trades Union Council (TUC) (1976) *Report of Equal Pay and Opportunities Campaign*, TUC.

Trades Union Council (TUC) (1977) *Report of Equal Pay and Opportunities Campaign*, TUC.

Treiman, D. and Terrell, K. (1975) 'Sex and the process of status attainment', *American Sociological Review*, **10**.

Trudgill, E. (1976) *Madonnas and Magdalenes: The Origins and Development of Victorian Sexual Attitudes*, Heinemann.

Tusser, T. (1557) *Five Hundred Points of Good Husbandrie*, W. Payne and S.J. Herrtage (eds.), English Dialect Society, **21**, London, 1878.

UK Census (1961) Appendix, HMSO.

Wainwright, H. (1978) 'Women and the division of labour', in P. Abrams (ed.), *Work, Urbanism and Inequality*, Weidenfeld and Nicolson.

Walby, S. (1982) 'The concept of patriarchy', paper presented to the BSA Sociological Theory Study Group.

Wallerstein, I. (1974) *The Modern World-System: Capitalist Agriculture and the Origins of the*

European World-Economy in the Sixteenth Century, New York, Academic Press.

Wedderburn, D. and Craig, C. (1974) 'Relative deprivation in work', in D. Wedderburn (ed.), *Poverty, Inequality and Class Structure,* Cambridge University Press.

West, J. (1978) 'Women, sex and class', in A. Kuhn and A.M. Wolpe, (eds.), *Feminism and Materialism,* Routledge and Kegan Paul.

West, J. (ed.) (1982) *Work, Women and the Labour Market,* Routledge and Kegan Paul.

Westergaard, J. and Resler, H. (1977) *Class in a Capitalist Society,* Penguin.

Whitehead, A. (1981) ' "I'm hungry, Mum": the politics of domestic budgeting', in K. Young *et al.* (eds.), *Of Marriage and the Market,* CSE Books.

Wild, P. and Hill (1970) *Women in the Factory: A Study of Job Satisfaction and Labour Turnover,* London, Institute of Personnel Management.

Wilde Committee (1973) The Institute of Bankers' Educational Policy Review, *Part 1; The Institute's Future as a Qualifying Association: A Report by the Wilde Committee,* Institute of Bankers.

Willis, P. (1978) *Learning to Labour,* Saxon House.

Wilson, C.S. (1963) 'Social factors influencing industrial output: a sociological study of a factory in North-West Lancashire', unpublished Ph.D. Thesis: University of Manchester.

Woodward, D. and Chisholm, L. (1981) 'The expert's view? graduate occupational and domestic roles', in H. Roberts, (ed.), *Doing Feminist Research,* Routledge and Kegan Paul.

Wrightson, K. (1981) *English Society, 1580–1680,* Hutchinson.

Young, K. and Harris, O. (1976) 'The subordination of women in cross-cultural perspective' in *Papers on Patriarchy,* London PDC and Womens Publishing Collective.

Young, M. and Willmott, P. (1957) *Family and Kinship in East London,* Routledge and Kegan Paul.

Index